THE ENVIRONMENTAL MEMORY

OTHER BOOKS BY THE AUTHOR

Ritual and Response in Architecture
Monuments of Another Age: The City of London Churches
The Art of Government and the Government of Art
Alvar Aalto: A Critical Study
Reima Pietilä: Architecture, Context and Modernism

THE ENVIRONMENTAL MEMORY

▲

MAN AND ARCHITECTURE IN THE LANDSCAPE OF IDEAS

▲

MALCOLM QUANTRILL

SCHOCKEN BOOKS / NEW YORK

First published by Schocken Books 1987
10 9 8 7 6 5 4 3 2 1 87 88 89 90

Library of Congress Cataloging-in-Publication Data
Quantrill, Malcolm, 1931–
The environmental memory.
Bibliography: p.
Includes index.
1. Architecture—Human factors. 2. Architecture—Environmental aspects. 3. Architecture—Psychological aspects. I. Title.
NA2542.4.Q36 1986 720'.1 86–6419

Design by Richard Oriolo
Manufactured in the United States of America
ISBN 0–8052–4016–0

All photographs are by the author with the exception of Plate 16, Alvar Aalto's Academic Bookshop, Helsinki, Finland. This photograph is reproduced with the courtesy of the Finnish Ministry of Foreign Affairs, Helsinki, Finland.

Published in association with the Graham Foundation for Advanced Studies in the Fine Arts, Chicago, Illinois

For my wife,

ESTHER

and

HOLMES PERKINS

my teacher, counselor and friend

CONTENTS

I L L U S T R A T I O N S

P L A T E S

Following Page 142

Page FIGURES

PREFACE

Man is the only animal who is conscious of his own mortality. This consciousness of a limited life span, that begins in such frailty and is of uncertain duration, causes us to construct frameworks of relationships and continuity in which we can have only a fleeting part. Attempts to understand the shifting patterns of civilization against the continuity of existence itself constitute a significant part of the history of ideas. This history is not a single tradition that we pass from generation to generation by word of mouth. It comprises, rather, two echoes of experience that, in spite of natural and man-made disasters, we continue to inherit and pass on. One is the tradition of the written word that records myth and legend, pragmatism and poetics, scientific fact and philosophical speculation, as well as the ephemera of music, drama, and dance. The other is man's tradition of representing those ideas in stone and brick, wood and plaster, metal and glass, paint and clay. The first offers evidence of man's consciousness of himself and his condition in the form of discourses, plays, and poems; the other mirrors the consciousness of passing generations in buildings, paintings, pots, pans, and jeweled remembrances. It is this second tradition that interests us here, with particular reference to man's relationship to the world of forms and images that he constructs, and to the ideas that he represents and remembers in architecture and the city.

This study is concerned with both the conceptual basis of architecture and urban form, and also with our perception of how such theoretical constructs affect our senses. Paul Frankl wrote: "There exists within every space something that appeals to emotion and something else that appeals to reason."[1] The ideas discussed here look at how we experience and memorize the spaces, forms, and details of environments; and how, in turn, this *environmental memory* enables us both to understand existing buildings and cities, and also helps us to invent new ones. "Environment" refers here to the physical objects that surround us in terrestrial space, their relationships to each other, the forms they impart to that space, and the way our existence is informed by those objects and forms. The *framework* of an environment does not depend upon its visible, perceivable elements alone: there may also be an underlying metaphysical or ritual order that is not immediately apparent in the form, that is carried by its hidden or "fourth dimension" of mythical or cultural memories.

Our experience of physical environments depends upon changing perceptions of patterns generated by solid and void, light and shade—patterns which reveal forms in space as we move among them and change our position in relation to them. It is this direct existential experience, combined with the imagery we perceive in our surroundings, that offers the basic material of environmental memory.

If all evidence of our traditions were to be systematically destroyed tomorrow, any scholars, scientists, historians, and poets who survived such a disaster would surely attempt to reconstruct our present scope of written knowledge and culture from memory. As daunting as such a task would be, the probability is that at least some of that information could be recovered and made available once more. The likelihood is, however, that by far the largest quantity of missing data would be in the category of pictorial information, and it would be quite impossible to reinvent our tradition of buildings and artifacts without abundant supporting visual evidence. In fact the case would be more extreme today than it was in the midnineteenth century, for we depend a great deal more on photographic evidence now than did the early Victorians. A hundred-and-fifty years ago artists who recorded the world about them would have remembered what they had previously drawn and would have been able to recapture essential forms and details. In the eighteenth and nineteenth centuries, ordinary men and women still committed extensive passages of literature to memory, and images of their surroundings to their sketchbooks. The subject or object of their scrutiny became part of their consciousness by the direct process of recording its characteristics.

In the preface to his *Venetian Architecture of the Early Renaissance* (1980), John McAndrew recalls having coffee with two German scholars at Florian's in the Piazza San Marco some years ago, when one of them announced: "Too bad that no one can work on the later architecture of Venice." His colleague agreed, explaining that there were no photographs of it available in the Cini Library. McAndrew was rightly disturbed by this exchange because, as he put it, "It exposed a sinister belief that work with photographs is essential and work with actual buildings is not."[2]

This study has been undertaken in the hope that it will increase interest in the "second tradition" of which architecture and the city are part, and reveal that its value equals that of our written heritage. The art of building, just as much as the theorem or the sonnet, is an essential part of man's collective memory and therefore of his identity with place and time. Yet while we hear constant outcries against the loss of literacy to television and the computer, our crisis of environmental memory goes virtually unnoticed. Both the crisis and our blindness to it arise because visual awareness and sensitivity to our surroundings have long since been condemned to the shadows of indirect experience.

Memory begins in our first room, we climb into it on our first stair, we nourish it with views from our first window. Images of these beginnings of consciousness are the basis for our dreams and aspirations. The room, the stair, the window seat, the fields and mountains beyond, the city streets and squares with their jostling facades, the museum where we have conversations with history, the church with its changing imagery of the seasons, and not least the school where our curiosity about this architecture of memory is stimulated—all this is the education of our visual memory, the development of our consciousness, the honing of our sensitivity to the outer world, and the awakening of our inner selves dreaming in that world. Environmental memory begins in our first house, our first field, our first street and library; then it is fostered by parents, teachers, and friends, to ensure that the images about us shine through the windows of our soul. *Otherwise environmental memory is blunted and allowed to decay!*

Malcolm Quantrill
Texas A&M University, 1986

ACKNOWLEDGMENTS

I coined the term "environmental memory" in a lecture given at Liverpool University in 1972. A revised version of that text is included in *Ritual and Response in Architecture* (1974), and I must thank John Taylor of Lund Humphries, London, for his encouragement by the publication of my first explorations of the problems of creativity in architecture.

My earlier notes were indebted to such divergent authors as Arthur Koestler, Christopher Alexander, George Steiner and Georges Simenon. When I recommenced my explorations of Alvar Aalto's work in 1978, however, I came to realize how closely my concept of environmental memory is connected to my long interest in the architecture of this modern Finnish master. After I completed *Alvar Aalto: A Critical Study* it therefore seemed natural to pursue my interest in this idea. I was encouraged to do this by a number of colleagues and friends; notably Reima Pietilä, Kenneth Frampton, Emile Capouya, Holmes Perkins, Robert Kennedy, Michael Bakewell, James Fitzsimmons, Tom Rosenthal, Christian Bergum, Bruce Webb and Gerald McSheffrey. In 1984 I was awarded a Fellowship by the Graham Foundation for Advanced Studies in the Fine Arts, Chicago, to allow me to complete and publish this study.

I am grateful to David Woodcock and Donald Sweeney of the College of Architecture at Texas A&M University for creating the opportunity to present some of this material in lectures at the University, and in Vienna at the invitation of Professor Timo Penttilä and Professor Anton Schweighofer.

I should like to express my gratitude to MIT Press for permission to quote extensively from Aldo Rossi's *The Architecture of the City,* and to Ohio University Press for permission to redraw and reproduce plans from *The Architectural Planning of St. Petersburg* by Iruii Alekseevich Egorov. My thanks are also due to H.R.H. Princess Alia al Hussein and Miss P. Vickers, who kindly drew the maps of Petra.

My editorial colleagues at Schocken Books, Merope Lolis and Millicent Fairhurst, brought to our collaboration an admirable combination of enthusiasm, tolerance and good humor. Through her persistent enquiries and patient criticism, and the valuable suggestions she made during our final editing of the text, Molly McCormick persuaded me to make substantial revisions in search of accuracy and clarity. The many hours she spent reading the manuscript, and on corrections and retyping are also much appreciated. I am grateful for her incisive critique of my ideas.

Finally, I must acknowledge my indebtedness to my wife, Esther, and my two young daughters, Francesca and Alexandra: in Jordan, Montana, Texas and Finland they sacrificed many hours of family life to these enquiries.

MALCOLM QUANTRILL
Texas A&M University
May 1986

INTRODUCTION

Our present-day sense of architectural and city form, and of space and distance—our sense of the physical limitations of existence—has been dramatically changed by twentieth-century modes of travel and communications. Speedy travel on land and intercontinental travel by air perfected during the past half-century have joined with television and telecommunications to give us a radically different perspective on space–time relationships from that possessed by our forebears. These changes in perception are dramatic in the true sense that our participation in the theater of environment is now much more extensive in scope and much less intimate in detailed involvement.

Today, as we travel from place to place we are increasingly cut off from our environment and our surroundings. More and more we find our sensitivity to places and environments is diminished by the speed at which we travel to or through them. Walking pace coincides rather well with our ability to identify and respond to phenomena around us. Running is more concerned with goals than paths: we want to catch that bus at the end of the street. Climbing the hundreds of steps within an ancient tower, we find ourselves becoming detached from our present exertions and more connected to the dreams of those who built the tower—hoping their construction will survive our assault. In the elevator, however, we are simply suspended in time and space as though in a vessel that transports us from one world to the next. Similarly, from the airplane our view of the world below, unrolling effortlessly, might just as well be the videotape that accompanies the music piped into our ears.

In short, our world is being synthesized. In the media, by travel, in the supermarket, and in the department store, the distinguishing elements of environments—the *genius loci* with its particular contrasts of form and effect, the landscape framework, and man's complementary pattern of geometric coordinates—all are being replaced by the endless tube. Whether it takes the form of aircraft, mall, or warehouse is unimportant. The space–time tube extrudes a universal synthetic environment in which both reality and the dream are controlled by the media or conditioned by the uniform theater of marketing. Under sophisticated commercial lighting the "corporeal similitudes"[1] of our increasingly uniform selves present few surprises: there is too much glare to allow us to focus on details and particulars. Thus, little is memorable for more than a few hours. The symbolic quality of images, which imparts "magic" or "energy"[2] to a place, is bleached out by the generalizing artifice of light and color, speed of passage, and loss of contact and dialogue.

Cut off from experience, we find it more and more difficult to relate to buildings and also to the spaces within and between them. In effect, we have laid aside the tools of civilization and entered a traveling theater of technical props. In consequence we no longer give a true value to architecture and the city: instead, we have relegated these essential artifacts of civilization to a purely ceremonial function. They are no longer part of our existential world. Unlike the Greek orator and the medieval scholar we do not see buildings as part of memory patterns, and therefore we do not invest them in turn with our own memories. The loss of the architectural and urban framework from our memories is an enormous one, because it has literally reduced the amount of traveling we can do in the mind. When we read a poem we cover enormous distances with the aid of our mind's eye: we travel by invoking and inventing images of people, things, and places. Our familiarity with things and places greatly enriches our source of images, because even when the thing or place we are trying to imagine is unfamiliar to us, we can make a model of it in our minds, using bits of the things and places we do know to construct that model.[3]

The real terror that characterized *1984* is coming to exist in the nearest shopping mall. In fact, we are condemned to a fixed moment in time, a sort of eternal present that has no meaningful reference to history or precedent and in which there are few poetic images or none. Without real understanding of the precision and articulation of geometrical coordinates, with virtual indifference to the structure of spoken and written language, we seem determined to wipe out the art of memory altogether, content to replace it with a staring eye that sweeps across a view of science and technology on the one hand, and a facade of cultural bric-a-brac on the other. We appear so intent upon inventing the world de novo that we are prepared to do so without the wisdom and experience of the ancients. The Renaissance Humanists sifted through eclectic sources in order to seek an underlying wisdom, a philosophical and metaphysical cause for the human condition. Our present siftings, however, are directed toward finding some amusing eclectic effects. Will the farce distract us from the reality that man is reducing himself to a creature without memory?

Frances Yates warns us of this state of affairs: "If a building has an immaterial existence in the mind of the architect before it is built, it has also many immaterial existences in the memories of those who have seen it. . . . Possibly architectural memory, which depends upon detail, will die out as buildings and cities grow more uniform, and air travel blurs the distinction between places."[4] Yet why should we fear a world of increasingly uniform patterns when such uniformity provides one of the principal stimuli for our capacity to challenge convention? The great potential of modernism, after all, was its drive toward a new and vital imagery, particularly in poetry and painting. Modern architecture and urbanism, however, have not fully explored this imagic potential. Breaking with convention, or opposing it, implies an understanding of what that convention is, and requires the capacity to build upon rather than derive from that convention. Lacking that understanding and capacity, many architects today have returned either to an eclecticism eschewed by the founding modernists as sheer parody, or to a rationalism based not on industrial techniques but on the *memory* of some rational forms from the past.[5] Thus, at the end of the twentieth century the poetic imagination has become impoverished and we are struggling once again with elementary problems of grammar and syntax. There simply is no poetic image or symbolic structure beneath the eclectic surface of appearance. Gaston Bachelard's phenomenological critique, *The Poetics of Space* (1969), illuminates this problem brilliantly:

> If there be a philosophy of poetry, it must appear and re-appear through a significant verse, in total adherence to an isolated image; to be exact in the very ecstasy of the newness of the image. The poetic image is a sudden salience on the surface of the psyche . . .
>
> The reader of poems is asked to consider an image not as an object and even less as a substitute for an object, but to seize its specific reality. . . .
>
> To specify exactly what a phenomenology of the image can be, to specify that the image comes *before* thought, we should have to say that poetry, rather than being a phenomenology of the mind, is a phenomenology of the soul. We should then have to collect documentation on the subject of the *dreaming consciousness*.[6]

In the spirit of Bachelard's illumination, my own study is an exploration of imagic memory and our "dreaming consciousness" as the basic tools of the creative, poetic imagination. My interpretation of "dreaming consciousness" may diverge, however, from that of Bachelard who says, "The poetic image is independent of causality," and again, "The poetic act has no past."[7] In exploring environmental memory, we must allow for the process of assimilating poetic depth as well as our being "receptive to the image at the moment it appears."[8] Since "poetry, rather than being a phenomenology of the mind, is a phenomenology of the soul," it must follow that poetic imagery cannot depend upon surface effects alone but must also strike deeper resonances. Indeed, the test of a successful poetic image must not only be that it hits the target first time but that it remains embedded in our memory and therefore our consciousness.

Thanks to the house, a great many of our memories are housed, and if the house is a bit elaborate, if it has a cellar and a garret, nooks and corridors, our memories have refuges that are all the more clearly delineated. All our lives we come back to them in our daydreams. A psychoanalyst should, therefore, turn his attention to this simple localization of our memories [to which] I should like to give the name of topoanalysis. . . . At times we think we know ourselves in time, when all we know is the sequence of fixations in the spaces of the being's stability. . . . In its countless alveoli space contains compressed time. That is what space is for.

The topologist starts to ask questions: Was the room a large one? Was the garret cluttered up? Was the nook warm? How was it lighted? How, too, in these fragments of space, did the human being achieve silence? . . . Memory—what a strange thing it is!—does not record concrete duration, in the Bergsonian sense of the word. We are unable to relive duration that has been destroyed. We can only think of it, in the line of an abstract time that is deprived of all thickness. . . . Memories are motionless, and the more securely they are fixed in space, the sounder they are.

—GASTON BACHELARD,
The Poetics of Space

PART ONE

▲

ARCHITECTURE AS THE TOOL-KIT OF MEMORY

Architecture fulfills cultural functions without which civilization is impossible; it is part of our man-made environment which remembers and gives order to human action. This it does by having a durable structure of suitable proportions.

—Frode Strømnes, "On the Architecture of Thought"

ONE
▲
THE HOUSE OF MEMORY

Frances Yates opens *Giordano Bruno and the Hermetic Tradition* (1964) with some observations that, two decades later, comment even more poignantly on the progressive ideas of modern man:

> The great forward movements of the Renaissance all derive their vigour, their emotional impulse, from looking backwards. The cyclic view of time as a perpetual movement from pristine golden ages of purity and truth through successive brazen and iron ages still held sway and the search for truth was thus of necessity a search for the early, the ancient, the original gold from which the baser metals of the present and the immediate past were corrupt degenerations. Man's history was not an evolution from primitive animal origins through ever growing complexity and progress; the past was always better than the present, and progress was revival, rebirth, renaissance of antiquity. The classical humanist recovered the literature and the monuments of classical antiquity with a sense of return to the pure gold of a civilisation better and higher than his own.[1]

Giordano Bruno and the Hermetic Tradition was the first of three books Yates wrote about aspects of memory.[2] In them I find drawn, with extraordinary erudition and great lucidity, a complex web of signs, symbols, numbers, and concepts that reaches back into antiquity like a multidimensional ladder, a lattice of mnemonic codes constructed by a succession of mystics and scholars. Throughout the centuries their purpose, allowing for interruptions and waverings in the Middle Ages, remained constant. Yates reveals how they wanted to create a pattern of ideas and language that linked the limits of the known world with the seemingly limitless unknown beyond human experience. We can see that their purpose was to extend man's consciousness not only of things but also of concepts into that realm where the mind encounters another more elusive self whose typological classification is less matter of fact. Indeed, I detect that seeds of the psychoanalytic distinction between ego and id were sown already in the fifteenth century. The essential difference between these proto-Renaissance explorations of knowledge and modern ones was the desire of scholars then to weld the "phenomenology of mind" and the "phenomenology of soul" (in Bachelard's terms) into one coherent whole. Modern psychology, in contrast, has cleaved the conscious ego from its psychic partner the id, so that the shadowy ego stands outside the marriage observing the divorce of thinking self from feeling self.

Ethical problems characterized the writings of the early Renaissance. The Humanist search for rigor and for beauty has been well described by André Chastel in *The Myth of the Renaissance*.[3] When Petrarch (Francesco Petrarca, 1304–1374) wrote his *Secretum* in the early 1340s, he confessed to vague desires, leaning more toward introspection than toward wisdom, which nonetheless he could not bring himself to abandon. How was he to overcome this problem? Then in 1345 he made a discovery important for the proto-Renaissance, when he came upon Cicero's letters to Atticus, in which the complete man was revealed. There he saw that Cicero combined an interest in the problems of public and private life, of both politics and ethics, while also devoting himself to the study of philosophy and the mysteries of life and death.

When Leonardo Bruni translated the *Nicomachean Ethics* in 1417 he wanted to remove from Aristotle the Christian bias that had been introduced by the Scholastics. This correction of the Scholastics' misinterpretation of the ancient texts took root and led to Neo-Platonism. Cristofore Landino's dialogue, *Disputationes Camaldulenses* (c. 1475), idealized the active life in a eulogy put into the mouth of the great

Florentine humanist, Leon Battista Alberti (died 1472), while the life of contemplation was championed in the person of the young Lorenzo de'Medici. The underlying questions in this dialogue are: "Is man born to know or to act?" and "Can the question of the true aim of life be avoided?". For Renaissance thinkers, these questions characterized both their spirit of enquiry and also their moral dilemmas. These changing attitudes toward man and his ideas, and particularly toward the heritage represented by classical texts, lay at the heart of the Humanist revolution we call the Renaissance, a revolution that truly heralded the birth of modern rationalism.[4]

In the first place, Renaissance scholars found that by looking beneath the surface of pagan poetry a layer of high moral significance was revealed. Only the pagan myths and heathen imagery obscured this truth. Or perhaps they did no such thing? After all poetic imagery and symbolic representation are our principal means of glimpsing the world behind physical appearance. Had not classical mythology described in graphic detail the struggles between the soul and the phantasmagoric underworld of the mind? The Renaissance poet, seeking insights into his own joys and sorrows, found it difficult to better the imagery of the mythical labors of Hercules or misfortunes of Orpheus, a burden that continues to haunt poets to this day. To reveal inner truth, double meanings became commonplace in Renaissance poetry, just as they were in the imagery of Renaissance painting, sculpture, and architecture. This duality produced two fundamental changes in man's consciousness: a new, underlying belief in the basic commonality of religious ideas, and respect for the importance and sacred significance of Eros as the universal symbol of love. For a true understanding of the Renaissance, we must grasp the impact made upon art and life by the spread of these two radical ideas.

As a parallel to Landino's question "Is man born to know or to act?" the translation of Plato's *Symposium* raised the question "Can the soul have life without love?"[5] Love, as the source of all objective beauty as well as of the soul's subjective response, was taken to be a complex phenomenon that, of religious necessity, had to be graded from coarse to fine. Naturally, the mixture of love and religion offered the most precious potion, to be compounded as the result of man's successful struggle to overcome his sensory, animal being and his strivings to achieve that level of intelligence where body and soul coexist in perfect harmony. The importance of this Renaissance marriage of Christian *caritas* and a finely graded manifestation of Eros is its new accent on the concept of beauty and its correspondence with a growing awareness and appreciation of the representational arts—painting, sculpture, and architecture. Thus, feelings, emotions, and passions that had been largely sublimated during the Middle Ages once again found overt expression as a result of the rediscovery of classical texts and pagan ideas. Petrarch's *Secretum* may be seen as the beginning of this process, bringing a medieval man's innermost, nonspiritual rumblings to the written page, to be followed later in the fourteenth century by Boccaccio's *Decameron* and Chaucer's *The Canterbury Tales*. Before the invention of printing these revelations were still very discreet, and their circulation extremely limited. Belief in a basic unity of all religions, and the concept of Eros as a component of the soul, both of which enjoyed wide currency by the end of the fifteenth century, not only radically affected the forms and imagery of painting, sculpture, and architecture, but also promoted a philosophical eroticism in literature that blurred the boundaries between the pagan underworld, the sinful world we inhabit, and the Christian heaven. Many Italian writers, for example Marsilio Ficino, Count Giovanni Pico della Mirandola, and Celso Maffei, sought to stress the gap between our earthbound, rational existence and the utmost limits of sensibility; they sought to bring immortal love into mortal beauty, and mortal love into immortal beauty. Eventually, painters, sculptors, and architects of the Baroque period combined their talents to put heaven and earth together on the same stage.

It was all part of a surge of enquiry, an exploration into the very depths of mind and soul, the philosopher's task in which was to explain the processes of conscious thought, the means by which the soul comes to grips with the scheme of things, the phenomenology of language, images, and ideas. Again we find the roots of those peculiarly modern phenomena, psychology and psychoanalysis, in the fifteenth century. Ficino translated and closely studied *De insomniis* by the Neo-Platonist Synesio, who expounded the theory of dreams. He described "a *pneuma* or subtle entity, acting as a subliminal mentor and forming the substratum of our dreams."[6] Synesio conceived of a "pneumatic envelope" of the soul, distinguishing between *phantasia* as a faculty of the rational soul, and imagination as a faculty of the sensitive soul, and believed that "the imagination is privileged domain midway between soul and body."[7] From this privileged position, according to Synesio, it is possible at every moment for the imagination to interpret our "inner states" in terms of both their astral symbolism and their sensory relations to musical harmony. This dual role of the imagination, as conceived by Synesio, is an unmistakably Neo-Platonist idea. The Neo-

Platonist ideal sought to unite all aspects of the mind as integral parts of a coherent whole, which accounts for the success of Neo-Platonism and the abhorrence of it by many bishops. George of Trebizond summed up these fears when he wrote of the appearance of Plethon of Mistra at the Council of Florence in 1440:

> I heard him with my own ears, when he came with the Greeks to Florence for the Council, declaring that soon the whole world would adopt one and the same religion, share the same feelings, the same ideas, and believe in the same doctrine. When asked "That of Christ or that of Mohammed?" he answered "Neither of them, but a faith identical with that of the pagans."[8]

At the heart of this surge of enquiry was a network of mysticism inherited from the classical world and known as the Hermetic tradition. This tradition was an extraordinary cipher of secrets—some divine, some magical, and others seemingly nonsensical—through which philosophers hoped to achieve a perfect understanding of cosmic order and meaning. During the Middle Ages all elements of magic embraced by this tradition were outlawed by the Church as heretical and diabolical. When the Borgia Pope, Alexander VI (1492–1503), came to the papal throne, however, these Hermetic enquiries were permitted again. The significance for us of the Hermetic tradition is the part it played in perpetuating memory patterns that link the categorization and celebration of cosmic forces with the use of number, dimension, order, and space in architectural or environmental memory. Yates makes a convincing case for a link between Hermetic principles, the secrets of the medieval mason, and the immaterial dimension of their buildings.[9]

Of course "the pure gold of a civilization better and higher than his own" (as Yates said in opening *Giordano Bruno*) literally implied for the classical Humanist that precious metal which the alchemist sought with his necromancy. Furthermore, the pagan ideas of the classical world had not been eliminated when Christianity became the official religion of the Roman Empire following the Edict of Milan in 313 A.D. They had simply been embalmed in libraries awaiting resurrection and rebirth in the fifteenth century. Almost immediately following their rediscovery, translation, and elaboration of Marsilio Ficino and Pico della Mirandola came the invention of printing around 1470. Significantly, Ficino's *Pimander* (his translation of the *Corpus Hermeticum* brought to Florence from Macedonia by a monk around 1460) was one of the earliest printed works, its first edition dating from 1471, with fifteen further editions before the end of the sixteenth century. Thus, the occultism, astrology, and alchemy that had been purportedly recorded by Hermes Trismegistus, of whom Roger Bacon wrote as the "Father of Philosophers," was made generally available to scholars and educated amateurs. Indeed, since the *Corpus Hermeticum* had been acknowledged by the early fathers of the Church to be older than Plato, Cosimo de'Medici commanded Ficino in 1463 to set aside his translation of the Plato manuscripts so that Cosimo might have the Hermes to read before he died. It is quite inconceivable today that such a key work as Plato's *Republic* could have taken second place to the *Corpus Hermeticum,* but it irrefutably demonstrates the Humanist thirst for astrology and alchemy, which were known to be older sciences than Greek philosophy.

In spite of their suppression in the Middle Ages, interest in alchemy and magic lived on. Although Albertus Magnus specifically censured some of the works of Hermes for their diabolical magic, interest in the black arts persisted. The memory of evil, damnation, and eternal punishment was celebrated by medieval sculptors as much as the holy virtues, salvation, and the promise of Paradise. Whereas the concept of man's fall from grace and his subsequent salvation through Christ the Redeemer was almost universally accepted or enforced, nagging doubts certainly remained in the minds of some thinking men. Indeed, Ficino's translation of Hermes in *Pimander* unveiled the Egyptian Genesis, wherein man reveals himself to nature as God. As he leans down from heaven to earth, man recognizes his own image in nature reflected in the water. At that moment he falls in love with nature and wishes to dwell with her, a wish immediately accomplished. In this way man assumes "the irrational form."[10] Clearly, such a description of man's relationship to his maker conflicted radically with Christian orthodoxy.

Interestingly, Pico della Mirandola's appearance on the scene brought the division of magic into the "natural" and the "Cabalistic." Natural (or scientific) magic, lacking the respectability of a Hebrew origin, was thought of as the weaker of the two. The Cabala, being connected to the Mosaic tradition of language and law through the Hebrew alphabet, Hebraic word codes, demonstrably derived more closely from the ancient sources of wisdom and virtue. Since their formal constitution in the early seventeenth century, the Masonic Orders have traced their endeavors back to the building of Solomon's Temple, and therefore implied that their origins have some connection with Jewish law and religious inheritance. Pico's preference for the Cabalistic strain, a snub for Ficino whose Hebrew was largely nonexistent, also underscores the revival of pagan eclecticism, reflected in the diversity of sources tolerated in tracing the roots of wisdom and knowledge. This eclecticism helps to explain, how Renaissance church design so readily adopted the plan types and models of pagan temples, and how the iconography of classical mythology came to be so quickly blended with Christian hagiography. For the moment, evidence of Egyptian mythology was still buried in the desert sands—the Egyptian myths that reemerged in fifteenth-century Florence having been transformed at the hands of Greek authors. But one thing was soon abundantly clear: all that was pagan, pre-Christian, and throughout the Middle Ages considered to smack of the devil, was now released into the Christian consciousness. Representations of this older, golden, and occult way of life not only challenged Christian orthodoxy, they coexisted with it.

The rediscovery of the Hermetic tradition gave Renaissance scholars an opportunity to examine an alternative theology and cosmogony to that presented by Christianity. Thus, in the evolution of the Humanist, Neo-Platonist tradition, these two diverging representations of consciousness flourished side by side and even intertwined. In this way the conflation of pagan and Christian symbols and mythologies, which had characterized the early centuries of the Church within Roman society, was reenacted in the Renaissance, in reverse. But this reenactment was not a perverse exercise or one simply based upon diabolic interests and pursuits. It is not at all a mystery of occultism and of superstition. Rather, it is the history of the Humanists' determination to relearn the undoubted wisdom of the ancients in the unfettered pursuit of knowledge. They wanted to reexplore the systems of consciousness that had been largely forgotten during the expansion of Christian society in the Middle Ages.

To do this the Humanists had to locate those ancient ideas and methods that had remained known to only a few, or had been buried in private and monastic libraries, but in any case had gone out of currency and were no longer in general circulation. This break in the continuity of thought and practice had been a gradual process, and the ideas and traditions of the ancient world were slow to die. Indeed, the emergence of the Church and its evolution through the latter stages of the Roman Empire, and then on into the Byzantine Empire, necessarily entailed a blending of the old with the new. In their assemblage of many fragments, the famous mosaics of the Ravenna churches and of

San Marco in Venice symbolize the bringing together of diverse pieces into a composite picture of reality. These pictures represent the intermarriage of two traditions, the pagan Roman with the Christian, to form the new Christian Imperial world. Within the Byzantine Empire these composite mosaics of tradition remained intact until the fifteenth century (shortly before the invention of printing), although from the tenth century onwards the Byzantine world had become increasingly remote and isolated from developments in Europe.

When Byzantium fell at the end of the fifteenth century, the standards of order and civilization achieved by the Romans had also long since fallen into disrepair. Parts of Italy still had substantial Roman remains, and through the persistence of Byzantine influence from Ravenna up to Venice the north-east coastal plain evidenced continuing architectural links between past and present. But these Byzantine "memories" preserved a frozen tradition, a *mosaic* of pagan and Christian societies recorded in the act of merging. Technically, the mosaics themselves reflected Roman practice as carried on by Byzantine architects and artists, but they did not represent ancient ideas per se. Even though the Byzantine world was essentially static and backward looking, nevertheless it did not actually offer a mirror of the ancient world. In the Byzantine world of the fifteenth century, in spite of fragmentary links to antiquity, there was no overall picture of continuity with ancient traditions, values, and wisdom. In contrast, the evolution of Western monastic orders created a new source of continuity between Christian ethics and Greek philosophy, with the Dominican friars in particular being influential in this sphere of knowledge. Two of their number, Albertus Magnus and Thomas Aquinas, are of special interest to us as links in the chain of philosophy and memory. It was Aquinas, after all, who enlisted Greek ethics to answer heretics and turned Aristotle from a potential enemy into an ally of the Church. Yet the memory of the ancient world remained very incomplete in Europe during the Middle Ages and, as we know, the Scholastics' interpretation of classical texts had a distinctly Christian bias.

What might at first have seemed to be an attempt to trade Christian orthodoxy for the dubious values of pagan occultism was to lead, within two centuries, to the founding of new societies concerned with exploring the secrets of existence. These new societies were not only secret ones, however, but also a new genre of serious scientific foundations such as the Royal Society chartered by King Charles II in England and the Académie des Sciences in France. The establishment of these societies in the seventeenth century created a climate favorable to generating the structure of our modern world of ideas and inventions. What the Renaissance demonstrated is that the remembrance of things past can hold the key to the future, but only if this remembrance involves exploration of both the rational and the irrational forces within us.

The irony is that when the Renaissance Humanists sought to regain ancient wisdom they inevitably reintroduced magic and myth into the consciousness equation. Christian doctrinal theory opposes pagan superstition, yet we know that such superstition continued to thrive throughout the Middle Ages and indeed has remained embedded in many branches of the Church until recent time. Although the Church in the Middle Ages taught only "religious truth," keeping dangerous manuscripts hidden from all but a few religious scholars, nevertheless an oral tradition persisted that assured the transmission of distorted versions of the Cabala and garbled bits of *Hermes Trismegistus*.

Since myths are humanity's attempts to explain world order, and magic and religion are efforts to bridge natural and supernatural elements of existence, people cannot long deny their intrinsic interest in the "magical" or the "miraculous." Indeed, we often speak of "magic" in our discussion of present-day events. We may find the performance of a play or a recital by a musician "magical," meaning that it had some extraordinary or poetic quality beyond our normal experience of the theater or music.

In visiting a place we sometimes become aware of an extraordinary atmosphere that we find difficult or impossible to describe in rational language: we are simply conscious of that place adding up to more than the sum of its parts and having an additional, inexplicable dimension. Indeed, when we find a place to be "memorable" it is usually the result of our having remarked that extra something. Architecture serves as a memory system for ideas about human origins, a means of recording understanding of order and relationships in the world, and an attempt to grasp the concept of the eternal cosmos which has no fixed dimensions, with neither beginning nor end. Yates's discussion of the classical ideas about the role of memory in consciousness and knowledge, and particularly the part played by architecture in the ancient memory system, is therefore of great interest to us here.

Simonides of Ceos, the Greek poet who is credited with inventing the art of memory, reputedly did so by identifying for relatives the mutilated corpses of the guests after the collapse of a banqueting hall roof.

This he apparently did by recalling precisely where each guest had been seated at the banquet table. That is, he pictured who had been sitting next to whom. His ability to make this recollection led him to conclude that a sense of order is essential to a good memory, for without his *visual picture* of just who had been sitting on either side of whom he would not have been able to perform this feat of memory.

Order is, of course, also the essential prerequisite of architectural space. How Simonides came to invent the art of memory is told by Cicero in *De oratore*. Cicero goes on to describe the device of *loci* and *imagines*—that is, *places* and *images*—used by Roman orators as the basic technique for memorizing public orations. As part of the art of rhetoric, then, the art of memory was passed down through the European tradition, and according to Yates was remembered as such until relatively recent times.

The first step of the mnemonic technique, which some call mnemotechnics, was to store in the memory a series of *loci* or places. The commonest type of mnemonic place system employed by classical orators and rhetors was the architectural one. Yates quotes Quintilian's *Institutio oratoria* as the clearest source of this process. A spacious and varied building is recommended for the purpose; the orator (or rhetor) is to include the forecourt, living room, bedrooms, and parlors as well as the statues, ornaments, and decorations. In other words, the entire environment of the building is to provide the storage system for memorizing an oration. The speech to be memorized must then be labeled with images, so that a precise visual idea corresponds to each part of the text. These images are then placed in imagination upon features and details of the building that has already been committed to memory. Subsequently, when the orator comes to make his speech, he is able to revisit the building, "seeing" again in his mind's eye the images that recall the salient parts of his text because he will "find" them in the memorized parts of the building where he has previously placed them. As the orator moves around the remembered building in his imagination, he will find all the points of his speech in the correct order, since that order is fixed in the sequence of spaces in the building. Yates emphasizes the importance of trained memory for the ancient world, which had no printing or even paper on which to take notes: "Ancient memories were trained by an art which reflected the art and architecture of the ancient world, which could depend on faculties of intense visual memorization that we have lost."[11]

More important than the observations of Cicero and Quintilian for our understanding of this art is an anonymous textbook compiled at the beginning of the first century B.C. by a teacher of rhetoric for use by his students. It is called simply *Ad Herennium,* in honor of the man to whom it was dedicated. Its importance derives from four characteristics: (1) it is based on Greek sources of memory teaching, and probably on Greek treatises on rhetoric that have vanished without trace; (2) it is the only complete source of the classical art of memory as practiced by the Greek and Latin worlds; (3) it was therefore the main transmitter of this classical art to the Middle Ages (during which period it was believed to be the work of Cicero himself) and the Renaissance; (4) all subsequent treatises on the art of memory inevitably draw upon *Ad Herennium.*

The author of *Ad Herennium* discusses the five parts of rhetoric: *inventio, dispositio, elocutio, memoria,* and *pronuntiatio.* He declares memory, however, to be "the treasure-house of inventions, the custodian of all parts of rhetoric," and says that memory is of two kinds, *natural* and *artificial.* We are born with a natural memory, he tells us, while the artificial memory is one improved by training. Thus, the art of memory is the art of training our natural memory by artificial means so its performance may be heightened.[12] Significantly, those following Simonides chose architecture—an art of order and cultural representation even more ancient than the art of memory—as the spatial and formal framework to use for remembering their critical images.

Our anonymous author speaks of the locus as a place that is easily grasped by the memory—for example, a house, a colonnade, an arch, or a corner feature—while *images* are forms, marks, or *simulacra* of what we wish to remember. He describes the art of memory as a sort of "inner writing" like making inscriptions in one's head, and suggests that the places are rather "like wax tablets or papyrus, the images like the letters" of the alphabet, "the arrangement and disposition of the images like the script, and the delivery is like the reading" of those notes.[13] He suggests that deserted or solitary places offer the best loci, an unfrequented building providing special advantages, as he believes that passing crowds of people confuse the spatial order and weaken impressions of its form and details. Also, the loci should be varied in character: not so large as to make them difficult to grasp, or so small as to become "overcrowded" with the images placed on them. In addition, the loci must not be too brightly lit (for fear of losing the image in glare) or too dark (for fear of losing the image in shadow). Formation of the loci is of the greatest importance, because a good set may be used again and again for remembering different material; material no longer required can be effaced, while the loci, resembling wax tablets, remain ready to be "written on" once more. Our unknown author stresses the ordering of the loci, and suggests that each fifth locus be given a distinguishing image and each tenth locus receive further emphasis.[14] Thus, the whole architectural world of space, form, light, character, dimension, and number is brought into the mind as the structure of memory and, therefore, of thought.

If buildings, environments, and even whole cities can be used as the frameworks for learning such as memory training, then we can begin to understand the complex role of architecture in the whole structure of human consciousness and the continuity of knowledge. For it becomes clear that architectural form and detail not only embody memories of some event, myth, or article of faith, but are intrinsically memorable themselves. As mnemonics they become those "wax tablets" that are capable of receiving additional "inscriptions" of memorable information.

This understanding of architecture and the city allows us to perceive not only their passive roles as memories of cultural history but also to accord them a significant function in our own consciousness of passing through time and space. Through our oral and written traditions, it is possible to transfer knowledge and ideas from generation to generation. At an early stage humanity decided that architecture is itself a kind of magic. Once imbued with representations of myth and belief the built works become architecture of thought, creating in the natural environment a complementary artificial landscape of ideas.

Whatever Albertus Magnus did to discourage the theory and practice of magic, he helped carry the mnemonic techniques described in *Ad Herrenium* through the Middle Ages by teaching the principles of artificial memory to Thomas Aquinas and others. In the second portion of the second part of the *Summa,* Aquinas describes the role of images and "similitudes" in the artificial training of memory. His purpose is ethical and spiritual, of course, when he writes: "It is necessary in this way to invent similitudes and images because simple and spiritual intentions slip easily from the soul unless they are as it were linked to some corporeal similitudes, because human cognition is stronger in regard to the sensibilia."[15] But his reference to corporeal representations to enhance the memory and his acceptance of the sensibilia as an inherent component of human cognition must be remarked. This cognitive aspect of the senses was explicitly recognized by Aquinas elsewhere in the *Summa:* "The senses delight in things duly proportioned as in something akin to them; for, the sense, too, is a kind of reason as is every cognitive power."[16] In *Gothic Architecture and Scholasticism,* Erwin Panofsky suggested that the high Gothic cathedral resembles a scholastic *summa* because its arrangement is "a system of homologous parts and parts of parts." Frances Yates comments, as follows: "The extraordinary thought now arises that if Thomas Aquinas memorized his own *Summa* through 'corporeal similitudes' disposed on places following the order of its parts, the abstract *Summa* might be corporealized in memory into something like a Gothic cathedral full of images of its ordered places."[17]

This is truly an extraordinary suggestion, because it reminds us not of the points of difference that distinguish a Gothic cathedral from, say, a Roman bath, but of the shared disciplines of order and harmony in the constructional and expressive systems of both. It is all too easy to think of Gothic architecture, the geometry and proportions of which are elusive, as something that anticipates modern organic design. Antonio Gaudí's work might be quoted as providing a bridge between Gothic and organic forms, exaggerating, as it does, the embodiment of natural forms found in medieval architecture and imagery. Of course, when an architectural system does not clearly demonstrate its formal, geometric origins, we have more difficulty in identifying the connection with its "roots." As Summerson suggests: "The porches of Chartres are, in distribution and proportion, just about as classical as you can get, *but nobody is ever going to call them anything but Gothic.*"[18] In other words, our memory of what is classical or Gothic is conditioned by custom which affects our judgment. Let us call Christopher Wren as a witness here. In his *Discourse* Wren observes:

> I have found no little difficulty to bring Persons, of otherwise a good genius, to think anything in Architecture could be better than what they have heard commended by others, and what they had viewed themselves. Many good Gothic forms of Cathedrals were to be seen in our country, and many had been seen abroad, which they liked the better for being not much differing from ours in England: this humour with many is not yet eradicated, and therefore I judge it not improper to reform the Generality to a truer taste in Architecture by giving a larger Idea of the whole Art, beginning with the reasons and progress of it from the most remote Antiquity.[19]

Wren had only a brief meeting with Bernini in Paris in 1665, with merely a glance at the Italian architect's designs for the Palais du Louvre, yet the Englishman, on his only visit abroad, clearly felt himself capable of memorizing the basic architectural ideas and outlines of a project he saw for only a few minutes. It was apparently not Wren's habit to go around with a sketchbook, recording the buildings that interested him with his crayon, but he was able to take good mental notes of compositions and plans which he could later disgorge with the aid of verbal and graphic descriptions. He later wrote to a colleague, "I had only Time to copy it in my Fancy and Memory: I shall be able by Discourse, and a Crayon, to give you a tolerable account of it."[20] His visit to France was of immense importance to Wren because, apart from Inigo Jones's few architectural works in London, he had seen no built examples of the Renaissance style from which to learn his newly acquired profession. As we know from his *Discourse,* Wren was eager to override the English memory for Gothic architecture and move his nation forward, in the Renaissance sense, by going back to the true roots of architecture. His brief glimpse of the Bernini design for the Louvre therefore represented a significant moment in Wren's career.

Wren's prevailing obsession, as expressed in the central idea of the *Discourse,* was to put the classical framework of ideals and forms back into the practice of architecture. Inigo Jones had already undertaken this task with some effect in completed projects for the Queen's House at Greenwich, St. Paul's Church in Covent Garden, the Banqueting Hall of the projected Whitehall Palace, and the exterior remodeling of St. Paul's Cathedral. But Jones was an artist, a painter, and stage designer, whose perceptions of architectural form, although derived from Palladio, were rooted in surface effects and appearances. Wren, on the other hand, was a scientist, a geometer, and an astronomer, whose interests quickly came to focus on the structure of the plan and elevations. He found it necessary to grapple with the geometric constituents of form, and then to order his architectural solutions according to architectural principles. It was most probably for this reason that he could memorize Bernini's basic ideas of plan and elevation so readily. On the other hand, it is almost certain that the more complex "hidden" geometric system of a Gothic cathedral would have eluded the architecturally inexperienced Wren. Even so, in the wake of Restoration emphasis on science, and the establishment of the Royal Society, of which he was a founding member, Wren was in a better position to translate classical ideals into English than Jones had been in the climate immediately preceding the Revolution and the creation of Cromwell's Commonwealth.

Some developments in psychology have confirmed aspects of ancient understanding of memory. The Norwegian psychologist, Frode

Strømnes, traces memory research back to the work of Hermann Ebbinghaus on cognitive functioning in the 1870s. To ensure that material to be learned was "new" (free from the influence of previous learning) Ebbinghaus devised his so-called "meaningless syllables," by which he concluded that the degree to which any material is forgotten is a function of how well it has been practiced.[21]

Commenting on experiments in the United States in the late 1950s, in which subjects learned extremely long lists of word pairs by responding to instructions that they should form *images* which linked the meaning of the two words, Strømnes found it was possible to show that this outstanding power of the image could be used in other situations as well.[22] Researchers seemed to have stumbled upon a new and significant trait of human memory. Perhaps images, being easy to remember, might also be the basis for memory?

As Strømnes points out, research during the 1970s showed that the spoken or written text is seemingly retained in short-term storage for only a few seconds, and thereafter an extracted "meaning" is stored in the brain. He asks whether this implies that meaning is to be equated with image.[23] This hypothesis should certainly interest the architect because he works with images: his creations are visible ones. If what we see is of central importance in psychic functioning, then this relationship between image and meaning, if demonstrated, would greatly enhance the value of the architect's work.

Strømnes reports Janellen Huttenlocher's research into problem solving by children, with the resulting conclusion that the children solved the problems by using imagery. He comments:

> [I]t was formerly held that "thinking is speaking in one's head." Now someone was telling us that thinking, at least in children, is seeing images in one's head. . . . Attempts were made to explain the results by assuming how the children would have had to speak "in their heads" if they were to solve the problems. But later research has been able to show that "speaking in the head" hypotheses cannot be correct: it really seems that people can think by using images in their heads.[24]

The implications of this rediscovery are clearly important to all of us, especially to architects. As Strømnes observes, if an architect wants to inform his public about a plan, a building, or an environment, he makes a scale model. The more the details of the model resemble the details of the real building, the more information the model contains.

Thus, an object resembling another object can contain information about that object, and the closer the resemblance, the more information is stored. If the resemblance or isomorphism is total, all the information contained in one object can be stored in another. On the other hand, if there is no structural resemblance, then no information is stored about the other object. This fact must surely be important in architectural language, both in terms of its roots and its derivatives, for it affects the entire nature and quality of representation (see chapter 5).

Imagery must be essential to our understanding of the world about us, for words themselves have practically no resemblance to the objects and events to which they refer. The word "cow" is entirely useless as a model for a cow; its physical structure contains no information about a cow. On the other hand, the brain must of necessity include a structure which really holds information about cows. Since structures which are models can do this, we naturally find that the brain uses such structures to store images.

Strømnes concludes that thought must necessarily embody architectural models of the world that are contained in our brains. In consequence he argues the existence of "the architecture of thought." He goes on to elaborate this important metaphor:

> An isomorph of a complex event, like a model of a house, is built up from parts—component isomorphs—which are then combined spatially according to a set of rules. . . . When trying to communicate our thoughts verbally to each other—our inner visions, models and environments, which are isomorphs in the visual modality—we must have a common set of rules for combining the component images into sensible wholes. The system of rules for verbal communication is therefore to be understood as the architectonics of imagery.[25]

Furthermore, through his research Strømnes has suggested the basis for distinguishing between Western psychology which categorizes the world in a linear or vectoral fashion, and non-Western psychology whose cultural expression centers on the timelessness of the world and existence:

> [T]he main model-building rules for Finnish, a Ural-Altaic language, and Swedish, an Indo-European language, were found. These rule sets have been used in easily repeatable laboratory experiments, . . . [and] the results were as clear cut as anyone

> could want them to be: Finnish-speaking people really have learned and used another rule system for image-combination—model building in the mind—than Swedish-speaking subjects. The Finnish rule system is a simple topological system, while the Swedish system is a simple vectoral one. This means that when a Finnish-speaking person combines parts of an intra-psychic model, he takes note of the relations between the borders of the parts. The Swedish-speaking person, on the other hand, combines the parts of the image according to the relations of their movements, the vectors involved.[26]

In the light of this culturally differentiated model-building, and with Finnish technology increasingly borrowed from Indo-European societies, Finnish architects could fruitfully ponder the role of movement in the built environment, Strømnes suggests.[27] It could be argued that most Finnish architecture has little interest in movement and, as the purpose of most buildings is increasingly to serve a technological goal in a movement-bound culture, this conflict of intentions might be disastrous.

In his general conclusion, Strømnes summarizes the function of architecture within the cultural framework of environmental memory. He argues that in order to create culture and civilization we must extend the abilities we have. Thus, given the hand and its muscles, human tools must suit the form and principles of the hand and muscles which are already there. We must remember that the ultimate value of a tool is its ability to increase or change the potential inherent in human thought and action.

Architecture can therefore be seen as a tool of physiology. But architecture is a tool of the brain, not the hands. The brain receives information, stores it, and uses it to help the organism and the species survive. This can be accomplished only by regulating action, so that action can be repeated in a certain context. Strømnes points out that architecture vastly increases the dependable regularity of human action beyond what can be accomplished by a mere animal brain without the help of this tool.

Our human tendency and need for structured social interaction, which has an extremely high degree of dependable replication over time, cannot be accomplished by thought alone; nor can we make implements and musical instruments just with our hands.[28] Architecture can therefore be seen not only as a product of civilization, but also as an indispensable tool in its making.

TWO

▲

THE CITY AS A MIRROR OF CONSCIOUSNESS

The idea and description of the Creation, the beginnings of the world and life, the birth of man himself as a select being who is in direct contact with his Creator, all are essential components of human myth. There are many common features in the mythic accounts of Creation formulated by the ancient Egyptians, the Babylonians, and the Jews. As soon as language became capable of describing concepts, rather than just things and actions, then man's consciousness of the great mystery of the Creation and his relationship to the cycle of life and death was explored and recorded in these myths. The separation of the dry land from the water, of the earth from the heavens, of light from darkness, and of the Garden of Eden from the wilderness are represented as an allegory in the book of Genesis. In this allegory the Garden is the Creator's domain but it is, above all, a place where the Creator and the created can meet. Although it is the Lord's private domain, he has invited Adam and Eve to share it with him. But this idealized relationship between God and man is short lived. Man challenges the authority of his maker—and as a consequence his membership in the Garden Club is revoked.

That clearly brought about a serious state of affairs because this Garden did not simply contain the fruits of the Creation, that is, vegetation for shade and trees for food; those twin symbols of Genesis itself—the Tree of Knowledge and the Tree of Life—were also planted there. Driven from that perfect garden and simultaneously denied access to both ultimate knowledge and perpetual life, man found himself in somewhat primitive circumstances: "The Lord God made garments of skin for Adam and his wife and clothed them. . . . He drove out the man; and at the east of the garden of Eden he placed the Cherubim, and the flaming sword, which turned every way, to guard the way to the tree of life."[1]

Human life may be seen as man's struggle to put together an alternative framework of life and meaning. The allegory of the Garden of Eden and man's expulsion from it reveals a consciousness of the discrepancy between two states of affairs: (1) an ideal, theoretical state, that may exist as in the Garden of Eden, but not in this place and time; and (2) the present state of affairs, which is far from perfect but which provokes man to seek some improvement in his condition by experimentation and innovation.

The ideas of shelter, of house, of hearth and home reflect man's struggle to regain some of the protective features of the Garden. On the other hand, the cultivated garden which extends habitat out into the uncultivated wilderness is but a *memory* of man's original relationship with nature. As we read in Genesis: "The Lord God planted a garden in Eden, to the east, and he put there the man he had formed. The Lord God made to grow out of the ground all kinds of trees pleasant to the sight and good for food. . . ."[2]

The city, however, seems to represent a different case, because it offers man not just a memory, the remembrance of a lost dream, but an opportunity to create *de novo* a progressive framework that allows him to extend his present consciousness into the future. In the Old Testament, the Jewish legends reveal how this consciousness was *represented* in built forms.

The first construction mentioned in Genesis is not a house but Noah's ark: "And God said to Noah, . . . Make an ark of resinwood; make it tight with fibre and cover it with pitch inside and out. This is how you shall make it: the length of the ark three hundred cubits. Make an opening for the ark and finish it a cubit from the top. Set a door in the side of the ark; make it with a bottom, second and third level. . . ."[3] References to the fiber caulking and pitch waterproofing are certainly taken from marine craft building, although the "door" and the "bottom, second and third level" suggest a residence rather than a boat. In any case it is clear that Noah could not have conceived of such a vessel had he not been well versed in carpentry.

The Jews had, of course, begun their days as nomads and tent-makers, but already in chapter 4 of Genesis we read that:

> Cain turned against his brother Abel and slew him. Then the Lord said to Cain, "Where is your brother Abel?" . . . What have you done? The voice of your brother's blood cries to me from the ground. And now cursed are you in the soil which has opened its mouth to receive your brother's blood from your hand. "When you till the soil, it shall not give its fruits to you; a fugitive and a wanderer shall you be on the earth."[4]

Echoing the plight of Adam and Eve, Cain was to be denied the benefits of cultivation and condemned to wander in the wilderness. Cain was afraid for his life and asked the Lord's protection, which he received: "And Cain went out from the presence of the Lord and dwelt in the land of Nod, to the east of Eden. Cain knew his wife, and she conceived and bore Enoch; Cain was the founder of a city which he named after his son Enoch."[5]

From the translator's notes we learn that "Nod" is an unknown place but that the word is uncommonly like *Nad,* the Hebrew word used in a previous verse to describe Cain as a wanderer. Cain's founding of a city clearly represents his "settling down" and establishing family and tribal life, for there is no reference to his "making" or "building" the city as Noah does the ark. We go on to read of Cain's progeny that:

> To Enoch was born Irad, and Irad became the father of Mahujael, and Mahujael the father of Mathusael, and Mathusael the father of Lamech. Lamech took two wives, the one named Ada and the other Sella. Ada bore Jabel; he was the forerunner of those who dwell in tents and have flocks. His brother's name was Jubal; he was the forerunner of all who play the harp and flute. It was Sella who bore Thubalcain, the forerunner of those who forge vessels of bronze and iron.[6]

Thus, the emerging pattern of Cain's tribe becomes clear: Jabel founds the line of nomadic shepherds, with their tents and flocks; while Jubal, the progenitor of musicians, and Thubalcain, the progenitor of craftsmen, represent the fruits of that more settled life that announces the dawn of civilization. This is, of course, where our present interest in Cain's progeny truly begins. But let us look at the implications of the allegories in Genesis so far.

Man, it seems, soon learned to modify his behavior on the basis of experience. If we accept that eating of the Tree of Knowledge brought Adam into our harsh world of reality, then we might correlate his knowledge of nakedness and his sense of shame with what we call consciousness. But Adam did not complain about being expelled from the Garden of Eden (as Cain was to protest to the Lord about losing his status as a farmer and his relegation to the nomadic life), because he was not yet able to fight back and enlist his omnipotent God in his struggle against the vicissitudes of reality. Adam and Eve were condemned to the desert, wearing their animal skins, an image of primitive man we can readily conjure up. In contrast to Adam's passivity, Cain protested: "My punishment is too great to bear. You are driving me today from the soil; and from your face I shall be hidden. And I shall be a fugitive and a wanderer on the earth, and whoever finds me will kill me."[7] "Not so," says the Lord, and he gives Cain his reassurance that he will not perish. The reassured Cain digs in, founding both a city and a dynasty.

If Adam became conscious of nakedness and shame when he ate the fruit from the Tree of Knowledge, then *consciousness* must be synonymous with *awareness*. But did Cain's behavior in a situation where he was similarly guilty suggest that he had learned, as animals learn, from genetic inheritance? Does Cain's behavior also imply that learning and consciousness are one and the same? Rather, Julian Jaynes suggests, it might be more helpful to regard consciousness as a metaphysical imposition, some sort of spiritual link between man and his Creator which, in the hierarchy of nature, makes us more equal than animals. Jaynes challenges the concept of consciousness as a product of evolutionary continuity.[8]

At this point it may be appropriate to contrast the allegorical account of the origins of man's consciousness as knowledge from God, with the evolutionary view of our origin through natural selection. In reaction to the Christian idea of human consciousness as a metaphysical imposition from the Creator, there grew up through the early period of evolutionary thinking an increasingly materialistic view. This assured us that consciousness does nothing at all, and in fact can do nothing. As animals evolve, nervous systems and their mechanical reflexes increase in complexity. When some unspecified degree of nervous complexity is reached, consciousness appears and begins its futile course as a helpless spectator of cosmic events.[9] This explanation did not solve the problem of consciousness, because nobody could really explain precisely when it had emerged or in what species, nor whether it required the support of a special kind of nervous system.

That "helpless spectator" notion of consciousness would seem to have more to do with Adam fleeing from the Garden of Eden than with Cain's ability to bounce back and found the city of Enoch. When clad in animal skins, Adam's behavior regresses to that of an animal cowering at his master's angry voice. Throughout the Genesis story, in fact, Adam's behavior is still characteristically animal. Forbidden to do something he does it, clearly *unconscious* of the consequences; and then, not yet conscious of the idea of forgiveness, he accepts the punishment meted out by the Lord God. In this allegory, of course, Adam eventually becomes *conscious* of the fact that the Lord God requires absolute obedience, and conscious also that disobedience inevitably brings dire consequences.

Thus, a moral sense is planted in Adam's primitive consciousness; which is, of course, the whole point of the allegory of the Garden and the Tree of Knowledge. At the same time, God expresses caring concern for man, whom he had created "in his image," for, just as he is expelling the disobedient creature from his Garden, he "made garments of skin for Adam and his wife and clothed them."[10] This might be taken as a further symbol of possible reconciliation.

Clearly, what is recorded in this allegory is not simply a tale of crime and punishment. By clothing Adam and Eve at the very moment he expels them from the Garden, the Lord God indicates that although man must suffer he will not perish in the wilderness. And it is precisely Cain's consciousness of this caring concern that leads him to protest that his punishment is "too great to bear" and that as "a fugitive and wanderer on the face of the earth" he will surely perish. But after further conversation, Cain becomes *conscious* of his special spiritual relationship with his God. He finds the courage to stand his ground, with the result that six generations later his descendants are playing upon the harp and flute, forging bronze and iron vessels, and doubtless spinning and weaving fine cloth to cover their nakedness. In the end it is not Adam, the natural man, so much as the murderous Cain, enlightened and emboldened by consciousness, who becomes the inventor, the innovator—in fact, the father of modern man.

One certain way of solving the problem of consciousness and its role in nature is to deny that it exists at all, which is exactly what the behaviorists did. As Jaynes says, it is an interesting exercise to sit down and try to be conscious of what it means to say that consciousness does not exist.[11] But all behaviorism really offered was a refusal to talk about consciousness, and nobody believed that he was not actually conscious. On the other hand, what is our basis for believing that we are conscious? Although the metaphor of the blank mind can be found in the writings of Aristotle, it is really only since John Locke thought of the mind as a *tabula rasa* that we have emphasized this recording aspect of consciousness, and thus see consciousness as inscribed with memories that can be read over again in retrospection. There is clearly a link between memory and consciousness, and that link has something to do with information, with data based on concepts and experience. Let us apply this link between memory and consciousness to Cain's "invention" of the city.

When Adam and Eve were driven out of the Garden by the Lord God, they dwelt in the wilderness. But of their sons we are told: "Now Abel was a keeper of flocks and Cain a tiller of the soil."[12] So, in one generation, in allegorical terms at least, man had conquered the wilderness by shepherding and farming. Clearly, the shepherd by possessing livestock was deemed superior to the tiller of the soil; the farmer Cain envied his brother, the shepherd Abel, and slew him. Let us recall the punishment the Lord decreed Cain should suffer for the murder of his brother: "When you till the soil, it shall not give its fruit to you; a fugitive and a wanderer shall you be on the earth."[13]

It was back to the wilderness for Cain, and a dangerous wilderness at that, where other murderers lurked. The idea of forgiveness, which had been born when the Lord made Adam and Eve garments of skin, was invoked now in the consciousness of Cain, and the Lord relented and promised Cain his protection.

As a further safeguard, Cain founded a city: he established the idea of a community as a bastion against the wilderness and those murderous fugitives and wanderers who were lurking in the untamed darkness. This is the meaning of the Greek *polis*—a community gathered together in one place to promote and protect the interests of those *within* it, against those who are *without* its bounds. This is important, because the city is not just a *thing*, a physical form in space: it is a concept, an *idea* uniting common interests and the organization of those interests into a pattern of the symbolic and ritual functions of *communitas*. But just what does this mental grasp of an idea mean? And how can our consciousness of its hierarchical and material implications become operational in order to give that idea tangible, perceivable form? By what means do we set about understanding the relationship of human behavioral patterns to objects in space and time?

We read of the founding of a city in the early chapters of Genesis, not so much as the emergence of semipermanent physical form, as the emergent idea of community against a threatening wilderness, with its marauders and fugitives. A tribal hierarchy generated by the family sought to formalize itself through the establishment of recognizable institutions. But what about Cain? How did he stumble upon "the idea of the city"?

Mental responses, like motor processes, have as a prerequisite something that is akin to experience—something learned over a period of time by repeated practice—and that something is skill. Cain was clearly very willing to learn by acquiring skill. When the Lord God sent him out as a fugitive and a wanderer, what Cain said in effect was, "Look here, I don't deserve this. What I need is a second chance." He felt the need for a stable structure, a society which, by its corporate form and nature would bolster him against the desolation of the desert. His solution was to establish "a city," which would offer the companionship of his extended family and friends, and provide protection from thieves and murderers, counteracting the post-Garden sense of abandonment and isolation. Cain's city made possible an ethos of consolation, warmth, and hope within the collective concept of communitas.

Thus, with Cain's city there came into existence a more complex structure than the simple concept of hearth and habitat; and with it primitive man's basic need to protect himself from the elements and untamed nature was extended into one that recognized interdependence and its helpmate organization. The birth of communitas generated hierarchies with their attendant rituals: these in turn eventually required a sophisticated architecture and urban framework to represent both their functional position and symbolic role within the civic structure.

So, Cain would have thought of his *city* first of all as a concept, an idea. In his mind's eye he would have seen it not as a physical form but as a social structure. But the difference between an encampment of tents and this "city" is that the idea of city is associated with a particular place. Only a fixed place can be made safe and defended. An encampment is vulnerable to attack, but a communal settlement can mark and protect its boundaries.

In all probability, Cain's "city" was a transitional form of settlement which would still have included some tents for summer use, although it would have been located in a defensible place, such as a rocky fastness that provided substantial winter accommodation in caves. Indeed, Bedouin settlements are like that to this day, for example in Petra, in Jordan. Even today when a *sheikh* moves his tribal headquarters to the outskirts of a conurbation and builds himself a house, those who come to visit him are received in a ceremonial tent pitched in his garden.

From this point of view the Bedouin present an interesting phenomenon: they have lived, as they continue to do, in many parts of the Levant for some thousands of years, producing such artifacts associated with civilization as fine textiles, jewelry and cooking vessels, to all intents and purposes *settling* in certain areas, yet never representing their society in architecture. Their religion is sometimes represented by a primitive mosque, but otherwise they have remained faithful to cave and tent.

Cain would probably, therefore, have projected his "city" as a *place* where his people could gather. He would have thought of an enclosed place, ideally with natural "walls" that could be defended. A watercourse, or the possibility of collecting water, would also have been in his mind as a farmer. Conscious of these requirements, he would then probably have tried to understand the existence and operation of such a *place*.

Jaynes asks how we try to understand something. Like children trying to describe nonsense objects, so we, in attempting to understand a thing, try to find a metaphor to fit. Not just any metaphor will do: we need one that is familiar and easy to comprehend. Understanding can be achieved by substituting a metaphor for the unknown. The resulting feelings of familiarity may be equated with the feeling of understanding.[14] Thus, language grows, expanding our conceptual framework, by the use of metaphor. When we find it difficult to describe an unfamiliar thing or a unique experience, we naturally resort to comparison; we suggest, "Well it is like so-and-so."

In these terms, to project a mental picture of his "city," Cain would have needed a metaphor that embraced the following interactive elements: "safe place," "capacity to accommodate large numbers," and "capability of being easily enclosed and readily defended." As a farmer, Cain's lexicon of suitable metaphors would not have been large, and "cave" might have suggested itself most readily. But after all, the slain Abel was a shepherd. And what would have been more appropriate than to borrow from his brother's world? Indeed, given the shepherd–flock interdependency and the shepherd's concern to safeguard his flock, the "sheepfold" would have offered a perfect metaphor for Cain's notion of "the city."

Jacques Ellul sees in Cain's actions the real beginnings of mankind.[15] Just as history begins with a murder, so civilization begins with the city and all that it represents. With the establishment of the city of Enoch, paradise becomes a legend and creation a myth. It was Cain who would realize man's wisdom and transform *Homo proto sapiens* into *Homo faber*. "It may be said that before him, there was only God. But by Cain's act God became the one no longer adequate for the life, the will, the thought of man. Cain bends all creation to his will. . . . From this taking possession, from this revolution, the city is born."[16]

In Ellul's terms, this revolution is a revolt against the persistent memory of the Garden that God denied to man. Ellul argues that our scriptural texts, although themselves dependent on myths which came into being at the dawn of consciousness, are:

> [a]lso meaningful because they tell us what man wanted to do when he created the city, and what he was hoping to conquer, what he thought to establish. This narrative of the origin of the city is essential, for we see there in its purest state, and simply expressed, the feelings of the builders. Such feelings are no longer evident in our modern day when the prodigious complexity of the world hides the simple plans of the never-changing human heart.[17]

After Cain, the next builder of cities we hear of in Genesis is Nimrod. And in this allegory, the power struggle between the God of Adam and the sons of Cain continues:

> The whole earth used the same language and the same speech. While men were migrating eastward, they discovered a valley in the land of Shinar (Babylonia) and settled there.
>
> They said to one another, "Come, let us make bricks and bake them." They used bricks instead of stones and bitumen for mortar.
>
> Then they said, "Let us build ourselves a city and a tower with

its top in the heavens; let us make a name for ourselves lest we be scattered all over the earth."[18]

But when he saw this city and its tower, the Lord decided that he had tolerated enough of man's arrogance and assertion of his newfound independence, and he said, "Truly, they are one people and they have the same language. This is the beginning of what they will do. Hereafter they will not be restrained from anything which they determine to do."[19]

So the Lord resolved to go down and "confuse their language so that they will not understand one another's speech." And he "scattered them from that place all over the earth; and they stopped building the city. For this reason it was called Babel, because it was there the Lord confused the speech of all the earth."[20] This image of "confusing man's speech" clearly has to do with the Lord's counterrevolt, the idea that God's revenge might deprive man of the tools of civilization, the images and models with which he constructs his independent consciousness.

But we must not overemphasize the significance of the tower, which is only a part of the city, an episode in this allegory. Ellul explains:

> The point of the story is the problem of the name, and the city and its tower are the means of obtaining the name. How important a name was for an Israelite is well known. It is the sign of dominion and has a spiritual quality. God gave a name to the first man. Man in turn named all the animals. Thus a relationship is established in which the one named becomes the object of the one naming. To make a name for oneself has nothing to do with the modern expression referring to a reputation; it means becoming independent, and that is what their attempt at building meant. . . . Their revolt is ever so much more profound in this myth than in that of Prometheus to which it is often compared. It is much more than taking over God's power. It is the desire to exclude God from his creation.[21]

Clearly, then, the idea of the city had developed considerably from Cain's Enoch to Nimrod's Babel. The original constituent elements of safe place, capacity to accommodate large numbers, and capability of being easily enclosed and readily defended, now included a further significant characteristic of communitas, namely, identity. This *identity* would provide a physical representation of the spirit and aspiration of the citizens; it would literally *make* a name for them. The identity of the city would, therefore, become symbolic of the city itself, hence the importance in the allegory of "a tower with its top in the heavens." In the first place, the very idea of the form of the city becoming a symbol of itself already suggests erecting an image of an alternative god, "a graven image." Such a construction is quite clearly proscribed in the Ten Commandments found in the Book of Exodus:

> "An altar of earth you shall make for me, and upon it you shall sacrifice your holocausts and peace offerings, your sheep and oxen. In whatever place I choose for the remembrance of my name.
>
> . . . If you make an altar of stone for me, do not build it of cut stone, for by putting a tool to it you desecrate it."
>
> You shall not go up steps to my altar, . . .[22]

The fact that the tower is intended to be high enough to reach the heavens makes it a symbol of man's ingenuity, his intellect and skill, which is to be thrust in the face of the Lord! The Lord has no alternative but to disrupt the building of Babel, because Babel represents the first instance of a city that symbolizes not just a *community* under God but a man-made *institution.* And with it begins in Ellul's words, "the prodigious complexity of the world" which will come to hide "the simple plans of the never-changing human heart."[23]

Thus, in the evolution between Cain's Enoch and Nimrod's Babel the whole theoretical basis of the city is established. Cain's idea of the city was a simple one based on the benefits of communitas: in his earthly struggles outside the protective confines of the Garden he sought to gather together a congregation of his fellow men for the advantages of mutual companionship and protection. To Cain the murderer, the city represented a peaceful haven where man's tasks and tribulations could be shared. As Cain was to enjoy the Lord's protection, so his "city" was no offense to God.

In the establishment of the medieval monasteries we see the revival of Cain's model of *communitas.* By withdrawing from the complex and institutionalized City of Man, in St. Augustine's sense, a city which owes its genesis to Nimrod's Babel, the monks could create a simple City of God which regenerate's Cain's decision to bring *order* to nomadic life through the instrument of a structured community. The more one understands of monastic order, and the representation of that order in the monastic community and its architecture, the more fitting the comparison appears. In the Augustinian ideal, the monastic life resembles a *spiritual ladder* ascending to the Lord, and this is to be achieved by prayer, contemplation, and silence.[24]

But there is also a parallel ideal operating within the monastic community, and that is based upon self-sufficiency in all material things. Thus, the monasteries attracted to themselves fields for agriculture, pastures, vineyards and, within the architectural framework, an actual garden. In its regeneration of Cain's model, therefore, the monastic ideal of a City of God contributed an important variation on the original. This monastic ideal could not be realized in architecture alone: the abbey church, the refectory for the communal meal, the cells for private devotions, and the cloister for contemplative pacing, were not in themselves enough. The monastery must be both *city* and *garden.* Its purpose is not primarily to establish man's sense of identity with place, as attempted in Babel. Rather, it celebrates the idea of "an altar of earth" that the Lord required in his Commandments: "In whatever place I choose for the remembrance of my name." A monastery is, both in its concepts and in its architectural representation, what I have called "a view toward the Garden" (chapter 5).

It is also clear that without the *models* of Cain's Enoch as the statement of communitas against the wilderness and Nimrod's Babel as an early memory of institutional complexity, the monastic *theory* of a simple life which draws on the metaphors of both "the city" and "the garden" could not have entered man's consciousness.

For a *theory* is just that: it is a metaphor that offers an abstract point of view somewhere between an existing problem and a previously existing model. A theory, therefore, expresses a relationship between a model and a thing or a context which that model might represent. In itself a model is neither true nor false; only the theory may be so.

The Niels Bohr model of the atom is that of a proton surrounded by orbiting electrons, similar to the pattern of the solar system, which is its principal metaphoric source. Bohr's *theory* was that all atoms were similar to his *model.* With the subsequent discovery of new particles and complicated interatomic relationships, Bohr's theory has turned out not to be accurate, but the model still remains good.

We often speak of "mapping our ideas," by which we mean that we set out to *plot* the field of our speculations about a topic; and our purpose in doing that is to see what relationship, if any, our ideas about and views of that topic may have to one another. Our mapping might conveniently take the form of a diagram, which would have the advantage of specifying and testing those possible relationships. But is a map or diagram a model?

Although an *analog* is a model, it is a model of a special kind. It is not like a scientific model, whose source may be anything at all and whose purpose is to act as a hypothesis of explanation or understanding. Instead, an analog is at every point generated by the thing of which it is an analog. A map is a good example. Now, a map is not a model in the scientific sense—not a hypothetical model, that is, like the Bohr atom that relates an unknown phenomenon to a theory. Instead, a map is constructed of something well known but not completely known. Each region of a district of land is allotted a corresponding region on the map, though the materials of the land and the map are absolutely different, and a great many of the land features have been left out.

What is significant to us is that the relation between an analog map and the corresponding land form is a *metaphor*. Thus, the threads of our discussion of the city as a mirror of consciousness become even more closely interwoven. As Jaynes explains:

> Subjective conscious mind is an analog of what is called the *real world*. It is built up with a vocabulary or lexical field whose terms are all *metaphors* or *analogs* of behavior in the physical world. Consciousness is an operation rather than a *thing*, a *repository* or a *function*. . . . Or, to say it in another way with echoes of John Locke, there is nothing in consciousness that is not an analog of something that was in behavior first.[25]

To be conscious of something, then, we must be able to think about it, and that thinking requires a conceptual framework. And how do we construct such a conceptual framework "in our minds"? To be sure, we don't really know. According to the currently predominant semantic view explicated, for example, by Luria and Pribram,[26] our *memory* has a store of mental *images*. For fish navigating in Devonian seas, these were visual images, but over 350,000,000 years of evolution, those visual images have become encoded. Nowadays, when we talk to ourselves about those images we do so in concepts that somehow reflect the original visual impressions. In utilizing these concepts, we conduct an interior monologue in which we convert those verbal concepts back into visual imagery.

One conceptual framework within which we can be conscious is that of language. Indeed, we may argue that Descartes' proposition

"Cogito, ergo sum" should be translated properly as "I think, therefore I am *conscious*"! This would explain the unrivaled importance of myth and allegory not only in literary texts but in the history of ideas, and of course in the formulation of architecture and the city.

The origins of the city, then, involve a decision by a community or its leaders to inhabit a strategic place, where that community may thrive and prosper. Cain made such a decision when he founded his city because he was conscious of the threats posed to men who did not congregate in a safe place for mutual protection and advancement. Safely gathered together, like sheep in a fold, men would stand a better chance of survival than if they were living a nomadic life in the wilderness, where they would be exposed to savage beasts and human murderers. So the first premise of the city concerned survival. Its model was probably the family and mutual interdependency of the family (because Cain had himself violated that fundamental structure of society); its metaphor was possibly the fold of the good shepherd; and its theory was, perhaps, based on the advantages of extending family ties into those of the community—or, in Cain's terms, to set up a structure which promoted the family of man as alternative to the original family of God.

When we understand these natural origins of the city it is easy to see the difficulties inherent in establishing new towns: they simply do not have that all-important communitas, and their satellite dependency upon an established city nearby operates against the emergence of such a spirit within that new structure. Whether we consider the Venetian military satellite of Palma Nova (founded 1581) or English New Towns established after the Second World War, we encounter the same problems of civic credibility. Above all other considerations, the idea of the city must surely exist in the minds of its citizens: they must be conscious of its organizational and formal implications.

Although at first responding to the simple ideal of the family, the evolution of the city led to an increasing complexity of relationships. These patterns provided alternative centers of activity and influence: power, centralized resources, trade, negotiation, and diffusion of ideas. Most of these institutions, of course, are still with us. As manifestations of the community at work these forces came to demand an architectural *representation* of their symbolic function. The tower projected for Nimrod's Babel was one such representation, as the cathedral or the great mosque were to become. Others include the palace, the temple, the market, the law courts, and the school. According to their relative importance these institutions occupied locations of varying degrees of significance within the urban framework. Often associated with them was a piece of land, an open space. Higher value was signified by raising them up onto a platform from which they dominated common life and extended their influence into the surrounding district. Significant institutions and their buildings created domains—quarters or parishes elaborating and articulating the metaphor of *identity.* In this way the city became no longer one place, but many.[27] Mirroring the links of institutions to society, the city enacted complex and subtle relationships of inner sancta with their dependent outdoor rooms.

THREE

▲

THE CELEBRATION OF PLACE

Open spaces within the Greek and Roman city mirror an underlying structure reflecting origins and institutions as well as patterns of growth and change. The Italian *piazza,* and its various European and American transformations, provide an excellent model of urban space as a nucleus and focus of city life. During the late Middle Ages and the early Renaissance the Italian piazza reached the peak of its development. The emergence of the city–state in Italy, whose physical if not its political form was strongly akin to its Greek precursor, was strongly instrumental in this process. During the late Middle Ages especially, the form of the Italian piazza became decidedly organic. Civic structures linked the form and character of these open spaces to patterns of daily life as well as the rituals of more ceremonial public life. Thus, the Italian piazza is a direct physical expression of the new process of urbanization, *representing* both in its form and its surrounding architecture those changing emphases in city life and the rituals of its institutions.

Within the tightly packed agglomerations of buildings that formed these rapidly expanding cities, open space was essential to accommodate the collective, public functions of urban life. During the late Middle Ages, in the mild climate of Italy, theatrical performances were still held out of doors. In addition to accommodating important civic ceremonies and religious processions and rituals, the piazza was also a daily commercial focus which centered on the open-air markets whose produce was as varied as that of the modern Arab souk. Throughout the Middle Ages the construction of churches, municipal halls, guild halls and other public structures remained the primary building task, which leads us to suppose that all other activities must have taken place outside in the piazza. After the first quarter of the fifteenth century, many of these outdoor activities moved inside, generating the need for other specialized building types. The theater in particular took itself off the streets and generated a new building form. Until that happened, however, the piazza was literally a stage on which the daily and civic life of medieval city dwellers was enacted in full view. A piazza was the natural focus of the urban theater.

It is important to understand that the Italian piazza is not simply a leftover space; it was created to accommodate deliberate acts. In the medieval period this space was carved out of the mass of the city, which accounts for its informality and irregularity. Indeed, the form of the medieval piazza is essentially arbitrary but not entirely fortuitous.[1] The Renaissance, however, brought a significant change in the ordering of the piazza, as indeed it did in the organization of the city as a whole: new cities and the new or rebuilt parts of old ones were laid out according to more regular geometrical designs. Naturally, these new or redesigned spaces and sectors of cities conflicted in their geometrical ordering with the more random patterns of the old structures. Frequently they seem alien to the organic medieval forms that took their spatial energy from accidents of land ownership or undisciplined building activity.

The newly rich and powerful dukes of the Renaissance sought a direct expression of the secular character of their city–states. In many cases, then, the process of urban renovation resulted directly from the evolution of a new social structure. The Piazza del Duomo, for example, was no longer the only or even principal open space within a city. Vying with it in size, grandeur, and civic importance, the Piazza Ducale or the Piazza dei Senatori directly expressed the political, civic, and social aspirations of wealthy citizens. The architectural character of building facades was changing. Now the emphasis was upon symmetry, with the addition of centralized balconies from which the dukes and princes could view the ceremonies enacted for their benefit. The treatment of the floor of the piazza became more elaborate, with patterns in the paving, changes of level, and the addition of bollards, monumental sculpture, and fountains. All these innovations created an order that was in itself more interesting and varied than that of the old piazza. In many ways this new ordering was also more abstract than the old, because it depended upon an imposed order, an esthetic that had not grown organically with the city and the evolution of its rituals over the centuries, but had been brought into being speedily and with deliberation. In this sense, the newer *piazze* represent the height of artifice.

Thus the seeds of our own sense of disconnectedness from awareness of place were already sown in the Renaissance by this newly abstract ordering of space. Today our sense of "space and place" in relation to the placement and displacement of things in the city is only of the present. Our present-day institutions no longer address the public space: instead, they speak of a skyline without a supporting city form, a private abstraction that parodies the patterns of the computer printout. Houston is an example of this *mirage-city*. We now possess little sense of memory and even less idea of our position in the eternal cosmos. Although we find that the piazza, with the cafes and colonnades that cling to its edges, expresses an admirable idea, it is difficult to emulate this model with any authenticity. Traditionally, the open public space in the city has been the effect rather than the cause. Our basic lack of ritual, however, makes us adopt its form in place of a cause. Perhaps we should not be surprised, then, that the effect does not correspond with that of the model. For any two representations to be comparable, there must be some correlation in the ideas that they represent.

Today we arrive in the urban theater with front-row tickets and expect the performance to begin. But the script has been eaten by the word processor, and neither the architecture nor we ourselves seem to remember the plot.

Open space within a *building* framework has a ritual origin. The forecourt of the Egyptian temple, for example, can be traced back at least to the Eighteenth Dynasty (1580–1314 B.C.) and the system of courtyards associated with temples and related buildings in the central quarter of Tell El-Amarna. A clear example is the temple of Rameses II at Abydos (fig. 1). Through the courtyards the temple, which was essentially the domain of the priesthood, was given an extension toward the outer world of everyday life. These courtyards created a "valve" that mediated between the institution of religion and the public, secular domain. This architectural form represented an institution with a discrete membership to the world at large, and it accommodated those crowds who did not have access to the inner sanctum. Almost four thousand years ago in the temple enclaves of ancient Egypt, then, a prototypical hierarchy existed in the ordering of city form.

In a similar way, the early Church borrowed the atrium or open court from Roman architecture to provide an intermediate zone between the external pagan world and the church itself as the sanctuary which only those baptized in the Christian faith could enter. This court of the catechumens thus reached out to embrace those who were in a transitional stage between an unbelieving outer life and an inner life of full membership in the Church.

The idea of extending an institution beyond its private or ritual boundaries into a more public domain is clearly an important one. Translated into architectural terms it represents our consciousness of *within* and *without,* of the privileges of belonging and being included on the one hand, and of not belonging and being excluded on the other. This is poignantly described by Aldo Rossi in *A Scientific Autobiography:*

> I have always loved the typology of the corral and often proposed it in my work. The corral was the form of life in the houses of old Milan; it constituted the form of the country dairy farm and dates back to the Imperial agricultural villa which was enclosed like a little city at the end of the Pax Romana. I saw the corral in the old houses of Milan, together with the balcony which is closely related to it, as a form of life made up of the intimacies endured there, the bonds, the intolerances. In my bourgeois childhood, I felt excluded by these houses, and I entered the courtyards with curiosity and fear.[2]

Several thousand years earlier, but with the same impulse, the Egyptian temple celebrated the division between the initiated and uninitiated. Nonetheless, Egyptian religion penetrated and informed every aspect of life. As Rundle Clark explains,[3] the Greeks were the first to discover spheres of activity independent of religious conditions that could, therefore, be expressed in nonreligious terms. Since the Greeks, Western man has become accustomed to divide experience into dualities: Church and state, clerical and lay, religion and science. As part of the pre-Greek era, the Egyptians understood no such dichotomy. They anticipated the Christian ideal, because for them the

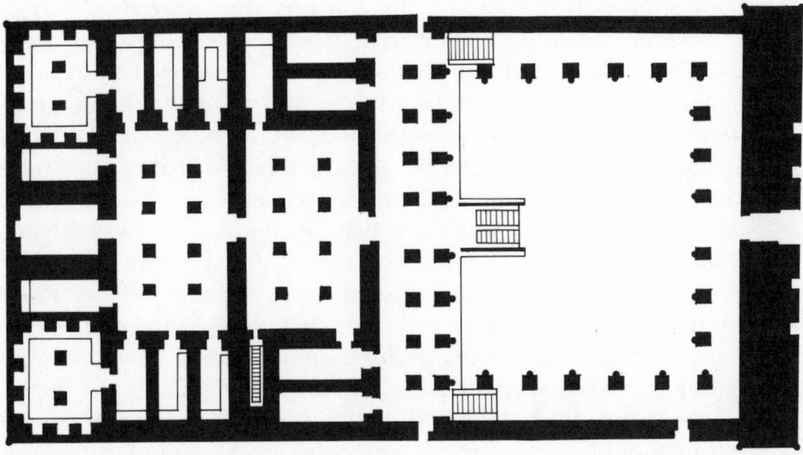

Figure 1. Abydos, Egypt; Temple of Rameses II, c. 1305–1224 b.c.

gods were everywhere. The pharaoh was the supreme priest, and under him all acts of daily life were played out against a background of divine patterns. Gods, men, animals, plants, and physical phenomena all belonged to the same order; there were no distinct realms of being. Conception, germination, sickness, or chemical change were as much god-directed as the motions of the stars or the beginnings of the world.

These theological ideas of the first great Western civilization were represented in Egyptian society and its architecture with ritual as the first and most characteristic mark of the religion. Ritual was built around a few basic ceremonies: a dedication rite known as "Opening the Mouth"; the treatment of the gods in their shrines; the offering of Mayet, the Goddess of World Order, at the end of certain rites; the liturgy of offerings; the enthronement rites of the king; and the *pyroyet* or public procession of the god. These various rites determined the calendar, primarily an arrangement of festivals, which was structured with reference to the phases of the moon and governed by reference to the observation of the dog star, Sirius. The physical disposition of the celebrants in these rites was the governing factor in the design of both temples and tombs. Architectural form derived, therefore, from the ritual coordinates that generated spatial order in religious ceremonies.

Life in ancient Egypt revolved around religious ritual. Religious acts were not at all perfunctory; on the contrary they were deeply symbolic, referring to things other than themselves, things which belonged to that other world of the gods. It was these other things that Egyptian religious rites and architecture represented and therefore attempted to explain. The shrine of the god, for instance, was "the Horizon," the land of glorious light beyond the dawn of civilization where the gods had their dwelling. The temple was an image of the universe as it now exists, while the land on which the temple stood was the primeval mound which rose from the waters of the primordial ocean at the creation of the earth. At the close of the daily temple service when the priest raised a small figure of Mayet once again in front of the divine image, this act asserted that rightness and order had been reestablished, but it also repeated an event that had taken place at the beginning of the world. It was vital to the spirit of Egyptian religion that all symbolism should be twofold. A ceremony was meaningless without both mythical and theological references.

From the cult of the dead and its architectural representation comes most of the evidence of Egyptian civilization that we possess. The need for permanent structures was the stimulus for erecting the first buildings of dressed stone, and these in turn represented man's relationship with the infinite powers of the unseen world beyond.

Nevertheless, Egyptian ideas about the next world were not very precise, and embraced two quite distinct and conflicting fates for the soul. The first permitted the deceased to join his ancestors who had already gone to their resting place in a cemetery on the edge of the desert, a place where life was very much like that on earth but carefree. The second concept allowed the soul to soar up to the heavens where it would join the stars, sun, and moon in their eternal process. Nearly all Egyptian art and architecture is symbolic and represents the relationships of god to king and man to life and death. Rundle Clark's description of this symbolic representation makes us aware of the relative poverty of our own symbolism:

> The architectural arrangements and decoration were a kind of mythical landscape. This was worked out down to the last detail of the furnishing; everything had a meaning or could be made to have one. Columns, capitals, walls, window-lattices, drainage

> outlets, gateways, screens and shrines all had significant traditional shapes with decoration indicative of mythical or theological schemes. The great temple halls, for example, with their papyrus-shaped columns simulated a Delta swamp in which the god's boat floated when it was carried out of the inner shrine in procession. . . . If we say that the architecture provided a background for the ritual, that is to make the one subordinate to the other; but in fact the visual arts, mythology and ritual were facets of one reality. An Egyptian temple appealed to the eye and the imagination at the same time. The full sensuous impact of a great ceremony must have been very impressive indeed. . . . But all had a deeper meaning, part mystical, part reasonable.[4]

Thus it seems that the two prime characteristics of Egyptian society—its theocracy and its preoccupation with the afterlife—were represented in Egyptian mythology. This mythology, in turn, not only supported the political, social, and religious structure of Egyptian society, but also created an extension of reality through memory and imagination. The concept of an afterlife extended the limits of existence, so that all Egyptian art and architecture, ritual, and literature *represented* the great natural cycle of life, death, and organic renewal. While that process retained its sense of wonder and mystery, yet it sprang from the earth. Firmly rooted in the mind of every shepherd and farmer, such knowledge confirmed that when nature feigns death it is only part of a necessary seasonal renewal, so that the Garden may flourish again and bear next season's fruit. In this way, too, the Egyptian calendar of rites celebrated the rebirth of the sun each morning as we begin life again after the refreshment of sleep. As Rundle Clark explains:

> The mythology had therefore to serve two purposes. It was to give steps whereby the universe was arranged, leading up to the final triumph of Horus and the coming of the pharaonic monarchy. The other purpose—only gradually understood—was to provide a series of symbols to describe the origin and development of consciousness. The theory of divine kingship was the stimulus of the one, the cult of the soul was the stimulus of the other. This may sound like the verdict of a modern psychologist, but it was already realized by the Egyptians themselves, although

not in modern terms. When they mythologized they knew what they were doing.[5]

The mythology of Egyptian religion celebrated the essential duality of creation, of the universe, and of life itself, by representing the paired opposites of order and structure in nature and society: day and night, morning and evening, sunrise and sunset, present life and afterlife, this world and the world beyond, the tangible and the intangible, what is accessible and what is inaccessible, what is within and what is without. In other words, it represented the ancient Egyptian's understanding of earth and sky, of space and form, of garden and desert. Consciousness of the real world and of a realizable world beyond was twofold, with both set within a landscape of ideas.

In accordance with the pharaonic prescription for a fixed and static society in this world, this landscape of ideas had natural boundaries like the edges of the desert. Just as, according to one theory, the dead lived a carefree earthly life beyond the edge of the desert, so man would come to a full realization of some of the ideas *represented* in the earthly landscape of religion and architecture only when he passed beyond the edge of that desert, *representing* the boundary of this life, to the eternal garden beyond. It is easy to understand the impact of the fertile Nile Delta on the landscape of ancient Egyptian ideas and mythology. Our interest here is to consider how their theory of contrasts affected the organization of building form and space, and the part this symbolic ordering played in generating urban structures that are centered on institutions.

The whole idea of place as an essential element of world order also emanated from Egyptian cosmology. However much they may vary in matters of detail, every Egyptian creation myth makes a common assumption: that before the beginning of the things the primordial abyss of waters was ubiquitous, stretching to infinite boundaries in all directions. These primeval waters were not like a sea, for that has a definite upper surface, and they had no such demarcation: they were continuous and admitted neither air nor light. Within this all-embracing liquid cosmos, there was neither time nor distance because all measurement was veiled by darkness and silence. To the Egyptians, our present cosmos was but an enormous cavity, not unlike an air bubble, mysteriously placed within those unfathomable primeval waters. And beyond the limits of the known, beneath the earth, above the sky, and at the ends of the world, those waters still concealed space and time.

Thus our seas, our rivers, the rains, and the floods they bring, were all part of the eternal ocean. For the Egyptians, as for the Hebrews, the sky was but a "firmament" that "divides the waters from the waters."[6] In this division, according to Egyptian cosmology, the universe is an abode of light surrounded by an infinity of thick darkness, a bubble of clarity and order enveloped in the eternal night of the primordial ocean. We can therefore understand all Egyptian legends that describe the origins of the earth as attempts to explain how our region of light and form came into being amidst the ineffable watery infinity of timeless darkness. Water is formless. It has no positive features and assumes no shape of itself. The primeval waters being infinite, all dimensions, directions or spatial qualities of any kind are therefore irrelevant. Nevertheless, the waters are not actually nothing. They are the basic matter of the universe, and all living things depend upon them. Without the rain and the flooding of the river, plants and animals could not live. In this sense, then, the waters represent the waters of life, and the primordial ocean, known to the Egyptians as Nun, is the father of the gods. The emergence from the waters has four aspects: it signifies the coming of life, light, land, and consciousness.

What is of particular interest to us here is the way in which the Egyptians linked the idea of creation with the creation of place: the very sacredness of *place* derives from its association with the Creator. Once again we find that the origins of these associations in Egyptian theology are found in Egyptian mythology.

When we visit Heliopolis today, it is difficult to imagine that this unprepossessing suburb to the north of Cairo was the greatest theological center of ancient Egypt. This was the site of the chief temple of Re, "the High God as the sun," or, to give him his original name, Atum, the Complete One. From the twenty-eighth century B.C., in the reign of Zoser, the doctrines formulated in Heliopolis became the closest thing to an orthodoxy known by the ancient Egyptians. The Pyramid texts, the largest single collection of religious writings so far recovered from that early period, must have been mainly the compositions of Heliopolitan priests. They contain the oldest references to cosmogony in terms of Atum, who originally "rose up as a High Hill." Thus Atum is revealed (in Utterance 600) as being the primeval hill itself, the first manifestation of land in the great separation of the earth from the waters.[7]

There was apparently no fixed form for the primeval hill. In the Pyramid text it is engraved as a simple hill slope, an idea that could easily have been derived from the mounds that emerge every year when the flood waters of the Nile recede. These mounds of fertile mud are soon covered with weeds and teeming with insect and animal life: they would have offered a perfect microcosmic image of the Creation, of Atum, the complete and all-containing one, in ancient Egyptian consciousness. As Rundle Clark tells us, the image of this mound was soon formalized into an eminence with sloping or battered sides, or a platform surrounded by steps on each side, and this became its most usual symbol. This is also probably what the stepped pyramids represent.[8]

So we have the suggestion that the emergence of the first land mass, the creation of place in the primeval waters of nowhere and nothingness, also represents God in earthly form. And the coming into existence of this island in the waters, this mound that establishes place—literally a landmark—also leads eventually and inevitably to the widespread idea of the "high place" that is more prominent and therefore offers a greater sense of proximity to the Creator. By connecting the concept of this first land mass—Atum, the all-containing one—with its architectural *representation* in the stepped pyramids, Rundle Clark advances a prima facie case for the symbolic origins of architecture.[9] The coming of life, light, and land out of infinity was established as a precept in Egyptian theology and planted in man's consciousness the concept of dimension, order, and form—the very basis of our spatial perceptions and of architecture itself. Throughout almost three millennia ancient Egyptian architecture responded to man's consciousness of the phenomenological world, *representing* a landscape of his ideas about cosmic order and its relation to his visions of both temporal and eternal life.

FOUR

▲

IMAGE, MEMORY, AND SPIRIT OF PLACE

To Plato true *ideas* were perfect and lucidly refined *notions*. Since the visual arts are not only subject to semiotic rules of conceptual order, but also interpenetrate without subjective frameworks of perception and creative imagination, Plato excluded them from the realm of ideas. In modern terms, the way we perceive visual ideas or images depends very much upon conditioning that governs the degree and nature of our exposure to those frameworks of which those ideas and images are part. Lengthening the "time-exposure" to frameworks and images clearly generates greater familiarity with these contexts and relationships, compressing space–time experience into memories of greater density and complexity.

Plato maintained that even if the objectives of artistic endeavor were achieved to the best of human ability, works of art could never be accorded a higher acclaim than that of the image. In other words, they would fall short of the realm of ideas in which notions have reached a state of absolute lucidity and perfection. Seen in these terms, the image is something of a halfway house between the projection of a notional concept and the actual representation of an ineffable idea.[1]

An image, then, is not the realization of an idea, but merely the visualization of it, a *representational* stage between a concept and its perception. As Plato pointed out, these visualizations are clearly not the ideas themselves, but merely appearances or visible clues to ideas, those parts of ideas which can be visualized.

The coexistence of things in time and space imparts a particular quality to those phenomena. Environmental quality could be said to suggest an aura or presence, while the detailed images that make up the whole impression could be thought of in terms of identity. On first acquaintance we gain a general impression of a place or a building in terms of its form and color as revealed in light and shade. If we are able to examine that place or building more closely our first impression will be modified as we become aware of the detailed images that make up the impressionistic whole.[2] Normally our perception of imagery works from the general toward the particular—quite the opposite from the way the human brain processes vision. Details are nevertheless essential components in structuring our consciousness of things and our memory of wholes.

We speak of the phenomenological aspects of an environment as its *genius loci,* the spirit of place.[3] That genius loci will possess both general characteristics, what we have called its "presence," and more detailed features, or what we have called its "identity." The very concept, spirit of place, depends upon the particular relationship of things to each other in a particular place. Being in the same place, in the same physical, environmental framework, things set up an interaction by that very coexistence so that they become intelligible to us not only as isolated phenomena but also as integrated parts of a unique whole. We may *conceive* environmental frameworks that conform to an underlying order of things according to natural or culturally ritualistic principles. However, we will *perceive* those frameworks in terms of certain characteristics of form, material, color, directional emphasis (horizontal or vertical), pattern, texture, and so on, which give a distinctive set of images to a particular building or place. Architecture, like all environments, is perceived as having both this general "presence" and a more particular "identity."

It is important to consider the concept of syntax at this point. Syntax posits a *structural relationship* between the idea (intention, meaning) and the image (expression, manifestation of the idea). The classes of architectural elements (walls, columns, roofs, and openings) must be seen in terms of their meaningful ordering in syntactical relationships. The syntactic hypothesis allows us to understand how relationships of plans and building forms may become transformed by cultural or regional variations in the use of those architectural elements. In Rossi's terms, *the typology is a general design that becomes the basis for cultural action which generates a particular architectural form.* How is it that architectural expression reaches points of ultimate refinement in particular places at certain times? According to the structural linguists, such "precision" is generated by the operation of syntax on forms. The artifice of syntax imposes increasingly demanding rules of order upon the architectural process. Whenever an architectural language is adopted without attention to the finer points of detail it degenerates into a regional dialect. As such it may present but a faint shadow of the original, yet its images will continue to stir a remembrance of its sources. Considering architectural evolution, identifying *types* and *models* (Rossi's *forms*), as Rossi has done,[4] allows us to categorize the architectural process.

We can only accurately recall comprehensive images of those things with which we have been on personal terms. A photograph of a building is a useful aide-mémoire but it is no substitute for having witnessed the original object. We shall distinguish between encounters with the *body of architecture* through direct experience, and second-hand recollections of the *body of knowledge* we have about architecture.

The very complexity of architecture—the composition and interaction of forms in space and light—makes it virtually impossible to witness except in *time,* which is truly the indispensable "fourth dimension" of space. A photograph can reproduce an elevation accurately, but it only captures a vague impression of form in space. Even a model, however accurately it replicates form and details, cannot substitute for the experience of actually moving through a building's volumes. This is a problem of scale. Only vivid or repeated personal encounters with the complex relationship of space, form, and detail in light will give real depth of exposure, allowing us to assimilate composite experience into our environmental memory. An environmental framework is not only one of space and form, it is also one of time: there are no short-cuts by which we can truly synthesize those composite encounters. To record them effectively the environmental memory depends upon a "time-exposure." Familiarity with places, spaces, and their details therefore increases the potency of our remembrance of them. Time is compressed into memorable images of space, generating an architecture of spatial consciousness.

Another aspect of the time component of environmental memory is our need or desire to relate to previous periods, societies, and cultures and our attempts to understand the social patterns and rituals that characterized them through their monuments and artifacts. One of the principal attributes of form—architectural form, city form, landscape form, or interior form—is that it is capable of connecting us to the deep well of human consciousness, keeping open the channels of historical continuity by the myths, ideas, rituals, and events which it represents.

The devastation of the Second World War necessitated a great deal of reconstruction in Europe. In rebuilding, we discovered that where order was given to new urban structures only on a functional, abstract basis, then those rebuilt cities functioned only at that level. Without the spirit of place that links sensory immediacy of experience to underlying cultural and ritual resonances, an environmental framework is sterile and barren. Yet neither architecture nor the city can mirror what is not the case, what is not supported by existential, phenomenological resonances. Imagery that does not connect with the depth of human consciousness will have little resonance in the environmental memory.

The spirit of place—Norberg-Schulz's *genius loci*—which gives an aura or presence to a particular environment is composed of the total character of the things that make up that place.[5] We may say that in the natural environment the supernatural extends itself into our consciousness through that presence we call the genius loci. In turn, man responds by implanting the spirit of his aspirations into the man-made environment. The ancient Greeks realized that through this *spirit of place* man meets with his spiritual other self. By creating the Sacred Way, the Greeks gave expression to the uniquely beautiful location of Delphi as an ideal rendezvous for man and his gods. The concept of genius loci necessarily involves a meeting, and merging, of existence with spirit. In such a place, our existential or concrete awareness extends into the spiritual or abstract dimension. An interaction between existence and spirit expresses the multidimensionality of human aspiration. The expression or presence of this multidimensional aspiration is the necessary prerequisite to a true work of art; it is the quality that imparts a memorable energy to the whole, that establishes a poetic dimension.

In order for a work of art to express the spirit of man there must be something beyond visual imagery; the surface structure must be underlaid by a deeper structure. The something beyond surface appearance is a link with man's subconscious, a link between existential appearance and imagic memory. A syntactic framework may describe the ordering of an environmental grammar and outline the rules for its elements. But such a system of signification is still abstract. Human responses, however, depend upon the way in which the signals arranged in a conceptual framework are actually received. The conceptual or theoretical framework, the semantic rules of a work of art, must also embrace a perceptual syntactic framework: together they must connect with the consciousness of the perceiver.

Existential space being a number of places, a series of loci, with which and within which man interacts, it stands to reason that if this space is limited then one's code of environmental references will also be restricted. Similarly, no one place exists in isolation. These loci are not simply dotted about the terrain, and the directions or paths which connect them are not confined to a lattice of horizontal routes. There is also a vertical scale of environmental relationships.

We can measure the complexity of man's building activities by his use of the vertical scale. Use of this vertical scale against the natural terrain represents not only wishing and dreaming, but a conversion of today's into tomorrow's reality. The poverty of our present-day urban vision is demonstrated by the shoddy way in which we so often treat the level ground in relation to the vertical aspiration. The sense of sacred place or precinct within the city is being forgotten. The art of constructing habitations for our memories has been lost.

The vertical dimension may represent our aspirations, a vision of a *higher place,* but it is the horizontal flow of space that accommodates man's concrete world of action. The displacement of the exterior horizontal pedestrian domain by the mechanistic vertical sandwiching of work areas, serviced by elevators of ever-increasing efficiency, has left deserted voids and chasms in our major cities. The removal of human contact, association, and communication gives an abstract character to urban life.

It should also be recognized that our late-twentieth-century return to dependence on historical form or decoration is a reaction to the insecurity implicit in the minimal geometry of the modern city and its architecture. Minimal geometry offers few sensory echoes: to the child, a piece of graph paper provides merely the roughest framework for his scribbled patterns. In the city, the gridiron plan is only a pragmatic outline to describe the basic division of land use. When the built form complies with the rigidity of the outline completely, then the abstraction of the gridiron becomes the urban reality.

The urban locus—the piazza, park, or square—is most successful when it does not prescribe precise patterns of use but rather provides a loose framework that will accommodate variety and freedom of activity and interpretation. Thus, the urban locus, whether it be piazza or park, is the valve that allows an energy exchange, a change of mood and environment, an interaction of a fixed space with changing users and their different dreams and desires.

We may journey between spaces vertically, but it is only in the horizontal, visually dynamic path that we can retain continuity of consciousness. Our existential patterns require a path, and in the city where the pedestrian has freedom of movement, this path is established at or near ground level. The effect of the elevator and the high-rise building has been to remove the dynamic quality from horizontal circulation within the city. For this reason, the ground level, the horizontal space between buildings, has become a desert, a no-man's land.

When this path is untrodden—when our horizontal space loses its *human energy*—then we also lose our way, as though we have no sense of direction other than some vague vertical ambition. In the environmental chess game today, we are in danger of abandoning the horizontal dimension altogether, of losing contact with the elementary forward and backward moves, as though we had no concern for what is ahead or behind. The path, the way forward and backward, is a basic property of consciousness. A path gives us continuity in space and time, for it demonstrates the basic existential pattern of interaction between place and time: it represents a continuum of what is, what was, and what could be.

Our scale of expectation spans from the minimal to the optimal. Environmental imagery is composed of both remembrance and anticipation: it structures an appreciation of the natural environment and man's desired social, spiritual, and physical goals. What is minimal produces disappointment and dissatisfaction; what is optimal, and poetic, gives us unexpected joy.

The essence of the elevator is the convenience and speed with which we can move from level to level. Of course, the elevator is a link between floors, but it is not a direction or path. Its function is a restricted and mechanical one. The elevator shaft is not a locus, as a linking piazza would be in the horizontal plane: it is simply not a place at all. "Elevation" is not a compression of time, but a functional movement in which time predominates. When traveling at speed, we have great difficulty in accommodating, simply because we are not located in a space which can accommodate our topoanalysis.[6]

The urban locus derives from the model of the temple court, the agora, the forum, the piazza: it is the meeting place of routes and streets; that is, directions and paths. In traveling the straight street, the focus is limited: time predominates. When we arrive in the piazza or square, the predominance of time is compressed by the sudden expansion of space. In the urban locus, the visual order is necessarily complex. It is unnatural to hurry across the open space at the same speed with which we travel the straight and narrow street. We become distracted by the complexity of visual images and human intercourse: we ourselves "dissolve" and fuse with the urban house of memories.

The elevator is similar to the straight street in one respect: it permits rapid transit. But the uniqueness of the elevator is that it achieves its purpose by suspending space in time. Therefore, the consideration of ground level—the principal point of arrival and departure—is of paramount importance to the high-rise building. Descending from a height of anything up to a hundred floors, it is not enough merely to arrive. One must arrive "somewhere." A space of arrival must compensate for the displacement of spatial experience induced by the elevator. After journeying, one needs time to adjust to the environment of the point of arrival, an environment in which the time scale recedes and the relative vastness of space takes over. If we are to take advantage of the recession of time in the urban locus, then we must also exploit that nonawareness of time, in motionless, dreaming consciousness.[7]

The city itself is a chain reaction of a series of arrival points, an interminable process of comings and goings which converts human and mechanical energy into a totally fluid pattern of life. In mechanical terms, it is a number of independent valves, each inducing its own level of pressure. Metaphorically, the elevator is itself a valve. Released from the pressure of its time valve, the human being needs to expand into a nonpressurized space. Such a space must accommodate a different tempo, a different mood, a contrasting idea of being.

Clearly the essence of the urban locus is its nonspecific orientation: it will have low determinism and high accommodation properties. The piazza, with its cafés and its nonspecific space, its capacity to break down the barriers of time with the multiplicity of its environmental images, is the paradigm of the urban locus. On the other hand, the enclosed garden, which is the focal point of the English square, is the antithesis of the urban locus. The French *place,* an essentially open space, often framed by pollarded trees which act as a buffer between the buildings and the paved center, is a model of the urban landscape mix of the pragmatic function and the poetic gesture.

The market square in European countries functions as a focus for social intercourse only when it is also the focus for commercial exchange. A market has its social function equally within enclosed architectural space as in open urban space: both are community spaces. In contrast, the so-called supermarket is deprived of the social content of the true market because it is specifically a seller's operation, a buyer-seller exchange. There is no dialogue in the supermarket: the products have to "speak" for themselves. Hence the exaggerated role of marketing techniques, substituting role-playing for the real human drama of comedy, necessity, and tragedy.

We can enclose the market and retain the urban locus, provided that we also retain the social exchange. Similarly, the square becomes an urban locus if the private garden is opened up to the public, with public footpaths crisscrossing through it. The fact is that all open focal spaces—points of arrival and interchange—within the city are true urban loci. But the shopping mall is not an urban locus. It has no typological basis in the memory of the city; it is not *street*, or *square*, or *market hall.* Its model is the industrial shed: in wartime we camouflage the shed, in peacetime (according to Robert Venturi) we should decorate it: neither treatment affects its interior space. Within buildings life is inclined to be conformist. Particular architectural spaces or specific forms dictate the range of human speculation; we are required to conform to the limitations of specific functional spaces, whereas, outside buildings, we are liberated into the nonspecific interstices of the city. In looking at these common or community areas in our cities, we might therefore ask: What is their capacity to accommodate the dreaming consciousness of the citizens?

The surface of patterns and images is the medium: it conveys signals that impart certain basic information, the purpose of which is to engage interest and excite curiosity. In order to develop an environmental dialogue, however, the recipient of those initial messages seeks for an underlying meaning which will connect to the deeper structure of his consciousness. The critical question is: "Will the surface effect yield a deeper resonance?" It is an existential question, since the surface structure of signs and the deep structure of meaning are interdependent; the one being apparent and the other beyond mere appearance. Beyond the existential reality of surface we seek *being and somethingness.* The something we seek is evidence of the spirit of man.

It is that something which, added to our existential being, raises our expectations beyond those of mere existence. This distinction is of particular importance within the environmental framework, since we leave traces of that extra something on the things and places we value, those phenomena we cherish. For a space or building to symbolize something beyond surface effect it must possess its own authentic sense of being, or what we might call its spirit, an imprint of our very souls.

This quality or presence that elaborates our consciousness of things, of the world about us, of existence itself, seems to have something to do with a mnemonic energy that "stores" collective human experience so that it is available to generation after generation in our landscapes, our monuments and the complex web of spaces and images that make up our cities.[8] Aldo Rossi, whose admiration of Max Planck's *Scientific Autobiography* led him to borrow that title for his own book of personal explorations, underlines the great impression made on Planck by the discovery of the principle of the conservation of energy in physics. Apparently, Planck always associated this principle with his schoolmaster's story about a mason who succeeded in heaving a great block of stone high on a rooftop. This mason reflected that the energy he had expended was not lost, but remained undiminished and stored for many years as latent energy in that block of stone. Then, one day that block eventually slides off the roof and falls on the head of a passerby, killing him instantly. Rossi observes:

> [T]he principle of the conservation of energy is mingled in every artist or technician with the search for happiness and death. In architecture this search is also undoubtedly bound up with the material and with energy; and if one fails to take note of this, it is not possible to comprehend any building, either from a technical point of view or a compositional one. In the use of every material there must be an anticipation of the construction of a place and its transformation.[9]

In turn, the things and places we cherish leave their traces upon our environmental memories. It is not difficult to imagine John Ruskin looking back to an hour, close to sunset, that he had spent among the broken masses of pine forest that skirt the course of the Ain, near the village of Champagnole, in the Jura.[10]

But Ruskin regrets how a sudden blankness and chill were cast upon it when he endeavored *to imagine it,* for a moment, as a scene in some aboriginal forest of the New Continent. For he found that the flowers lost their light, the river its music, and the hills became oppressively desolate:

> [W]hile a heaviness in the bower of the darkened forest showed how much of their former power had been dependent upon a life that was not theirs, how much of the glory of the imperishable or continually renewed, creation is reflected from things more precious in their memories than it, in its renewing. Those ever springing flowers and ever flowing streams had been dyed by the deep colors of human endurance.[11]

Ruskin's conclusion was that: "It is as the centralization and protectress of this sacred influence, that Architecture is to be regarded by us with the most serious thought. We may live without her, and worship without her, but we cannot remember without her."[12]

Ruskin suggests that a convincing image of an environmental framework is one that has "been dyed by the deep colors of human endurance." His environmental framework relates man's consciousness and historical continuity to the condition of nature and his response to her charms. Yet he is unable to project his appreciation of perceived phenomena to another, *unknown* place. In attempting to uproot familiar images and relocate them in unfamiliar terrain he finds himself deprived of the evidence of "human endurance" which is available to him in the Jura. Ruskin's attempt at environmental transformation indicates how dependent our perception of environmental frameworks is upon the remembrance of other such frameworks. As Rossi comments:

> In the summer of 1977 I was staying at the Osteria della Maddalena when I came upon an architectural definition in the course of a conversation that was otherwise not very memorable.
>
> I have transcribed it: "There was a sheer drop of ten meters from the highest point of the room." I don't know the context that this sentence refers to, but I find that a new dimension was established: is it possible to live in rooms which drop off so suddenly and so precipitously? Does the possibility exist of inventing such a project, a representation which lies beyond memory and experience?[13]

Rossi explains how he tried in vain to draw this project, this hypothetical room, but that his drawings always stopped short of that "void which cannot be represented."

When we look at a distant landscape, or experience a particularly memorable sunrise or sunset, we often find ourselves in the presence of something magical. This impression, or feeling, derives from a set of general characteristics which we cannot actually reach out and "touch": it is an impression that depends upon our being distanced from the detailed phenomena that make up the whole. We can see what it is, and we know how it is made up, but its appearance depends upon our generalized perception of form, mass, color, and light: we have no knowledge of its detail. As with a stage set in the theater, a distanced view allows us to grasp the overall effect of a scene. Closer exploration reveals details, *images* that generate new pictures of reality. Some of those pictures may help to explain the whole, while others may call the whole in question, often showing us to have been the victims of trompe l'oeil.

A landscape image—an image of a natural landscape—differs from an architectural image in that it is not drawn together from a series of detailed parts. Of course, a landscape image has a conceptual framework of parts, but it is perceived either as an impression of a whole or in terms of its component details. From a distance it is plain, desert, valley, forest, or mountain range: in other words, we experience its entire composition from its general characteristics. Close up, however, we are more aware of its detailed features; individual rocks, trees, indentations, or water courses become more important. Those two pictures of reality, the general and the particular, are not necessarily supportive one of the other, and within the environmental memory they will not merge.

What would happen to our perception of that same landscape, however, if it were to become populated by man-made architecture, if buildings formed particular groupings or patterns dotted about the terrain? In all probability, the first consequence of such re-forming of the landscape would be that the natural terrain, which is difficult to perceive in terms of distance and scale, would become overlaid by a structure of measurable forms. The presence of architectural features introduces a relativity into our appreciation of the total landscape, so that the general impression of land formations in light is seen and understood in relation to remembered forms of walls, roofs, and towers. This modification of the *landscape image* will result directly from our memories of architecture because, as Ruskin found, architecture seems to be an integral part of our memory of space and form and therefore of existence itself.

Exposure to many complex patterns of form and detail will allow us to remember an entire building or group of buildings. The semantic part of our brain will allow us to determine whether that amounts to a cohesive framework, or just an unrelated collection of fragments. Our sense of the wholeness of a building or an environment will relate to the interaction of form, detail, color, and light that achieves a coherent identity from those component parts. Such cohesion imparts a material existence but also gives a spirit to the form of the thing or place. A craftsman endows an object with being but he also gives it something else beyond that being, because craftsmanship involves storing human energy in a material thing, imbuing monuments and objects with the human spirit.

FIVE

▲

A VIEW OF THE ROOM— A ROOM WITH A VIEW

All landscapes exist within frameworks—frameworks holding the forms and ideas that give shape and meaning to the landscape. Architecture is itself a frame for landscape, just as landscapes frame architecture. In composing a building within a landscape the paramount idea is pictorial. Similarly the architectural frame of a space captures a slice of reality as a picture. What is observed and how it is seen sets up a relationship between space and the objects within that space, and this in turn creates a particular framework of reference that we may call a representational matrix.

The difference between the relationship of architecture to landscape and a pictorial representation of landscape, however, is that the former offers a spatial experience in which we are the prime movers and to which our response is complex, sensory, and direct. In contrast, the picture plane represents experience by "freezing" a single, mental image (literally a "frame," as photographers say). This frame abstracts the space/form/light/color assemblage that unfolds itself to us and through which we pass. By this selectivity, a picture or photograph steals away the multiplexity of direct experience, substituting for it a univalent pictorial world of its own.

A picture of something or some place we know is more meaningful to us at first glance than an image of the unknown. If we have actually taken the picture ourselves it is still more meaningful, because we have framed the original image in our minds. Similarly, drawing rather than photographing an object or scene imprints the image more deeply on our remembrance, because the act of drawing is a kind of time-exposure that allows the image to develop more completely in our memory through longer experience with it.[1]

Painting and sculpture are quite different from photography in their ability not only to represent an object or scene but also to reconstruct its content and form, so that symbolic elements may be emphasized while others may be played down or even eliminated. Architecture is clearly more like painting and sculpture than photography, in that it represents ideas rather than pictorial facts, constructing environmental needs not only as *shelter* but also as *dream houses.* Like the painter and the sculptor the architect fuses technical skill to an extraordinary point of view, a poetic vision. With this vision the architect operates within the landscape of ideas, linking his new constructions to the landscape of memory.

The excitement of experiencing architecture, like that of studying paintings or sculpture in detail, lies not in viewing the surface of form and imagery but in exploring the structural totality and its representation of ideas. Beginning with a journey through architectural space, we leave behind material form and explore a path through the labyrinth of reconstructed memories into a new poetic landscape which is as much symbolic as it is real. Such an extraspatial dimension of architecture, by opening windows on a landscape that extends beyond perception, unleashes the latent energy store of architecture—its *expression of consciousness.*

But how can we connect with that extraspatial dimension? What is the link between ourselves and the labyrinth of architectural consciousness in which architecture exists beyond space and form? What enjoins us to journey through our minds, seeking to link our own remembrance with the timeless passage of architecture as it reconstructs humanity's collective memories and dreams?

Michael Graves asks: "Is it, then the decoration that represents us in architecture?" He believes that is part of the story, at least. However, it is also imperative that the *argument* in our architecture be familiar

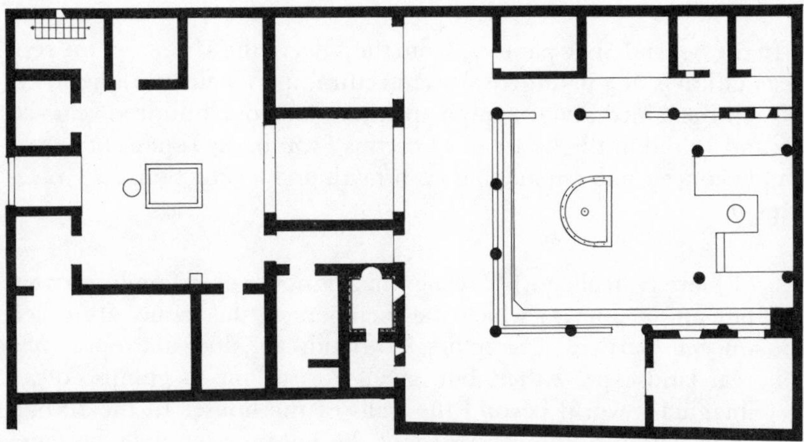

Figure 2. POMPEII, ITALY: Plan of the house of Trebius Valens, first century B.C.

enough to allow us to appreciate and accept "necessary abstractions," "because we are really dealing in architecture with analogies or replicas, levels of symbolism within the body of the work. . . . When the abstract code takes over, when it becomes too elaborate or difficult, it starts to deny us access to the language and to exclude us, ourselves, from the argument."[2]

The "argument" we are concerned with here addresses not the dimensions of spaces but rather the linguistic dimension between spaces: the dialogue between real spaces, how that dialogue connects us to a spatial framework, and thence to those spaces in the landscape of ideas that stretch beyond the material limits of form. Michael Graves draws our attention to two paintings related to the idea of the Pompeian house (fig.2), one of the Second Roman Style (pl. 1) and the other of the Third Roman Style (pl. 2), both dealing with illusion.

> They attempt to open up the wall through painted imitations of architecture and hints of imaginary distant space—an illusion made necessary because the Pompeian house was primarily open to the sky. The rooms in a typical Pompeian house faced around

a central atrium, and in these closed conditions, there was an understandable impulse to allude to and extend the landscape in the wall decoration.[3]

In the Second Style painting from the Villa of the Mysteries, the representation is of a paradoxical architectural space painted rather literally. In the Third Style example, painted some one hundred years later and found in the house of Lucretius Fronto, the representation is highly conceptual, embodying both myth and abstraction. As Graves explains:

> [T]here is an allegorical scene which is not really a family portrait, but an allegory in which the members of the family are called upon to participate as actors. The landscape does not represent a real landscape, either, but an allegorical one, a glimpse of an imaginary world beyond the walls of the house. In the Second Style painting, the literalness of the images eventually becomes burdensome in the respect that, like a representational painting, it runs the risk of becoming a singular likeness. This is not so much the case with the later style painting where abstraction and representation play equal roles, allowing us to develop various narrations within the scene.[4]

What is significant in Graves's example is the artist's incorporation of pictorial representation within an architectural framework "to allude to and extend the landscape in the wall decoration." Graves demonstrates clearly how architectural imagery is not limited to the physical, material confines of space, but can be extended to suggest spaces and forms (and therfore ideas) that lie beyond those confines. Of parallel interest, of course, is the division of those extraspatial allusions into: (1) illusion: the explicit architectural representation of *another place*; and (2) concept: a more notional framework of an alternative environment beyond the enclosing walls. The first, in the Villa of the Mysteries, draws a picture of reality, while the second, in the house of Lucretius Fronto, opens up a range of possible vistas within an outside world or "extra dimension." We recall from chapter 3 that this representation of reality and its extension into another world is a characteristic of ancient Egyptian architecture. Graves says the key to this kind of extraspatial extension is embodied within the idea of representation, which he defines as "the ability of the wall surface to engage us through its narrative potential."[5]

Graves then goes on to give examples of well-known paintings in which "this idea is developed and expanded to include in the surface of the wall a description of our position in the landscape." Of Jan van Eyck's *The Marriage of Jan Arnolfini,* he says:

> It's important to know that Jan van Eyck painted this as a representation of the marriage. Because there were no marriage contracts, van Eyck was asked to paint a likeness of the two main figures and to stand witness by the act of painting. What's important about this is that the witnesses, seen in the mirror, are actually a portrait of the painter himself and presumably us. One finds the backs of the male and female and then the painter's likeness as well. As van Eyck stands with his image in the mirror so must we imagine ourselves looking back into the painting. What van Eyck is doing is forcing us not only inside the picture by virtue of the frame but also forcing us back out of the picture plane through the device of the mirror.[6]

In this way, Graves argues, the artist has established a foreground for the painting and a situation in which we ourselves inhabit that foreground, while the picture plane holds the middle ground, and the reflected images become at once the background and a link to the foreground.[7]

Clearly, van Eyck's conceptual interest has less to do with painting a portrait of Jan Arnolfini and his wife than in the creation of a complex environmental framework in which the narrative role of the room—its walls and furnishings—is equal in importance to that of the subject. Indeed, the room as object is more alive through its pattern of complex interactions and reflections than are the stiffly posed burgher and his bride. The result is that the subject of the painting, a contract between a man and his wife, exists only as it is reflected in the internal environment of the room. In van Eyck's masterpiece the idea of portrait is subservient to the architectural ideal, so that the figures themselves act as a frame to the centrally placed mirror which is the true focus of the picture's spatial concept.

Graves speaks of his interest in "the relationship of subject matter to the object, or intention of the building—the expression and the transformation of various cultural and psychological ideas, intuitions and traditions into architectural form,"[8] and in this context he has emphasized the "narrative potential" of a wall surface. As a further example of "the wall as a narrative" he cites Botticelli's painting *The Annunciation,* observing:

> Here we are given a facade, architecture if you will, as the device which establishes the diptych. What is significant is the role that the rather blank surface of this wall starts to play. It becomes a division between the inside and the outside, as in the templum. Cassirer defines the templum as a space that is cut into the landscape. Imagine that the landscape is fully forested and that a place is then cut for the temple, the idealized place. We are cutting away, and, as we use a template today, we are making a boundary around something. This describes the difference between in and out, between sacred and profane.[9]

Returning to Botticelli's painting, Graves stresses the importance of the wall elements as the architecture. In *The Annunciation* the wall is the barrier which establishes the division between two worlds: (1) man's post-Fall shelter, the architectural interior; and (2) the landscape view, with its memories of the Garden of Eden. The significance of the floor pattern represented in this painting should also be noted, for it delineates the vectors of the two worlds in its markings: the lines parallel to the bottom of the frame indicate the path or orientation of the Virgin Mary, while those that are perpendicular to them and drawn in perspective link us, by their convergence, with the outside world of "the garden" beyond the architectural, interior space.

In this delineation of the axes, which give orientation to (1) the sheltered space of man's *architecture,* and (2) the complementary unsheltered space that is revealed in a vista of the *garden* beyond the walls, Botticelli is following a convention already established in earlier paintings of the Annunciation such as that by Fra Angelico. This observation tends to confirm that the complementary ordering of these two axes, which represent the inhabited world of man (and the protected, introverted world of the Virgin), contrasted with the idea of the lost Garden of Eden, is a well-established convention in Christian consciousness. The Annunciation of the impending birth of the Messiah is, after all, held by Christians to be the beginning of the fulfillment of God's promise, made through the Jewish prophets of the Old Testament, that man would once again have access to the Garden of Eden. As part of the Christian's doctrinal memory it recalls the central thesis of Christianity, which focuses on the distinction between the material world of Caesar that we inhabit and the world of God inhabited by the spirit.

Perhaps this helps us to understand the essential nature of architecture as an expression of man's desire and intention through architecture—as through all art—to bridge between the material world of facts and the spiritual world of ideas. Not only did Adam and Eve feel naked and ashamed after they had eaten the fruit from the Tree of Knowledge but, evicted from the Garden of Eden, they would also have been aware of the vicissitudes of climate for the first time. In its most primitive form, shelter symbolizes man's humiliation after the fall from grace. It is through architecture that man aspires to frame views toward the lost Garden or toward alternative visions he structures in his myths, theology, and philosophy. Architecture is therefore a supremely optimistic activity. It frames new vistas that extend the spirit of man by providing him with glimpses of a world beyond himself.

Botticelli's *Annunciation,* with its blank wall penetrated by an opening which reveals the landscape beyond, is therefore a symbolic representation. It portrays the essential human need to extend the limitations of body and habitat through the realm of ideas. It also perfectly summarizes the role of architecture in its occupation of the *Zwischenraum* ("space between") the inside and outside, the private and public, the profane and the sacred. The architect literally draws the lines that will effect this demarcation and represent in space the frameworks of reality and of myth, of the mundane and the divine. In the construction of any aesthetic system, by far the most important element must be the definition of the field of art itself. As Christopher Gray observed: "This basic definition cannot be stated without implying even more fundamental assumptions about the nature of reality, the phenomenal world, truth, and even morality. In short, certain metaphysical assumptions lie behind any aesthetic system no matter how deeply concealed or violently disavowed."[10]

We must understand the potential of architecture as a conceptual framework which generates a sort of metaphysical energy between the material world of building construction and that world beyond ourselves which we inhabit with our ideas and spiritual values. Architecture offers a realizable framework of values and objectives, a sort of halfway house between inborn human imperfections and limitations and that reconstructed Garden of Eden with its heavenly mansions towards which we journey. It is not difficult to see in the great medieval cathedrals an expression of man's desire to reach up toward God. The outward reality of the high-soaring Gothic vaults is a representation of an inward abstract idea.

Piet Mondrian expressed a similar intention when he wrote: "Yes, this inward life will create an outward aspect: the abstractly realistic life will demonstrate itself in outward life and thereby in all outward aspects: the new man will then find his outward aspect and thereby his complete happiness."[11] For Mondrian as well, the *inner* conception and the *outer* projection—"inward life" and the "outward aspect"—connects with the idea of man's "complete happiness." To the artists of the De Stijl movement, perfection of form necessarily depended upon an inner theoretical and philosophical spirit or process. For, as van Doesburg himself proposed, "Style is created by achieving a well-balanced relationship between inwardness and outwardness, by means of common cognition of life."[12]

Indeed, we may perceive much common metaphysical ground between the medieval ideals in architecture and those of the De Stijl movement as expressed in van Doesburg's proposal for a new universality:

> The development of modern art towards the abstract and universal idea, i.e., away from outwardness and individuality, has—by joint efforts and common insight—made it possible to realize a collective style, which—beyond person and nation—expresses plastically the highest and deepest and most general desires of beauty of all nations.[13]

The abstract idea he describes was to find, however, briefly, a more universal application than any previous architectural "style." Indeed, the International Style became more widespread than any immediately preceding revivals of major historical styles—Egyptian, Roman, Greek, or Gothic. But a distinction must be made between an abstract idea and one that may be perceived to have a *universal* message or appeal. We recall Graves's comment on the limitations of abstractions: at its limits, abstraction becomes mute. Here again the difficulty arises in making the transformation from a conceptual framework to a perceptual form. It is once again a problem of language. Whereas the abstract *structure* of modernist concepts may be intellectually interesting and of wide appeal, the *representation* of these abstract concepts as perceived forms and compositions is less universal in its appeal than that of any previous historical style.

As we have seen, architectural frameworks can offer the means of: (1) extending our experience of interior space and form; and (2) opening up vistas of an exterior world within our interior perspective. They must do this by establishing and conforming to certain conventions. These conventions (as opposed to "styles") can be identified as significant to the evolution and theory of architecture when we can see that their occurrence in history has either (1) fundamentally changed the ordering of space and form, or (2) advanced a distinctive conceptual hypothesis, a theory of how space and form might be otherwise structured and understood. As examples of the former case we may cite the development of classical space through its Renaissance, Mannerist, and Baroque phases; while the latter is illustrated by Cubism and De Stijl.

At this point let us return to Graves's example of the Pompeian house form. The internalization of that house was, toward its central square atrium, while the architect attempted an externalization by painting on the internal walls "imitations of architecture and hints of imaginary distant space." In this example we are dealing with the classical framework of space where (1) an open-air "outside" space—the atrium—is itself framed by rooms of the house; and (2) those "interior" rooms also have an axial relationship to the exterior room of the atrium; while (3) the paintings that present architectural compositions and views of imaginary distant spaces imply a similar axiality in the relationship of inside to outside. All these relationships are very perspicuous within the vectoral framework of classical planning. We move from one space to another along a defined axis; we view the outside space of the atrium, from the surrounding spaces, as the umbilicus of the entire body of those spaces; our imagination of other architectural forms or distant space beyond the framework of the house interior is stimulated axially through the picture plane of the painted wall.

Spatial organization within classical architecture is more concerned with conformity than comfort. Egyptian, Roman, and Greek architecture derived from a strong ritual basis, and this gave its planning, its forms, and details a distinctly ceremonial flavor. This ritual or ceremonial origin generated axial planning relationships, which in turn favored symmetrical arrangements not only of rooms but also of doors, windows, pediments, and other features.

Symmetry speaks of authority, dignity, and aloofness: this probably explains why the Palladian model which inspired the plantation houses of Louisiana and other southern states of America did not provide the inspiration for the homesteads and ranch houses of the American West. The unsettled, frontier conditions of the Wild West made more immediate demands and prompted more casual responses in its buildings. It is perhaps difficult to imagine a greater contrast than that between the formality of the classical-style houses found in Virginia, the Carolinas, and Louisiana, and the homes built in the West by frontier immigrants, many of whom came from European farming communities. In this connection it is interesting to recall how the symmetrically ordered features of Frank Lloyd Wright's early houses—his own first house in Oak Park (1889), and those for George Blossom (1892), and W. H. Winslow (1893)—began to disappear by the end of the 1890s to be superseded by the more informal compositions of the Prairie Style.

Let us consider what would happen if the Pompeian house model were to take on the distortions of Italian Mannerism. What, for example, would be the consequences for the *x-x* and *y-y* axes of the classical Pompeian house plan? Physical access to the atrium could be cut off by a gallery running around the central open space. To ensure that there would be no axial alignments possible with the eye, the four arcades would be open only at the bays adjacent to the corners. That disorientation would not, of course, correspond to a Cartesian coordination but to a diagonal "counterlogic" which would generate a sense of unease and disorder in the surroundings. The wall paintings would similarly represent a world in disarray and disorder, even to the extent of undermining the apparent stability of the architectural framework itself, as we may experience in the "Hall of the Giants" at the Palazzo del Té in Mantua by Giulio Romano.

In Baroque spatial systems the perpendicular *x-x* and *y-y* axes are retained. The significant difference is that the spatial development and creation of foci of interest is not along classical axes but is organized instead to counterpoint the linear thrust that characterizes classical space ordering (fig. 3). If we were to transform the Pompeian house model into a statement of Baroque space hierarchies, we would find not the close packing of rooms around the square atrium but an elliptical courtyard around which the accommodation has been dispersed as though by some centrifugal force. The constant relationship of room to atrium set up by the Cartesian coordinates of the classical plan is clearly not part of the Baroque hierarchy. Instead, the rooms would relate to the courtyard radially, thus counterpointing and to all intents and purposes eliminating the primary *x-x* and *y-y* axes. The explosive nature of the plan also defies perspective analysis.

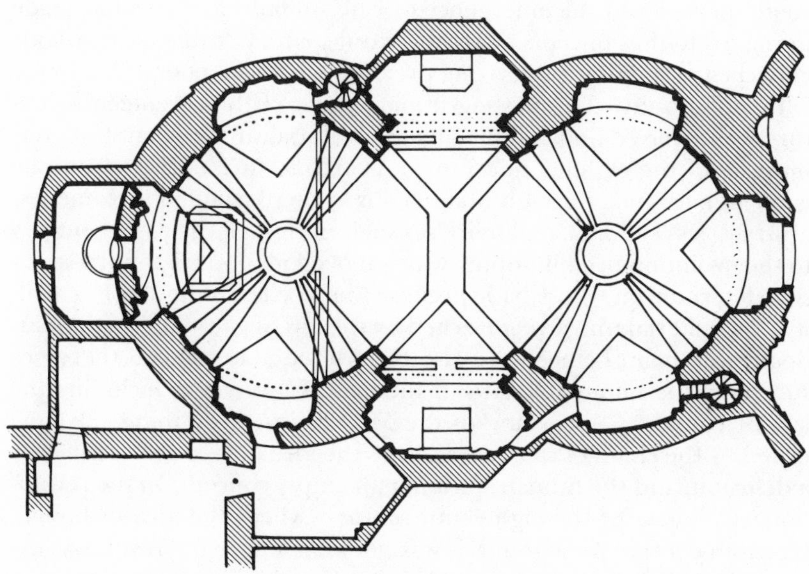

Figure 3. GUARINO GUARINI: Church of the Immaculate Conception, Turin, Italy, 1672–97

Within the Baroque interior, the classical view of the Garden—that *memory* of a world which stretches beyond the confines of the house—is displaced by a spatial system that has little to do with the spirit of man or the memory of his lost innocence. The Baroque view of space is closely connected to the cosmic world of science, as reflected in Guarini's transformation of scientific speculation into solid geometry (fig. 3). Furthermore, the Baroque spatial mode is not simply an architectural framework supported by painted imagery. Actually, in the Baroque mode the combination of spatial ordering and painted representation creates an entirely different world, in which architecture is no longer just a bridge between interior space and an external world, but becomes a theatrical framework within which any illusion of space and effect can be created.

From the end of the Baroque period there was a gap of some two-and-a-half centuries before any new spatial system was generated.

The advent of Cubism around 1907, and its evolution into the experiments of De Stijl and Constructivism, opened up genuinely alternative ways of structuring and perceiving space and form. Between the Baroque period and the emergence of Cubism little progress was made in regard to the concepts of architectural space. For the most part, architects marked time by reviving previous historical modes.[14]

In philosophy, the questing human spirit of the seventeenth century was diverted and confined by the Materialism, or scientific determinism, of the eighteenth century. As architecture evolved from the early Renaissance through Mannerism to the Baroque it became less abstract, less rational, and more sensual. In this it clearly ran contrary to the evolution of philosophy, which moved inexorably toward scientific determinism whose basic premise was a belief in the absolute reality of a material universe governed by the law of causality. Within this doctrine human beings were also considered material and therefore subject to the immutable laws of the material universe, including the law of causality. According to the Materialists, everything was governed by the chain of cause and effect, the idea of free will was merely a delusion, and the human spirit but an empty concept. In the revolutionary climate of the eighteenth century, where the idea of human freedom became paramount, it was not long before the revolt was extended to combat scientific determinism. In the nineteenth century, a counterphilosophy of Idealism took root.

Idealism took the preeminence of the human spirit as its fundamental assumption. What man knew and what he would imagine constituted the absolute reality for Idealists, while man's sensory perception of the material world was mere hallucination. The true domain of the human spirit was what we have called the landscape of ideas; only in the illusory world of material things was man a prisoner of causality. Clearly, the ancient battlegrounds of philosophy, both pagan and Christian, were being revisited by our Victorian forebears. This conflict reached a high point toward the end of the nineteenth century, when Symbolism emerged as the most advanced form of Idealism.

The Symbolists, particularly the poets, drew substantially upon the inspiration of Baudelaire and other Romantics, while their philosophy was more in tune with Hegel than Kant. Like Hegel, they rejected the idea of "the thing as itself" representing the ultimate reality, and substituted instead the concept of reality as a projection of the mind, with the absolute as the ultimate truth. Symbolists thus saw the absolute intellect evolving ideas and progressively revealing reality. In fact the material world, far from participating in this process, interfered with it; and the role of the artist was to pierce this barrier of material things and discover the pure essence which was the manifestation of the idea itself. This explains Mallarmé's concern that the artist should "paint not the thing itself, but the effect it produces." According to Mallarmé this could be done by invoking the idea of *correspondences,*[15] which assumes a direct relationship between the quality of a sensation and the type of emotional response aroused by it. Working within this concept would allow an abstract artist to eliminate all "literary" elements from his painting yet still control the full range of human feeling.

Mallarmé's concept thus offered the artist freedom from reference to natural objects in his efforts to express the human spirit in *concrete* forms. This idea is clearly of particular interest to architects, because much of architecture is necessarily abstract yet expressive of aspects of human feeling at the same time. It also connects with Graves's interest in "the relationship of subject matter to the object, or intention of the building—the expression and transformation of various cultural and psychological ideas, intuitions and traditions into architectural form" and the "narrative potential" of the wall surface in representing these ideas and feelings.[16]

But Symbolism was too extreme, the concept of "the perfection of the Absolute" remaining an unattainable goal for the artist. For that absolute exists only in pure intellect, with no recognizable characteristic to stimulate the senses: it cannot be painted by the artist, or reproduced by the composer, or interpreted by the poet.[17] Graves is right: it is through the "narrative potential" that we pick up the threads of abstract ideas; and that process, of course, describes the nature of the architectural task, with all its difficulty, its complexity, its capacity to make a bridge between dreams and reality. Architecture is above all the representation of a vision, and it must, therefore, make abstract ideas into perceivable and memorable entities.

Cubism, De Stijl, and Constructivism were all concerned with creating new frameworks for the visualization and realization of ideas. These movements were substantially influenced by the Symbolist revolutionaries, although they had to reject the negativism of Mallarmé's unattainable absolute in order to give form to their visions. The importance of Picasso in these developments cannot be overemphasized. From his arrival in Paris in 1901 he was in the forefront of experimentation with the new ideas that were focusing attention on French art. Soon his experiments began to center on a preoccupation with Symbolist ideas, which found startling expression in the work of his Blue Period. As Christopher Gray observed:

> From the very first the pictures of the Blue Period drew heavily on Symbolism. Pictures, such as Picasso's *Mother and Child,* are representations of states, or rather a single state, of the human spirit. There is a melancholy inward-turning, meditative mode in which the subject is withdrawn from all contact with the outer world into an inner world of the mind. The figures are composed into self-contained masses that emphasize the separation of the figure from all contact with surrounding space. . . . The features are delicate, ascetic, almost ethereal, while the eyes are either closed or fixed in a sightless, far-away brooding stare. There is no sense of movement, nor is there any suggestion of its potentiality. There is no sound. Even the light is unreal and seemingly divorced from any earthly source, and it, too, expresses a sense of timelessness.[18]

But even more important than the composition of the figures, the expression on their faces, and the sense of motionlessness is the color:

> A blue that makes one think of both the *Azur* by Mallarmé, and at the same time the dictum of the Symbolist poet Verlaine: "pas la couleur, rien que la nuance." The artist has skillfully combined many elements to create a work of art of great power. . . . It is symbolism in which each element is washed clean of every bit of dross, leaving only the pure, direct, primitive expression—"To paint not the thing, but the effect it produces".[19]

Is this not already evidence of what van Doesburg later described as "the development of modern art towards the abstract and universal idea, i.e., away from outwardness and individuality, . . . a collective style"?[20] For what Picasso has succeeded in painting in *Mother and Child* is not a portrait, and not *une tranche de vie* but a mood. And moods have no materiality; they exist only in the mind!

The French poet Guillaume Apollinaire was also to have a significant effect upon the development of the visual arts in the first decade of this century. In his *From Cubism to Surrealism in French Literature* of 1947, Georges LeMaître contrasts Apollinaire's use of words with that of Mallarmé, telling us that Apollinaire possessed the inborn gift of calling forth "spiritual entities beyond the grasp of our senses; that he was profoundly sensitive to the mysterious affinities between words, and was able by their association to evoke the most extraordinarily delicate shades of feeling, giving his words a miraculous ring that Mallarmé might have envied."[21]

Apollinaire's work made constant experimentation with abrupt word juxtapositions, setting ideas forth in bold relief, and appealing to fantastic, even hallucinatory effects in order to achieve a sense of what he called the "surreal," which prompted Jean Royère to write: "How I envy artists with a narrative style!"[22]

More than anyone else, Apollinaire led artists away from the cul-de-sac of Symbolism toward what he called New Dynamism. Although Picasso was not among the first of the artists who abandoned Symbolist inspiration for New Dynamism, his work is of profound importance. Already, at the end of his Blue Period, there is a distinct suggestion of turning outward, and he became increasingly interested in the idea of the human being in his environment. As Gray observes:

> Mood is no longer everything; there is the beginning of an awakening of a lively interest in purely pictorial problems. Perhaps the first sign is the aesthetic interest in the rich patterns created by the costume of Harlequin. Certainly by the time of *Woman with a Fan* of 1905, Picasso is interested in the exploration of aesthetic qualities of form and line for their own sake—interests that lead him into researches outside the field of his contemporary art into the art of Greece and Egypt, and later to Iberia and Africa.[23]

In the first decade of this century, Picasso set out to liberate modern art from introspection while avoiding the overworked model of nature. As he was to say later: "Art and nature, being two different things, cannot be the same." Therefore he sought out images and references in other, unexplored cultures, and thus rejected a purely abstract absolutism in favor of a more eclectic modernism. This concept was not to occur in architecture until much later in the twentieth century.[24] The search for new sources of inspiration is very much a characteristic of the group of painters that became known as the Fauves. Picasso's *Les Demoiselles d'Avignon* of 1907 has become identified with the beginnings of Cubism, although in fact there is no basis for distinguishing between Fauvism and Cubism at that time. *Les Demoiselles* is just one of Picasso's many new approaches to the problem of form. The problem is a very complex one for, as Kant revealed in his *Critique of Pure Understanding,* there can be no direct perception of form: only sensation interpreted by a logical understanding can give form, never sensation alone. The development of a logical approach is therefore central to the Cubist ideal. As Juan Gris believed: "Cubism was simply a new way of representing the world. By way of natural reaction against the fugitive elements employed by the Impressionists, painters felt the need to discover less unstable elements in the objects to be represented. . . . *In the beginning, cubism was a sort of analysis.*"[25] Apollinaire described how this analysis brings about a transformation in the representation of objects:

> To create the illusion of the typical is the social and peculiar end of art. . . . Without poets, without artists, men would soon weary of nature's monotony. . . . Wishing to attain the proportions of the ideal, to be no longer limited to the human, the younger painters offer us works which are more cerebral than sensual. . . . They express metaphysical forms.[26]

He goes on to assert that Cubism is not "an art of imitation" but "an art of conception," explaining "most of the new painters depend a good deal on mathematics, without knowing it" and stating that "geometrical figures are the essence of drawing."[27] Then he goes on to elucidate the central thesis of Cubist art:

> Until now, the three dimensions of Euclid's geometry were sufficient to the restiveness felt by great artists yearning for the infinite. . . . Today scientists no longer limit themselves to the three dimensions of Euclid. The painters have been led quite naturally, one might say by intuition, to preoccupy themselves with the new possibilities of spatial measurement which, in the language of the modern studios, are designated by the term: the fourth dimension. . . .[28]

Cubism is not concerned with nature and reality as it might be perceived but in the way it may be analyzed and explored as a conceptual framework. In other words, the Cubists wanted to remove their work from the limitations of three-dimensional space—the landscape of perceivable forms seen within the framework of perspective—and offer instead a bridgehead to a "fourth dimension"—the landscape of ideas.

The Roman architects and painters at Pompei allowed the imagination to extend its domain beyond the limited framework of the windowless wall. Christian painters of the late Middle Ages and early

Renaissance, such as Fra Angelico and Botticelli, further extended that vision by giving viewers a *memory* of the lost Garden of Eden. In the Mannerist period of the high Renaissance the coherence of the architectural frame itself was shattered, and the views depicting the world beyond the walls offered only further evidence of disorder. In the minds of men, the Lost Garden became populated with pre-Christian hypotheses, the ideas and images of classical mythology. This resulted from the impact of Humanist philosophy on man's ideas about himself, challenging the relationship of man to God and man to space and form that had been established by the early Church and worked out in Romanesque and Gothic architecture. The coherence of classical space–form relationships derives from the principle of axiality, and although this principle is still remembered in the Mannerist representation of the space it is in effect counteracted and negated by the calculated confusion of the moment.

Baroque architects and artists sought to overcome the disorientation represented by Mannerism: they were no longer interested in the manipulation of flat surfaces but in the sculptural dynamic of forms in space. In the Baroque world the old view of the Lost Garden is not so much restored as replaced. Although axiality exists in Baroque compositions, it no longer has the connecting power it possessed in classical and early Renaissance art and architecture. The aim of the Baroque is not a directional progression of space implied by the axis, but a variability of orientation and experience as one moves through it. Instead of Mannerist *dis*orientation, then, the Baroque aimed at *re*orientation: instead of offering a view of the Garden, the perfect estate of Paradise is represented as another world in outer space. The Garden as a symbol of lost innocence and the promise of redemption has been displaced by a view of heaven as a space among the clouds. Thus, the representation of the mystical idea that man occupies a *Zwischenraum* between the post-Fall shelter of architecture and a memory of the Paradise Garden has been replaced by a more scientific view of man's relationship with the heavenly bodies, a sort of futurama of the celestial world.

Along with the lost connection to nature, the "narrative potential of the wall" also went underground from the end of the Baroque almost to our own day. Thus, although Baroque architecture is a conceptual art, the essence of its concept is the immediacy of its surface effect. Its illusory nature is integral with its spatial system. The underlying structure of Baroque spatial concepts is therefore more difficult to perceive than, say, the formal classical systems of the Basilica of Constantine, Hagia Sophia, Sant'Ambrogio in Milan, Amiens Cathedral, or the Capella Pazzi in Florence. The underlying structure of Baroque architecture is veiled not in mysticism but by superrealism. The axial thrust that characterizes classical, medieval, and Renaissance space corresponds with ceremonial progression, ritual focus, and the convention of perspective. In Romanesque architecture we observe a restraint based on the close integration of weighty structure and taut surface. Gothic architecture is definitely more talkative, but retains the ceremonial axis. The Baroque is the first to break away and become gregarious. The dynamic sense of movement achieved in Baroque space results precisely from its abandonment of the classical axes. After that, no truly new concept of representing spatial relationships emerged between the Baroque period and the advent of Cubism. Even the Neoclassical ideals that were worked out by Karl Friedrich Schinkel in Berlin, Leblond and his successors in St. Petersburg,[29] and Engel in Helsinki[30] had an innovative impact only upon the form of the city itself. As a material change, however, the increased use of glass and iron in the early nineteenth century that culminated in the Crystal Palace was to affect radically the nature of the architectural enclosure in the sense that glass "dissolved" the traditional relationship of interior to exterior space. Glass architecture necessarily eliminated the narrative potential of the wall.

Michael Graves's work consciously attempts to reinstate the wall in its narrative role, but his interest in the narrative potential of the wall seems more painterly than architectural, his drawings and compositions more obviously kin to the wall as a two-dimensional surface than as part of the volumetric world. At Pompeii, as Graves observed, this emphasis of surface is invaluable because it informs the interior of the house by framing or suggesting the view beyond the enclosure of the room. When we paint the exterior of an architectural composition, however, the effect depends not on the color or form alone but upon the combination of materials, details, and the regional qualities of light and shade.

There is a distinction to be made between the narrative extension of an interior space in the pictorial sense, and a picture of an object painted or superimposed on a building's exterior, in the manner of gift wrapping a box. Andrea Palladio's Villa Barbaro (now Villa Maser) makes this point most effectively (pl. 3); its exterior is painted to enhance the architectural order (pl. 4), while inside, Paolo Veronese's trompe l'oeil murals offer a variety of views "beyond the walls" (pl. 5). Thus, the exterior of the villa is composed and painted as part of the landscape, while the interior walls have a different narrative role; the former is architectural and the latter illustrates pictorially the interior "family life" of the house.

Graves's idea of the wall's narrative potential is undoubtedly a valuable one. What is of equal importance, however, is the need to distinguish between the appropriate narrative roles of interior and exterior walls, of *within* and *without.* This also implies a necessary distinction between a view from the room and a view of the room—the composition of the room's enclosure within the wider landscape.

While not confusing these different roles theoretically, Graves appears to do so in his work. Philip Johnson has referred to Graves's Portland Building as "a highly successful drawing" (pl. 6).[31] Certainly, the graphic design of the exterior decoration for the Portland Building seems to represent Graves's architectural intention of a festive wrapper for this administrative office tower. Bachelard cautions that "over-picturesqueness in a house can conceal its intimacy":[32] in the case of the Portland Building, perhaps its *dignity* is also endangered. For, as Bachelard says: "For the real houses of memory, the houses to which we return in dreams, the houses that are rich in unalterable oneirism, do not readily lend themselves to description. To describe them would be like showing them to casual visitors."[33] The counterargument would suggest that it may have been Graves's purpose to have the building exterior express its inner warmth and friendliness. Without engaging in a medieval disputation on the expressive details of the Portland Building, we may nevertheless question their devaluation of narrative potential into a picturesque, not to say pictorial display.[34]

SIX

▲

THE CITY AND ITS HABITATIONS: THE ANATOMY OF MEMORY AND THE LABYRINTH OF THE SOUL

Giordano Bruno, whom we encountered at the outset of our journey, was in the vanguard of those advocating a comprehensive use of visual imagery to illuminate and perfect classical ideas that had been clouded by the medieval Scholastics. Among those who wanted to adopt and develop the visualizing techniques of antiquity, with the hope that a more methodological arrangement might provide a sort of universal repository of thought, was Giulio Camillo Delminio of Udine (circa 1480-1545). Camillo taught at the University of Bologna and then subsequently became attached to the court of Francis I of France. Between Bologna and the Val de Loire he spent a period as professor of *ars memorativa* at Milan.

Aldo Rossi's methodological ideas appear indebted to the work of Camillo, who was very much the Humanist scholar and archeologist of imagery. Rossi's possible debt to Camillo, as well as his own subjective nonneutrality as an architect is made abundantly clear in *A Scientific Autobiography:*

> Perhaps the observation of things has remained my most important formal education; for observation later becomes transformed into memory. Now I seem to see all the things I have observed arranged like tools in a neat row; they are aligned as in a botanical chart, or a catalogue, or a dictionary. But this catalogue, lying somewhere between imagination and memory, is not neutral; it always reappears in several objects and constitutes their deformation and, in some way, their evolution.[1]

Giulio Camillo Delminio was one of the most famous men of the sixteenth century, a fact confirmed by the entry devoted to him in the *Enciclopedia italiana.* Today his fame rests on incomplete recollections of those who knew his work and ideas, and upon fragments of his projected book *L'Idea della teatro* that were collected posthumously in his scanty *Tutte le opere* (Florence, 1550; and Venice, 1552, with nine subsequent Venetian editions between 1554 and 1584). In a letter written to Erasmus from Padua in 1532, Viglius Zuichemus described Camillo as an architect who had "constructed a certain Amphitheater, a work of wonderful skill, into which whoever is admitted as spectator will be able to discourse on any subject no less fluently than Cicero." Viglius then went to Venice, where he met Camillo and was actually taken into the amphitheater by the architect, so we can understand this project to have been a model of considerable dimensions. In a subsequent letter to Erasmus, Viglius described Camillo's theater:

> The work is of wood, marked with many images, and full of little boxes; there are various orders and grades in it. He gives a place to each individual figure and ornament, and he showed me such a mass of papers that, although I always heard that Cicero was the fountain of richest eloquence, scarcely would I have thought that one author could contain so much. . . . He calls this theater of his by many names, saying now that it is a built or constructed mind and soul, and now that it is a windowed one. He pretends that all things that the human mind can conceive and which we cannot see with the corporeal eye, after being collected together by diligent meditation may be expressed by certain corporeal signs in such a way that the beholder may at once perceive with his eyes everything that is otherwise hidden in the depths of the human mind. And it is because of this corporeal looking that he calls it a theater.[2]

It seems, according to Yates in *The Art of Memory,* that the "little boxes," or drawers, were arranged in tiered rows in the form of an amphitheater, and that each of the drawers was exhaustively labeled and indexed. This system of drawers was so designed that all the knowledge drawn from Cicero could be compressed and ordered, allowing planetary deities and mythological figures to rise up in corresponding tiers, with the various "orders and grades" of the cosmic and psychological, the supernatural and moral aspects of consciousness, echoing one another from top to bottom. Also, consistent with neo-Platonist Humanism, the amphitheater demonstrated in its complex ordering how readily Christian cosmogony could be superimposed and integrated within the emerging framework of universal knowledge and ideas.

Clearly, Camillo's *Idea della teatro* was an extension of the classical ideas of *ars memorativa,* of the rediscovered work of Cicero, Quintilian, and the unknown author of *Ad Herennium,* that were his main academic references as a professor. But it was more than that, because, in combining the classical orator's construct of an architectural framework for memory with the physical form of the theater in which the orator would actually deliver his oration, Camillo built a true model for metaphysical ideas in architectural terms. Camillo's "theater" is, however, not at all concerned with *l'idea della teatro* in the conventional sense, for in his amphitheater the "spectator" is on stage observing a representation of those "orders and grades" of cosmic, psychological, supernatural, and moral forces that make up a comprehensive picture of consciousness. In other words, Camillo's *teatro* expresses in material, corporeal form and spatial order the nonmaterial operation of consciousness, and ideas and values are thus brought forth as visible images arranged in an observable hierarchy. This dramatization of knowledge, coming soon after the invention of printing, not only constructs a model which physically displays images of consciousness, it also provides the original model for the development of dictionaries, encyclopedias, computerized databases, and all subsequent systems of information storage. The importance of Camillo's theater remains, however, in its physical representation of the imagic world of memory and consciousness, in its formal display of an *architecture of thought.* In this way, also, it anticipates the architectural ideas of Bachelard as well as those of Rossi.

Of course, Camillo's theater may also be seen to represent a symbolic humanist framework, with man on stage at the center of knowledge about the universe. Such an interpretation, however, would have to contend with the form of the amphitheater, that is, a semicircular or incomplete form. Clearly, since Camillo intended that his theater should embrace "all things that the human mind can conceive," some of the symbols displayed in those "little boxes" must have referred to aspects of consciousness which lie beyond our comprehension of space and time. Equally, any rationalization of knowledge, or of the repository in which such data may be stored, can only affect our rational being. Not all data is verifiable data, and unverifiable stimuli account for that invisible "other half" of the theater of consciousness. Perhaps inadvertently, Camillo's *Idea della teatro* represents this "hidden dimension" of consciousness. Thus, man could still be seen to occupy a central, Humanist position—a position spanning the worlds of accumulated knowledge and of the mind.

In selecting an image for the cover of a book it is often difficult to find one that is capable of representing the subject/object of the book unambiguously. Such an image may also represent a hidden or unconscious content. This is, I believe, the central difficulty of Rossi's work—a difficulty which also makes it both worthwhile and rewarding—in that it contains an essential ambiguity. This ambiguity reaches its most forceful expression, perhaps, in Rossi's interpretation of the *teatro del mondo* that he designed for the Venice Biennale of 1980.

Such ambiguity is already contained in the discrepancy between Rossi's view of the city's material existence as "verifiable data" and as an "autonomous structure." This concept echoes both Alvar Aalto's autonomous architecture of 1941 and Bachelard's foundations of New Criticism of 1958. The conflict between data and autonomy is literally the conflict between material determinism and the poetic representation of Apollinaire's "essence of the thing." As such it returns to the threshold of modernism, where, contemporaneously with the evolution of psychoanalysis, there was a desire to counterpoint the view of objective reality with a subjective framework of mood which Bachelard was to call our "dreaming consciousness."

Throughout *The Architecture of the City,* Rossi stresses the rational process of enquiry. As he explains in *A Scientific Autobiography:*

> I wanted to write a definitive work: it seemed to me that everything, once clarified, could be defined. I believed that the Renaissance treatise had to become an *apparatus* which could be translated into objects. I scorned memories, and at the same time, I made use of urban impressions: behind feelings I searched for the fixed laws of a timeless typology. I saw courts

> and galleries, the elements of urban morphology, distributed in the city with the purity of mineralogy. I read books on urban geography, topography and history, like a general who wishes to know every possible battlefield—the high ground, the passages, the woods. I walked the cities of Europe to understand their plans and classify them according to types. Like a lover sustained by my egotism, I often ignored the secret feelings I had for those cities; it was enough to know the system that governed them. Perhaps I simply wanted to free myself from the city? Actually, I was discovering my own architecture.[3]

He confesses that he later "clearly saw that the work should have encompassed a more comprehensive set of themes, especially in the light of the analogies which intersect all of our actions." *A Scientific Autobiography* is an equally clear attempt to redress the balance of Rossi's "feelings" with his earlier view, expressed in *The Architecture of the City,* that the only way to explore the irrational was by a rational examination, sabotaging his original dream of a "definitive work" in which "everything, once clarified" could be defined, an aspiration not unlike Camillo's claim that his theater could embrace "all things that the human mind can conceive." While attacking historicism—the modernist critique of history—Rossi's analysis of the city has much in common with the clinical approach of the modernists. Simultaneously, he also believes that "the Renaissance treatise had to become an *apparatus* which could be translated into objects." In fact, if we allow that the Renaissance treatise marks the genesis of modern rationalism, then we might see that Rossi's interest in history links him closely with those early Renaissance scholars who sought to find a way forward by retracing the steps of the ancients. *The Architecture of the City,* in addition to reflecting the method of Camillo's *L'Idea della teatro,* also recalls the pioneer interests of the Renaissance anatomists. As Eisenman correctly observes:

> The skeleton thus provides an analogue for Rossi's understanding of history, for it is at once a structure and a ruin, a record of events and a record of time, and in this sense a statement of facts and not causes. . . . [also] the skeleton's nature as a collective artifact allows us to understand Rossi's metaphor of the city as a giant man-made house, a macrocosm of the individual house of man.[4]

This metaphor of city as a large house and the house as a small city is, of course, borrowed from another great Humanist, Leon Battista Alberti. Rossi uses history as the skeleton in much the same way as the Humanist scholars used rediscovered classical texts; that is, as a structure for enquiry about form and purpose. In Rossi's terms, history is limited by continuity of function. Thus, if a building continues to be used for the original purpose for which it was constructed then it has *historical being*. But if there is a change of use—if a church or castle becomes, for example, a museum or prison—then its historical nature is transformed into *memory*. As Bachelard expresses it, "In its countless alveoli space contains compressed time. That is what space is for."[5] The entire skeleton of the city becomes its collective memory through the spatial memories of its constituent parts.

We find this component of time in the collective memory expressed by Sandro Chierici. He says of Sant'Ambrogio in Milan: "To speak of Sant'Ambrogio means to speak of Milan, and to tell the story of the basilica means to recount sixteen centuries of Milanese history, such were these bound together from the episcopacy of St. Ambrose (AD 374–397) to our own day."[6]

This example raises a question of Rossi's most celebrated transformation of the object into a typical manifestation, the "idea of type" or the *typology*. In Sant'Ambrogio we have a demonstration of the compound of object and memory, with the object embodying both an idea of itself and a memory of a former self. As defined by Rossi, Sant' Ambrogio still has a historical being because, in spite of its physical transformations it still represents continuity of use. It is a *form,* in Rossi's terms, or a *model* in our terms. In typology, the typo-*logic* of a type may predetermine form, but such a consequence is not necessarily predictable. An essential distinction to be made between a typology and a model is that the typology is part of a comparative ordering gauge of spatial elements, whereas a model gives a specific image of a particular spatial order, as Rossi said.[7] As we have observed (see Chapter 4), a typology is a general spatial ordering, shaped gradually over time, that through cultural action generates particular representations or forms.

In other words, the *typology* gives only an example of the *process* of spatial ordering. The *model* provides a picture of a particular piece of this process *in operation,* and that model may therefore be copied.

Rossi explains it this way:

> This overlapping of the individual and the collective memory, together with the invention that takes place within the *time* of the city, has led me to the concept of *analogy*. Analogy expresses itself through a process of architectural design whose elements are preexisting and formally defined, but whose true meaning is unforeseen at the beginning and unfolds only at the end of the process. Thus, the meaning of the process is identified with the meaning of the city.[8]

It is not the case, as Eisenman suggests, that "Prior to modernism, cities were thought to have evolved over time through a process which was an imitation of natural law." Indeed, the concept of the ideal city, which was in the forefront of Humanist thinking from the fifteenth century on, had its origins in classical times and flowered—particularly in its military applications—from Palma Nova (1581) throughout the seventeenth and eighteenth centuries.[9] These attempts to rationalize the ordering of the city and to represent it in an ideal, geometric form, came to a head in the eighteenth century, as we shall see in our example of St. Petersburg discussed in chapter 9. The fact that cities *did* evolve over time, and were transformed by history, ran counter to the way men "thought" about their order and form at least from the Renaissance on. Thus, although the Renaissance city does not exist *in fact,* as do such medieval examples as Siena or such Baroque ones as Rome, it has most certainly had an existence in men's minds.

What the modernists did, or attempted to do, was to reform the city so that it emphasized not so much form as social content. This might also help to explain the essential formlessness of the modernist city, as an inevitable consequence of abandoning the natural skeleton of history and the *ideal* or "ritual" forms invented by the Humanists and perfected by the rationalists. The ideological strategy of modernist planning theory, reflecting Marxist impatience with the historical process, treated both the historic city and the industrial city as dead. Unlike Rossi's urban "anatomist," however, the modernist ideologue views the corpse of the city as a butcher might approach a carcass. Indeed, zoning diagrams of the city and the maps of meat cuts displayed in butchers' shops, have much in common. The obvious characteristic of the butcher's approach to the city is that the various "cuts" become divorced from both skeleton and form, having no further need of either!

Rossi also sees the historic city as being visited by some fatal pestilence, which leaves the *skeleton* of its former self as a sort of symbolic ruin. This "ruin," as we know, has been brought about only partially by the utopian moralizing of the modernist planners; a substantial part of the credit for its decay must go to the unplanned revolution of the automobile. The formless and endless suburb is not at all an "American Dream" because it is not a product of "free choice." On the contrary it reflects how the vehicle of that free choice, the automobile itself, distances us from that necessarily complex repository of choices—the traditional city as defined by location, status, and evolutionary form.

For Rossi, then, the historic city has become, by dint of the death of many of its original functions, a "house of the dead." This means, simply, that it is no longer inhabited by the *spirit* of its original purposes and rituals—a spirit that had been nurtured previously by the continuity of the historic process, but is now made up of the habitations of memory, perpetuating the shell of a way of life that has ceased to be. Nevertheless, this skeleton of being that has had life and spirit, is of great interest to Rossi both as "structure and ruin" since it promises to reveal the typological genesis of the skeleton's parts as well as its whole. Rossi explains this interest as it relates to the interaction of type and model:

> With time, the city grows upon itself; it acquires a consciousness and a memory. In the course of its construction, its original themes persist, but at the same time it modifies and renders these themes of its own development more specific. Thus, while Florence is a real city, its memory and form come to have values that are also true and representative of other experiences. At the same time, the universality of these experiences is not sufficient to explain the precise form, the type of object which is Florence.[10]

In my terms, it is by rendering the "themes of its own development more specific" that the typology loses its more generalized typicality and becomes the more specific, and possibly unique form of the model. As Rossi continues:

> The contrast between particular and universal, between individual and collective, emerges from the city and from its construction, its architecture. . . . It manifests itself in different ways: in the relationship between the public and private sphere, between public and private buildings, between the rational design of urban architecture and the values of *locus* or place.[11]

Rossi makes it clear at the outset that the most important analytical method he will employ in *The Architecture of the City* is the comparative one. This returns us to the idea of the Renaissance treatise becoming an "*apparatus* which could be translated into objects"; which in turn suggests the origins of such a process in Camillo's *L'Idea della teatro.* The comparative method of architectural analysis also has a respectable history, beginning seriously with Durand's *Recueil* (1800) and *Précis* (1805), and developing through Banister Fletcher's work to the present. Before them, Palladio's *Quartro libri* is arguably the genesis of typological studies, which were furthered in particular by Durand's *Précis* and Milizia's *Principi di architettura civile* (1832).[12] Rossi is careful to explain that although his decision to make a comparative analysis involves emphasizing the historical method, the city cannot be studied solely from a historical viewpoint. He says:

> Instead we must carefully elaborate a city's enduring elements or *permanences* so as to avoid seeing the history of the city solely as a function of them. . . . I have sought to dwell particularly on historical problems and methods of describing urban artifacts, on the relationship between local factors and the construction of urban artifacts, and on the identification of the principal forces at play in the city—that is, the forces that are at play in a permanent and universal way.[13]

As a principal witness in his case for *permanences,* Rossi invokes the work of Fustel de Coulanges and that author's emphasis on "institutions as truly constant elements of historical life and the relationship between myth and religion." Rossi adds:

> I believe that the importance of ritual in its collective nature and its essential character as an element for preserving myth constitutes a key to understanding the meaning of monuments and, moreover, the implications of the founding of the city and the transmission of ideas in an urban context. I attribute an especial importance to monuments, although their significance in the urban dynamic may at times be elusive. . . . if the ritual is the permanent and conserving element of myth, then so too is the monument, since, in the very moment that it testifies to myth, it renders ritual forms possible.[14]

For those who have no childhood memory of a historic city or only a fleeting acquaintance with a great European city, it is useful to clarify what makes such an urban structure a memorable and even haunting experience. Rossi offers just such a tangible *model* at the beginning of his opening chapter:

> In almost all European cities there are large palaces, building complexes, or agglomerations that constitute whole pieces of the city and whose function now is no longer the original one. When one visits a monument of this type, for example the Palazzo della Ragione in Padua, one is always surprised by a series of questions intimately associated with it. In particular, one is struck by the multiplicity of functions that a building of this type can contain over time and how these functions are entirely independent of the form. At the same time, it is precisely the form that impresses us; we live it and experience it, and it in turn structures the city.[15]

For those of us who were born in one of the great medieval cities of Europe, the memory of such a "structuring form" returns quickly to mind. In my own case Norwich provides the model, the restored Norman keep of a castle fit for a giant: a larger than life memory of the city's evolution which, after its original function had become outmoded, was successively the city's prison and then its museum.

But for many Americans there is no such model in their consciousness. The nonspecific nature of suburban form and space generates no monuments to fuel the imagination, to crowd the memory. In America, in particular, where a conspicuous ritual of intimacy characterizes public life there is a proclivity for the secret, erotic moment, but this can hardly be celebrated within the confines of a suburban box. Suburbs have no *permanences,* none of the complex structures with which we build our profiles or urban consciousness. Our image of the endless suburb is equivalent to that of an underground skyline. Even the deserted classroom and the empty theater, like the outmoded historic city, still have their function of memory; and, in the spirit of Camillo we can label their salient features, their empty boxes, with appropriate identifying information. But the suburbs have no such identifiable structure of memory. In the random scatter of boxes, there is no structure, none of the collective evidence of life which represents the city, and it is unhelpful to label each box descriptively as "box." The European historic city may have become a city of the dead, but it is the suburbs that have equally become its unordered graveyard.

The construction of a suburban church highlights this problem.

How is it possible to represent a focus of collective spirituality in a nonlocus—a "no-place"? From what place, for example, does one enter into the church? The point of arrival and departure cannot be vested simply in the function "door." Introductory and dismissive rites also demand space and elaboration; they are an integral part of the "permanent and conserving element of myth" which the monument celebrates. Part of the problem, as Rossi elaborates, has to do with the newness of a structure, because a new building having none of "that richness of its own history which is characteristic of an urban artifact" possesses only an *architectural* presence. Having no residual memory it can only be analyzed and assessed in material, formal, and aesthetic terms.

This problem was already faced in the last century, when parishes in the City of London were disbanded, their fine Wren churches demolished, and new buildings intended to revitalize those parishes were erected in the rapidly expanding suburbs of Camden Town and Kings Cross. What the new buildings lacked—quite apart from a material memory of form, space, and architectural detail—was the contextural framework of the City of London, with its narrow, winding streets, and its *family of associations*; that is, the collective memory of the original building in relation to surrounding buildings. They lacked the time-honored, collective locus, what I call the sense of placement, for they had literally been displaced and deprived of all reference to the original. To this day St. Michael's, Camden Town, is a witness to unrelatedness, to the problem of placing all suburban churches.

At the very least it is necessary to create a composite urban fragment that incorporates an anteroom, forecourt, walled cloister, or atrium, or some other typology from the urban anatomy, to act as an accommodating framework for any locus in the suburbs, whether that locus be a church, town hall, library, or school (see chapter 10). Rossi confirms, however, that the "individuality of the urban artifact" will be absorbed into the collective locus only when it becomes part of a more complex, historic richness of place. Therefore, the individual architectural piece, an individual building, has only a limited role within the urban framework, depending for its full participation in the structure of the city upon an elaborate interplay with other buildings and spaces and the inevitable transformations of the historical process. Conversely, this means that the memory of an individual building or urban artifact depends not only upon the original intent of the builders, but on the complicity of later events—"complicity"

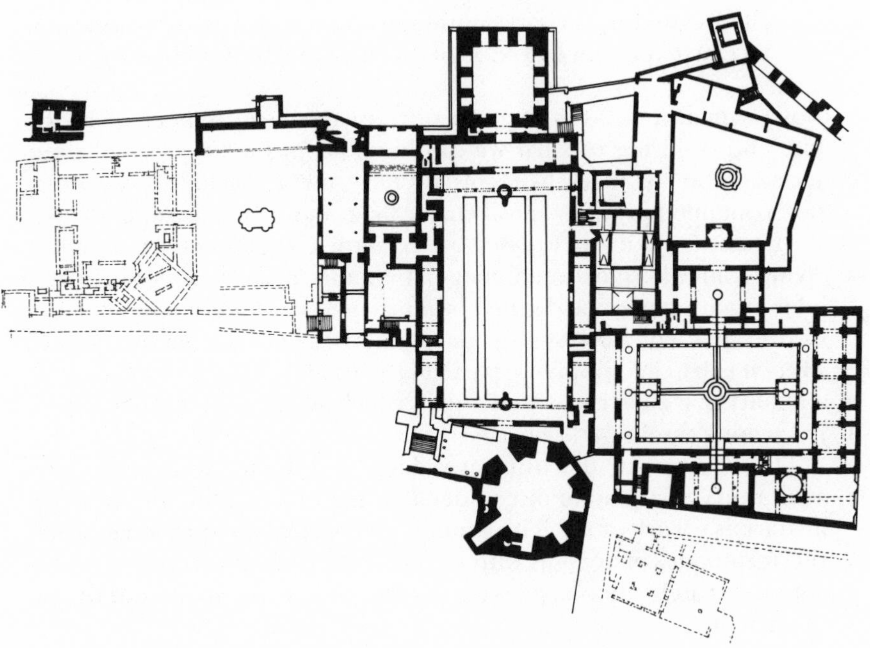

Figure 4. Plan of the Alhambra Palace at Granada, Spain, 1314–59

because the historical process is not always benevolent toward the original intent.

Rossi explains that *permanences,* therefore, have two aspects: an element of vitality and a pathological element. Repeatedly Rossi invokes the Palazzo della Ragione in Padua as a model because, although everyone basically thinks of this building as an art object, the fact that it still functions as a retail market at street level confirms its element of vitality. As an example of a pathological permanence Rossi selects the Alhambra in Granada (fig. 4) because, as he says:

> It no longer houses either Moorish or Castilian kings . . . [although] this building once represented the major function of Granada. It is quite evident that at Granada we experience the form of the past in a way that is quite different from Padua. In the first instance, the form of the past has assumed a different function

> but it is still intimately tied to the city; it has been modified and we can imagine future modifications. In the second, it stands virtually isolated in the city; nothing can be added. It constitutes, in fact, an experience so *essential* that it cannot be modified.[16]

Rossi's apparatus has as its prime purpose the measurement, quantifying, and ordering of what we can learn about the city, so that these facts may be "arranged like tools in a neat row" much like the information contained in "a botanical chart, a catalogue, or a dictionary"; but the necessity for it also to assess *quality* means that the resulting catalog "lying somewhere between imagination and memory, is not neutral." This quality cannot be defined other than to say it is vested in the sum of the parts. For Rossi such a concept derives in part from the work of French urban geographers, particularly Chabot: "for whom the city is a totality that constructs itself and in which all the elements participate in forming the *âme de la cité*."[17]

This concept of the unmeasurable, the infinite landscape of the soul, is essential also to our understanding of a building or an urban artifact as a work of art. The resulting reconciliation of rational, scientific techniques of analysis with an indefinable whole confirms the persistence of an irrational, poetic Rossi gleaming in the shadow of the rational man:

> As the present investigation is intended to establish and identify the nature of urban artifacts, we should initially state that there is *something in the nature of urban artifacts that renders them very similar—and not only metaphorically—to a work of art.* They are material constructions, but notwithstanding the material, something different: although they are conditioned, they also condition. This aspect of "art" in urban artifacts is closely linked to their quality, their uniqueness, and thus also to their analysis and definition. This is an extremely complex subject, for even beyond their psychological aspects, urban artifacts are complex in themselves, and while it may be possible to analyze them, it is difficult to define them.[18]

For the French architect Eugène-Emmanuel Viollet-le-Duc, the idea of restoration, as evidenced by Carcassonne, was to cancel out the historical process in search of some supposedly more original and pristine architectural intention. He is a Rossi hero because of his unambiguous view of "architecture as science" and his definition that "it was the principles of architecture together with the modifications of the real world that constituted the structure of the human creation."[19] It was Viollet-le-Duc, responding to Alberti's image of the city as a large house, who discovered that it is in fact the house which offers the best evidence of ritual patterns, customs, and aesthetic preferences of the population as a whole, because the structure of the house, like its order of functions, only changes gradually over long periods of time. By studying house plans, Viollet-le-Duc was able to use his penchant to reconstruct the past in the formulation of the principles of urban nuclei, extending those principles to describe such medieval artificial cities as Montpazier. He found, for example, that Montpazier not only had a regular planning grid but that all the houses were of the same size and with an identical plan. The citizens of Montpazier, who were compelled to take up their abode there, were on an absolutely equal footing one with another; an entirely different fate from that which awaited those who were forced to settle in St. Petersburg (see chapter 9).

Gaston Bachelard, wishing to explore our habitation of space and time and to describe frameworks for our "dreaming consciousness" of the real world, also selected the house as an ideal typology of man's memory and psyche. But Bachelard's "house" has its roots in Alberti's Renaissance house–image rather than in the house–typology that Viollet-le-Duc showed us and which has become a principal part of Rossi's skeletal apparatus. Indeed, if we accept Peter Eisenman's metaphor of the spiral as representing Rossi's intention in the "unfolding path" technique to reveal the "process of transformation," then we may certainly posit the labyrinth as the mythical and symbolic form of Bachelard's house.[20] For it is thanks to the house, as Bachelard says, that "a great many of our memories are housed, and if the house is a bit elaborate, if it has a cellar and a garret, nooks and corridors, our memories have refuges that are all the more clearly delineated."[21]

The idea of the "refuge" is the important image here, because it is the nature of the refuge not to advertise itself. Whereas Rossi's spiral path through the skeleton seeks to yield the transformational process between cause and effect, Bachelard's elaborate house with its corridors, secret nooks, and inaccessible cellars and garrets, conspires to hide and disguise the private retreats of the soul.

The urban labyrinth mixes public and private spaces in a confusion of delight. In contrast, the suburb is too simple and tediously repetitive, as though the *spiral* has been straightened out simply to measure its length! The suburban house, although repetitive, is not typologically structured: it does not generate the order Viollet-le-Duc proclaimed, the order of Montpazier. Instead, the suburban house seeks to display in miniature a mimicry of the grand villa, the great estate, the plantation house. The suburban box may be gift wrapped and decked with architectural trinketry, but it remains an empty box for all that: its basic form lacks the simple dignity of type and, within, it contains no memory of ritual habitation.

Bachelard explains that, whereas the urban geographer or ethnographer can describe the variety of dwelling types, it is the phenomenologist who must "seize upon the germ of the essential" and locate "the original shell" in every house. He speaks of "all the subtle shadings of our attachment for a chosen spot" but admits that there are many problems in identifying their "profound reality." Bachelard says that the phenomenologist must take these shadings as the "first rough outlines of a psychological phenomenon." The important thing to understand is that they can have no superficial representation, such as a coat of paint or a Doric portico. To fathom their profundity it is necessary to describe: "how we inhabit our vital space, in accord with all the dialectics of life, how we take root, day after day, in a 'corner of the world.' For our house is our corner of the world."[22]

Bachelard, like Rossi, is concerned not with ephemera but underlying rituals that persist "day after day." As I write, in a small hotel where I can look down on the west porch of San Marco in Venice, I am not at all reminded of Las Vegas. San Marco is no "painted shed," as Robert Venturi suggests.[23] It is an urban work of art that radiates its splendor as much at dawn and dusk as at high noon. San Marco resonates in the space of the piazza as a cornerstone of civilization; it has both a cosmic and a personal scale. And inside, it is certainly a house of memories that encompasses many moments, places, and occasions in the Byzantine world. Through what distortion of art, or history, or memory could Venturi see this monument as a source of comparison with the tawdry illuminations of Las Vegas? By probing the *permanence* of San Marco we may comprehend much about the mind, architecture, civilization, and the history of Venice itself.

Has Venturi simply failed to understand the "collective nature" of the ritual? The outward signs of celebration do not represent "the feast" unless they are a manifestation of the repetitive ritual that preserves the myth. In Venturi's typology, the "fair," the celebration, has become divorced from the "feast," the ritual day of memory. Las Vegas, of course, celebrates our transience. To acquire the meaning of ritual, gambling must be part of consciousness. Was not Cain gambling on the future when he invented the city, and Dr. Faustus when he played for time? Indeed, what makes Faustus a modern man is his belief that he can gamble with the future *and win.* But the only *permanence* generated by gambling today is the bank, which might perhaps explain why the bank rather than the church has become the ritual focus of suburban life.

As a house of memories, San Marco possesses what Bachelard describes as the "ultimate poetic depth of the space of the house." As he explains:

> By approaching the house images with care not to break up the solidarity of memory and imagination, we may hope to make others feel all the psychological elasticity of an image that moves us at an unimaginable depth. . . . I must show that the house is one of the greatest powers of integration for the thoughts, memories and dreams of mankind. . . . Past, present and future give the house different dynamisms, which often interfere, at times opposing, at others, stimulating one another. In the life of a man, the house thrusts aside contingencies, its councils of continuity are unceasing. Without it, man would be a dispersed being. It maintains him through the storms of the heavens and through those of life.[24]

By thus personalizing a composite house image, Bachelard accords to a particular house in one man's lifetime a fraction of the performance which it represents in the life span of the city. As he says, "a house constitutes a body of images that give mankind proofs or illusions of stability" and he describes two ordering, or connecting themes for these images:

> 1. A house is imagined as a vertical being. It rises upward. It differentiates itself in terms of its verticality. It is one of the appeals to our consciousness of verticality.
> 2. A house is imagined as a concentrated being. It appeals to our consciousness of centrality.[25]

Bachelard goes on to explain that the sense of verticality is "ensured by the polarity of cellar and attic" which make deep marks in our consciousness because they "open up two very different perspectives for a phenomenology of the imagination." He proposes the opposition of "the rationality of the roof to the irrationality of the cellar." The roof demonstrates itself as shelter and its slope gives clues about the climate, we are conscious of the pointed roof averting the rain clouds. Bachelard observes: "Up near the roof all our thoughts are clear. In the attic it is a pleasure to see the bare rafters of the strong framework. Here we participate in the carpenter's solid geometry."[26]

The cellar, on the other hand, will have its rational uses and its conveniences will be "enumerated." But Bachelard characterizes the cellar as the "*dark entity* of the house," connecting us with "subterranean forces" and irrational depths. He clarifies how the labyrinthine structure of his "house" is interwoven with its vertical polarity so its construct, or "mental image," is connected with the construction or "formal ordering" of the dwelling. "We become aware of this dual vertical polarity of a house if we are sufficiently aware of the function of inhabiting to consider it as an imaginary response to the function of constructing. The dreamer constructs and reconstructs the upper stories and the attic until they are well constructed."[27]

It is not the case that the subterranean forces and irrational depths to which we have access through the cellar have no function in this process of construction. Our consciousness of attic and cellar is no simplistic interior description of a positive and negative, a good zone and bad zone within the soul. It is rather a complementary construction that makes a close fit of opposites. Bachelard gives an example of the "positive" explorations generated in the imagination by the cellar:

> If the dreamer's house is in a city it is not unusual that the dream is one of dominating in depth the surrounding cellars. His abode wants the undergrounds of legendary fortified castles, where mysterious passages that run under the enclosing walls, the ramparts and the moat put the heart of the castle into communication with the distant forest. The chateau planted on the hilltop had a cluster of cellars for roots. And what power it gave a simple house to be built on this underground clump![28]

Indeed, as the idea of the cellar carries us off on irrational adventures in the primeval depths of the soul, so too can the clarity we sense in the attic be extended to give us a view of the landscape beyond the walls. The vehicle for this extension is, of course, the tower. By its very verticality it complements the underworld by stretching from earth to sky. According to Bachelard, a writer's description of a house with a tower "illustrates the verticality of the human being" and also "dramatizes the two poles of house dreams." As he elaborates:

> It makes a gift of a tower to those who perhaps have never even seen a dovecote. A tower is a creation of another century. Without a past it is nothing. Indeed, a new tower would be ridiculous. But we still have books, and they give our day-dreams countless dwelling places. Is there one among us who has not spent romantic moments in the tower of a book he has read?[29]

The images of the tower and of the underground cellars extend our consciousness of the house. But Bachelard argues that the consciousness imposes a sort of natural limit on this vertical extension. If I were the architect of a dream house, he says:

> I should hesitate between a three-story house and one with four. A three-story house, which is the simplest as regards essential height, has a cellar, a ground floor and an attic; while a four-story house puts a floor between the ground floor and the attic. One more floor and our dreams become blurred.[30]

Nooks and corners, the space immediately beneath the bare rafters of the carpenter's solid geometry—these are some of the most likely alveoli where time is compressed and memories stored. But there are other "refuges" for our dreams—the reservoirs of the imagination—for the house is furnished with "drawers, chests and wardrobes." Bachelard comments upon Bergson's consistently disdainful references to drawers, saying: "Our philosopher dislikes compartmented arguments." And he reminds us that the drawer metaphor, as well as others such as that of "ready-made garments," is used by Bergson to convey what he believed to be the inadequacy of a philosophy of concept. The significant questions here are: (1) Does the invention of categories to label and store concepts allow the poetic imagery of ideas to remain fresh in these containers of convenience? (2) Is the storage "system" constructed to allow individual ideas to emerge from their drawers and move freely about the house from "cellar to attic" so that they may become acquainted with each other on the staircase?

Bergson resisted the notion that memory exists in a "cerebral or any other kind of drawer," criticizing Kant for seeing science as merely the operation of "frames within frames." This is noteworthy because we see Bachelard—mounting Bergson's spiral staircase, returning from cellar to attic—dismissing that "simplicity, which at times is too rationally vaunted." Both French thinkers offer a critique of Camillo's *L'Idea della teatro* and Rossi's tool chest or catalog. Neither Bergson nor

Bachelard condemns the theory of concepts as such. But they resist the isolation of concepts from experience and the compartmentalization of experience into discrete categories. What Bergson rejects is the reduction of concepts to drawers for classifying knowledge, and the bad fit of "ready-made garments" which shrug off the individuality of knowledge derived from experience. Such reduction shrinks the concept into a kind of lifeless thinking, since it would become, by definition, classified thinking.

Much of the power and durability of Bachelard's imagery stems from his ability to hover between real environments, like that of our "first house," and the surreal world of dreams, visions, and ambitions. This quality also characterizes the work of the Belgian painter, René Magritte (1898-1985), for whom the denial of objective and pictorial categorization became a *cause célèbre.* Magritte's various pictures of a pipe, conspicuously labeled within the painting "Ceci n'est pas une pipe," reinforce the imperative distinction between an *object* and the *representation* of an object. The painting confirms that "This is *not* a pipe" but a *picture* of a pipe![31] Indeed, I propose that one of Magritte's masterpieces, *La Philosophie dans le boudoir* (1947), perfectly represents Bergson's idea of the philosophy of concepts as "ready-made garments," which conform to Magritte's insistence on representing not the object as an objective thing but as an idea which the image then counterpoints and elaborates. Bachelard resists the "drawer metaphor" itself, saying:

> It is even possible, when listening to certain lectures, to foresee that the drawer metaphor is about to appear. And when we sense a metaphor in advance there can be no question of imagination. This metaphor—which, I repeat, is a crude polemical instrument— . . . has mechanized the debates that Bergsonians carry on with the philosophies of knowledge.

And he goes on to caution that: "[A] metaphor should be no more than an accident of expression, and that it is dangerous to make a thought of it. A metaphor is a false image, since it does not possess the direct virtue of an image formed in spoken reverie."[32]

Bachelard quotes an episode from Henri Bosco's novel *Monsieur Carré-Benoît à la campagne,* in which the author uses the Bergsonian metaphor of the drawer in reverse, so that instead of characterizing the intelligence as a filing cabinet, the filing cabinet is represented as intelligence! Monsieur Carré-Benoît's filing cabinet has forty-eight drawers and is made of solid oak. It is his favorite piece of furniture because of its precision and meticulous utility. Anything filed in it can be retrieved rapidly; thus he sees it as replacing everything, even memory and intelligence, so marvelous is this tool! Indeed, M. Carré-Benoît attributes a sort of magic power to his set of drawers, which he comes to regard as "the foundation of the human mind." But hardly are these words out of his mouth when he opens the drawers of his "august cabinet" to discover that his maid has stored in them the mustard, salt, rice, coffee, peas, and lentils. As Bachelard says, poor Carré-Benoît's "reasoning cabinet had become a larder."[33]

In Bergson and Bachelard, therefore, we find the most effective undermining of the Tower of Babel erected by Venturi and Graves. Whereas Bergson rushed to judgment to burn the dry rationalism of Kantians, Bachelard is seeking a poetic rationale, which in turn illuminates the not-so-dry rationalism of Rossi.

As Rossi admits, the universality of the experiences which may be cataloged as representing Florence, is still "not sufficient to explain the precise form, the type of object which is Florence." The quality of Florence remains fresh because, like Bachelard's poetic image, it is immediate while retaining an essential elusiveness. Although Florence contains a number of identifiable typologies these do not, in total, constitute a recognizable urban model. The whole is interesting because of the pieces, and the pieces make up a whole; yet the whole cannot be defined except in terms of those pieces that I term the "urban fragments." And these fragments resolutely refuse categorization in collective drawers of analytical convenience (see chapter 10).

Similarly, the experience of interior space and imagery in San Marco may summarize the Byzantine experience, but it does not achieve this summary by being typical. As interior space it synthesizes, while within the framework of its piazza the basilica of San Marco is unique, uniquely Venetian. Its quality cannot be translated to another place—a problem encountered by Ruskin when he attempted to translate the quality of the Jura. The attributes of San Marco cannot be divorced from its placement.

The value of the typology as a measuring stick is its capacity to identify persistent architectural responses to conscious rituals. Similarly, the *urban artifact* teaches us about architecture and the urban work of art as true complexity—the compression of time and human energy into material form and space. For both Bachelard and Rossi, this coincidence of time and energy in compression is the soul of architecture and the urban work of art. The architect's task is to construct a skeleton, a framework between the subconscious cellar and the superconscious attic—a sort of material larder in which cultural energy and memory may be stored. By moving vertically through this spatial framework of consciousness, by ascending this evolutionary spiral of self-revelation, we find ourselves lifted up by memories of previous encounters with existence, confidently poised on our own staircase of experiential exploration.

PART TWO

▲

MORE A MATTER OF SUBSTANCE THAN OF STYLE

[H]uman lives are composed . . . like music. Without realizing it, the individual composes his life according to the laws of beauty even in times of greatest distress.

It is wrong, then, to chide the novel for being fascinated by mysterious coincidences, but it is right to chide man for being blind to such coincidences in daily life. For he thereby deprives his life of a dimension of beauty.

[D]reams are eloquent, but they are also beautiful. That aspect seems to have escaped Freud in his theory of dreams. Dreaming is not merely an act of communication (or coded communication, if you like); it is also an aesthetic activity, a game of the imagination, a game that is a value in itself. Our dreams prove that to imagine—to dream about things that have not happened—is among mankind's deepest needs. Herein lies the danger. If dreams were not beautiful, they would quickly be forgotten.

—MILAN KUNDERA, *THE UNBEARABLE LIGHTNESS OF BEING*

SEVEN

▲

MYTH AND MEMORY IN THE LANDSCAPE: THE NABATEAN MONUMENTS AT PETRA

In his unpublished *Discourse* on architectural theory, Sir Christopher Wren discussed the "two Causes for Beauty," the "natural" and the "customary." "Natural is from Geometry, consisting of Uniformity (that is Equality) and Proportion. Customary Beauty is begotten by Use of our Senses to those Objects which are usually pleasing to us because of other Causes, a Familiarity of particular Inclination breeds Love to Things not in themselves lovely."[1]

To Wren, therefore, the natural structure for beauty was the classical system of order, proportion, and rhythm; whereas some more commonplace but repeated experience, that "Familiarity of particular Inclination" to which we are accustomed elicits an unschooled, sensory response that gives ordinariness its customary delight.

In considering Petra, and in our efforts to come to terms with both its total environment and its monuments (fig. 5), we are at once confronted by Wren's double standard for beauty. Here our interest lies in both the calculated intention of Hellenistic classical order and the looser, sensual framework of Nabatean architectural games. For the

Nabateans who carved out Petra, that remote and awe-inspiring wilderness was familiar; it possessed a "Customary Beauty" they could manipulate with inventive ease.

Certainly, there is nothing commonplace about Petra, yet it undeniably appeals to our atavistic sensuality. Its geology and geomorphology, even without the imprints of the Nabateans, are quite astonishing. Each visit to this weird and extraordinary site refines and retunes one's earlier impressions. What already seemed remarkable from a first visit takes on yet another, even more dramatic aspect when seen later in a different quality of light. The rapid movement of winter clouds induces constant transformations of color, texture, and shape. In Petra we accede to a mysterious other world of light and form. With the exception of the Khasneh and its unique relationship to the Siq, it is not at all the stage set for classical architecture.

Familiarity with Petra reveals that it is not in the least a natural environment in Wren's sense, but in fact one of "Customary Beauty." Because the Nabateans were truly accustomed to this place, they could leave their marks upon its environment without destroying it. For the Nabatean monuments interpret not simply classical architecture but also the means, material, and place that are distinctively Nabatean.[2]

Petra has to be considered, first and foremost, as a unique natural site that offers an experience as varied and awesome as that of the Grand Canyon. It was this natural citadel and fortress which the Nabateans embellished and enriched, conforming to Ruskin's dictum that: "it is in becoming memorial or monumental that a true perfection is attained by civil and domestic buildings. . . ."[3] Having little evidence of free-standing Nabatean buildings (the Kasr el Bint being a notable exception), we are left today with a wild natural landscape of incredible scale and remarkable contrasts, rendered in a bizarre palette. Within this landscape the architectural evidence clings to the rockface of which it is part like a veil of civilization fused to the rugged terrain. Indeed, the longer one looks at Petra the more apparent is the integration of the carved monuments with their setting. Wherever seismic shocks have torn fragments off the monuments and tilted them at odd angles, these have quickly returned to the structures of natural formation.

Although the classicizing Khasneh (pl. 7) brilliantly terminates the journey through the Siq (and we shall see that there is nothing in the purely Nabatean architectural repertoire that would have achieved the same effect), the site of the Khasneh is unique. Wholesale inser-

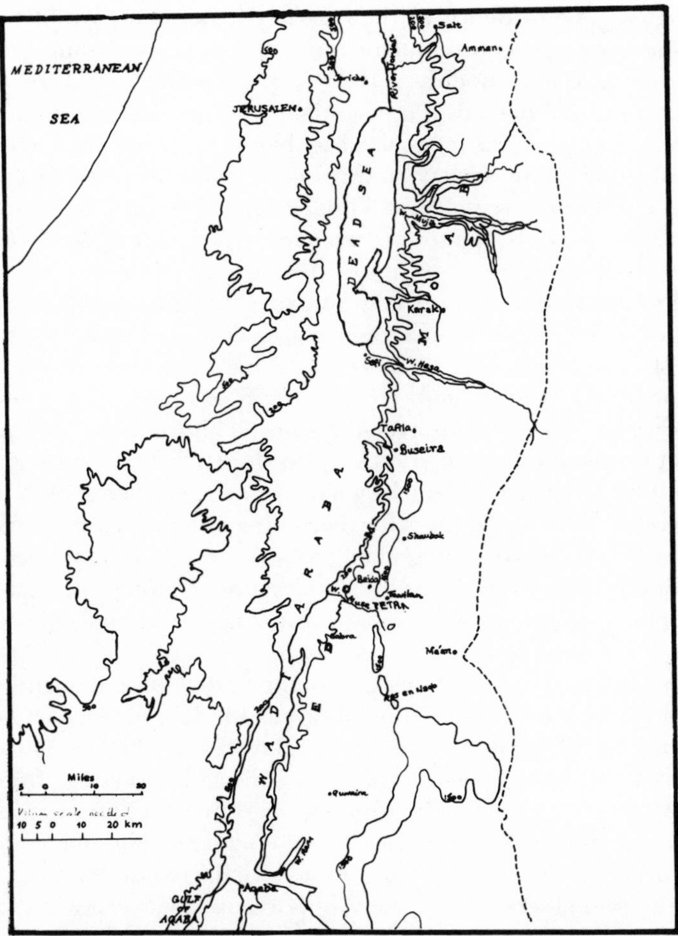

Figure 5. Map of southern Jordan, showing the location of Petra in relation to the Gulf of Aqaba (Red Sea), the Mediterranean, Amman, and Jerusalem (after Hammond, 1973)

tion of Hellenistic classicism into the organic context of Petra would, therefore, have been quite inappropriate. Fortunately, the Nabateans seemed fully alert to this discrepancy of style and context and avoided the temptation to separate the idea of monument from the nature of place.

What Wren thought of as natural was certainly not so to the Nabateans. The evidence of their earlier monuments is not that of craftsmen struggling to emulate classical ideals and failing because the experience and models at their disposal were second- or third-rate. Petra is well named: it is essentially an experience of rock. Even Nabatean deities were formalized as blocks of stone. The embodiment of stone in life, society, and culture was the authentic Nabatean response to the ethos of Petra. Thus, Petra can be read as the evolution of natural landscape toward architecture. The result is not an architecture of detachment of figure from ground, but of attachment. It is also an architecture of continuity. Although individual monuments or groups of monuments may appear at first glance to be isolated phenomena, the experience of taking the same route for the third or fourth time suggests that the architects planned a grand design of vistas and visual interrelationships. This is particularly apparent in exploring different routes up to the High Place (pl. 8), or in descending from that sacrificial plateau to the Garden Tomb, or to the Roman Soldier's Tomb. After becoming accustomed to the physical exertion required to negotiate the steep pathways, one becomes increasingly aware of the subtle interactions among space, movement, and panorama. Both Nabatean foresight and hindsight reveal themselves along the way.

To reach Petra one must descend to the wadi floor and negotiate its undulating course. This area is known as the Bab-el-Siq, that is, the "gateway" to the Siq itself. Once in the Bab-el-Siq, whether on foot or horseback, human impact on the rock walls and pinnacles of the approach track is immediately apparent (fig. 6).[4] The jinn blocks announce themselves dramatically. These enigmatic monuments to the spirits of the air arouse powerful emotions in the visitor. First and foremost, the jinn blocks display sheer opportunistic virtuosity in deploying detached rock formations to make a cultural and symbolic statement. Among the architectural dramatis personae of Petra, the jinn blocks serve symbolically as sentinels or even as representations of the stone gods. The traditional label of jinn block itself suggests that they were associated with spirits, perhaps with the warding off of evil spirits. Certainly they occupy an appropriate territorial position to do so; for it is quite impossible to approach the Siq without passing close to them.

All the jinn blocks are located outside Petra proper, most of them being found in the Bab-el-Siq area; and in all cases the details of their decoration have been eroded. Actually, in their present eroded condi-

Figure 6. Map of the central area of Petra, showing the location of the principal monuments (after I. Browning, 1973)

tion they do not appear particularly ominous (pl. 9). If we examine these monuments in the Bab-el-Siq a number of interesting things may be observed. First of all, there is the monolithic character of the jinn blocks themselves. Furthermore, the nature of their decorative carving would appear to have been strictly architectural and abstract rather than expressing any overt symbolism. What we are left with are cuboid masses, with clear traces of architectural treatment remaining on their sides. In some cases, the contours of the pilasters are still visible, framing central bays that are wider than the outer ones. Some contain tomb chambers, while others appear to have had a purely symbolic function. On the other hand, explicit representation is rare in Nabatean work. Exceptions are the Lion Tomb, the Lion Monument and the recurrence of the snake motif. There seems little doubt, however, that the abstract statement of the rock itself as a metaphysical force was a key idea in Nabatean monumental carving. An understanding of this abstract, interpretive cosmos, somewhere between nature and architecture, would seem essential in any comparison of Nabatean work with the classical tradition. The fact that such abstraction had no impact upon the pragmatism of the Romans meant that the Nabateans' days were numbered once their exotic fastness caught the Imperial eye.

The Bab-el-Siq was obviously an important area, since it not only approaches the Siq but is also contiguous with the extensive "suburb" of El Madras. The Bab-el-Siq was probably a processional way. This directionality would seem to be confirmed by the position of the archway that spans the entrance to the Siq. Once inside the canyon of the Siq, we find ourselves drawn relentlessly into its cool shade, attracted by some invisible promise, which only reveals itself at that very moment we have come to believe this awesome experience of enclosure to be endless. Suddenly, the natural rock canyon reveals a perfect picture of civilization, an architectural representation that is as urban as any we can imagine yet is firmly embedded in the cliff face: the Khasneh. One moment this revelation is just a slice of classical facade, the next the entire monument towers over us, and the invisible promise is confirmed.

Other indications as well specify the significance of the Bab-el-Siq area: the bilingual inscription and, opposite it, that curious conglomeration of the so-called Obelisk Tomb with the Bab-el-Siq triclinium beneath (pl. 10). Very shortly after we have encountered the jinn blocks our attention is drawn to what, at first glance, appears to be a two-story edifice. This is the Obelisk Tomb and Triclinium. Closer inspection shows that the two "stories" have been carved in distinctly different styles, and therefore belong to different periods. Also, it is apparent that the central axis of the lower, later "story" does not coincide with that of the one above. Any suggestion that this nonalignment is merely a clumsy gesture in classical terms is denied by an examination of the rock formation. One obvious difference between the two monuments, for this is what they are, is the fact that they have not been carved in the same plane. Having noted this, it becomes clear that the reason for shifting the central axis of the lower facade is to obtain greater height for the lower monument. On this cramped site this was, naturally, an important advantage. With its monumental simplicity, the upper, earlier facade seats four large obelisks or elongated pyramids on a broken podium containing the doorway. These initially had determined the architectural scale of the entire cliff wall. In adding the later, more elaborate and delicate facade of the triclinium below, the Nabateans had to contend with this predetermined and controlling factor.

They did so in a most ingenious and, one might say, classical way. It would have been relatively simple, after all, for such accomplished rock carvers to have cut back the cliff face below in order to fashion the lower facade on the same plane as that of the upper tomb. But, in competing with the visual weight of the upper facade, it was clearly helpful to keep the lower facade projecting forward from it. To have synchronized the axis of the lower facade with that of the one above would have resulted in a loss of height at the apex of the triclinium facade. Thus, part of the advantage of keeping the lower facade in front of the upper one would have been lost by less apparent mass. This appears to be the reason for adopting this subtle but effective shift of axis. Admittedly, the result is confusing. On the one hand there are two quite distinctly different facades, unrelated except by physical juxtaposition; a terraced development, as it were, that responds to the nature of the rock formation. Yet, on the other hand, the placing of the triclinium in this position cannot have been an accident: it was clearly a deliberate decision. But why was such an important statement of Nabatean classicism squeezed in beneath an existing tomb, when there were other more promising sites? After all, there is not a similar instance of this stacking of edifices in the whole of Petra, or for that matter at Madain Saleh.[5] (Madain Saleh was the other principal Nabatean site known to us. Located in present-day Saudi Arabia, it is also in a remarkable state of preservation.) All this points to a determination to insert the triclinium at all costs. But what lay behind this seemingly perverse gesture?

The Bab-el-Siq triclinium is an example of Nabatean architecture that refers obviously to a classical model. Browning traces the origin of this facade back to the Hellenistic Khasneh (pl. 7), through the Nabatean derivative of the Corinthian Tomb (pl. 11, right side), saying:

> [T]hey had to match the "pure lines of crystalline beauty" of the Khasneh. The only thing to do was repeat the upper part of the Khasneh elevation and incorporate it into a programme of native classicism. The result was the Corinthian Tomb . . . [which] gave rise to three other facades and, indirectly, to one more. The Bab-el-Siq triclinium is a straight copy of the lower part, less the two additional bays.[6]

In his exposition of the earlier periods of Nabatean architecture, Browning outlines the transformations of that predominant characteristic of earlier Nabatean work—horizontality.[7]

It was the carving of the Khasneh in the reign of the greatest of the Nabatean expansionists, Aretas III Philhellen (84–56 B.C.), that upset the preoccupation with those dominant horizontal cornices. The Khasneh is essentially a vertical composition. Its one continuous cornice, that runs behind the entrance pediment, in no way counteracts the vertical emphasis of the other architectural elements. Indeed, the Khasneh is not merely a facade in the manner of other Petra facades; it is much more a full-blooded architectural treatment that literally thrusts, with the depth of its portico and almost free-standing tempietto above, into the solid rock. Of all the subsequent Nabatean emulations of this Hellenistic model, only ed Deir was to approach the marked vertical emphasis of the original.

According to Browning, the Bab-el-Siq triclinium is "a straight copy of the lower part (i.e., of the Corinthian Tomb) less the two additional bays"; but it is clearly nothing of the sort. Rather, it refers back to the superimposed pediments of the Khasneh itself, although in the triclinium the lower as well as the upper pediment is broken. Even the spacing of the pilasters, with the pairs on either side of the entrance being closer together than the outer pairs, is a direct reference to the *in antis* portico of the Khasneh. Browning also says of the triclinium: "It was probably given its prominent position in the Bab-el-Siq as much for advertisement of the Nabatean classical as anything else."[8]

Given its obvious references to the Khasneh, however, it is more likely that the Triclinium's function was to announce the shape of things to come; that is, the Khasneh itself at the other end of the Siq. Perhaps this explains why the triclinium was compressed into that inadequate site. As an architectural composition, the addition of the triclinium beneath the Obelisk Tomb achieves a total ensemble that echoes the sculptural qualities of the Khasneh. The marked three-dimensionality of the obelisk forms adds an architectural weight and chiaroscuro without parallel in the other Petra facades.

Of the seven monuments carved during the so-called Nabatean Classical period, Browning writes that "each is of great individuality, denoting an amazing eclecticism and instability in the sphere of architecture."[9] Eclecticism one has to allow, but instability seems a misnomer for the almost reckless confidence with which the Nabatean designers conducted their often witty interpretations of established classical themes. Clearly, Browning adheres to Wren's prescription for the natural beauty of "Uniformity and Proportion," and this colors his assessment of Nabatean architectural intentions. Speaking of ed Deir (pl. 12), he concludes, with obvious regret, "In the design of the Deir, Hellenism has been brought to heel and made to serve the Nabatean tradition."[10]

It is of fundamental importance, in this context, to understand that the Nabateans were denied the essential refinements of the classical tradition of architecture because the sandstone of Petra, and for that matter Madain Saleh, was generally unsuitable for delicate carving. There is no question that the Nabateans were capable of fine detailing. The delicate profiles of their pottery, particularly the profiles of the bowl rims, are adequate evidence of extreme sensitivity in these matters. This sensitivity led, for example, in the case of the Kasr el Bint, to the development of sophisticated decorative plasterwork that has the small, domestic scale of Pompeian frescoes. Some of the Petran stone did permit finer carving, however. The Khasneh, in its uniquely sheltered position, is obviously a case in point. So also the capitals of the Corinthian Tomb (pl. 11, right), although much eroded by the elements, still retain rather fine detailing. In the case of the Corinthian Tomb this is clearly in emulation of the Hellenistic Khasneh—but those capitals have very idiosyncratic Nabatean leaf patterns; they are certainly not Corinthian! Also, these later examples are exceptions to the rule established earlier both at Petra and Madain Saleh.

The evidence of the earlier tombs demonstrates convincingly that the basic Nabatean intention was to retain a simplicity of form that is consistent: (1) with the scale and character of the context—the rugged, often harsh characteristics of the landscape; and (2) the fierce, burning desert sun that strikes the facades most of the year. Cliffs considered suitable for carving, because they appeared to be free of flaws, were first rough hewn to provide a working surface. We can have an idea of this preliminary process from the Quarry in the Wadi Siyagh. These prepared surfaces were then marked up and carved. From the Rectilinear through the Double Cornice periods, the dominant elements in the Petra facades were horizontal, relieved in the later periods by the verticals of simplified pilasters. The monuments in the Street of Facades (pl. 13) and at the foot of Um el Biyara, reveal the next stage in the progression from the quarry face toward an architectural expression.

The basic architectural elements of the Nabateans were the architrave and the cornice, the pilaster and the pediment. Their employment was in bas-relief compositions which usually, especially in the earlier periods, include references to preclassical architecture. We noted above that these compositions create a unique world between the nature of geological landscape forms and the human world of architecture. They may refer to established architectural traditions, but they also exist in their own right as an extension of the terrain. Clearly, there is a difference, both in cause and effect, between the builder's art—that of assembling masonry into a statement of house, temple, or tomb—and the art of carving monolithic, bas-relief monuments. As though to underline this distinction, and even perhaps to overcome the gap between the two, the Khasneh sets out to be not merely a bas-relief composition but a simulation of three-dimensional architecture.

Browning writes:

> [I]n the Deir we see how they stripped the Khasneh of all its Western decoration and presented the structural form in a powerful and moving way. Gone, too, is the *in antis* portico, for the lower half is a solid wall pierced only by the central doorway. The architect has learned from the Corinthian Tomb that, although the over-elaboration of lines was a mistake, the solid base

gave a much greater impression of strength and substance than any portico.[11]

That's hard to agree. It seems, rather, that the architect drew on the environmental memory of his own Nabatean tradition in Petra. The Deir (plate 12), while emulating the essential verticality of the Khasneh, did not achieve the same architectural assertiveness as its Hellenistic model. Although its upper story has some of the flamboyance of the Khasneh, ed Deir only projects out from the rock face, it does not also thrust into the mass of the rock itself. In its vertical emphasis the cornice of ed Deir is virtually eliminated, with its horizontal line broken above each pilaster to allow the continuity of the vertical theme. Verticality is, in fact, even stronger in ed Deir than in the Khasneh. This effect is achieved by fragmenting the upper facade into distinct slabs, and aided by the addition of a detached composite pillar at either end. Throughout the composition the vertical lines prevail, and Browning's reference to a "solid base" seems a misreading of this design.

It will be recalled that the Obelisk Tomb (plate 10), in contrast to most early Nabatean work, also slices the rock vertically. The raison d'être of these primeval shafts of stone, observed in the jinn blocks and the obelisks on the ridge below the High Place, achieves a purely architectural significance in the Obelisk Tomb. These vertical monoliths, and their integration within monuments, also represent the god Dushara. This enables us to interpret ed Deir not simply as a reworking of the Khasneh but also as a variation on that most fundamental of Nabatean themes, the upright stone monolith or *betyl* of Dushara (pl. 14). It is probable that what the Nabateans sought in carving their stone monuments was not an architectural ideal per se, but rather a symbolic, religious ideal that linked the enduring power of the rock (Dushara himself) with the transience of this life. Within this ideal, therefore, stone embodied both the cause and the effect, the means and the end: hence the form of Dushara as a phallic source of life.

At the outset we referred to the "sensual framework of Nabatean architectural games." Architraves and cornices, pilasters and pediments were not simply copies of external stylistic models but curious amalgams that do not appear together elsewhere. The bold concave *cavetto* molding, for example, which doubles for the cornice or the upper cornice in the middle period of work at Petra and provides a dominant theme at Madain Saleh, derives directly from Egyptian temple pylons, and is combined with elements associated with classical architecture. It probably suggested itself because the upward tapering of many early tomb facades has a direct affinity with the pylon form. As a terminal molding or feature the grace and powerful overhang of the giant cavetto is hard to beat.

Given the problem of architectural legibility in the fierce desert sunlight, the cavetto was a natural molding for the Nabateans to incorporate into their designs—once they became aware of it. Since strength of form to counteract the "bleaching" effect of the harsh light was of primary concern to Nabatean designers, they were on the lookout for similarly striking sculptural effects. The Nabatean style, then, seems to have evolved largely in response to: (1) a material that did not respond to fine detail, and (2) light conditions that required bold forms if bas-relief compositions were to appear as more than graffiti. This unity of material and place achieves a perfect fusion at Petra, and not unnaturally inspired the sensitive Nabateans to create a unique architectural expression. Although it freely embraced elements of other architectures, Nabatean work remained governed by its own rules of composition and symbolic emphasis.

We have noted that the Corinthian Tomb (pl. 11, right) did not have truly Corinthian decoration on its capitals. Nevertheless, the designer of the Corinthian Tomb made a conscious attempt to embody the spirit of the Khasneh. The tomb's anomalous weakness, therefore, is in its effort to reproduce the Hellenistic trinketry, whereas the strength of normative Nabatean work lies in its bold and vigorous interaction between materials, form, and ethos. Wren's "Geometry of Uniformity and Proportion," like Hellenistic gentility, would have stirred little response in the Nabatean soul. Before the carving of the Khasneh the fundamental concern of the Nabatean designers was not uniformity but variety, and not proportion but contrast. In achieving these aims they were undoubtedly aided by Egyptian masons, whose expertise in stone carving was legendary throughout the region, and who traditionally favored a simplicity of form and detail that stemmed from a not dissimilar desert environment. We do not need to ask where the cavetto molding came from, and it is not too difficult to guess who brought it to Petra.

The Egyptians were masters of bas-relief as has been no nation before or since. Also, the Egyptians progressed from bas-relief carving of tomb and temple to the Great Temple at Abu Simbel (ca. 1300 B.C.), the most stupendous of Egyptian rock-hewn temples, and an absolute model of surface preparation for the technique observed in

Nabatean work at both Petra and Madain Saleh. It would seem entirely reasonable that artisans of the later Ptolemaic period were attracted east to Petra and beyond.

Perhaps the most abstract aspect of the earlier Nabatean facades is the crow-stepping (or stepped-pyramid) motif that occurs above the concave cavetto cornice (pl. 15, top). This almost certainly derives from the Mesopotamians and appears on the majority of the monuments at both Petra and Madain Saleh, sometimes as a terminal feature over the cavetto but also in the form of bands, either one or two, at the top of the facade. The Street of Facades has many examples of this latter form. Although obviously out of key with the later, pilastered facades, this motif continued to be used as a capping feature. It is, of course, a pattern that is indigenous to many primitive societies; it persists today as an essential feature of Bedouin embroidery. Since it occurs as the top decorative feature of Nabatean monuments it would have been the first to be carved. This downward working method is confirmed by the Unfinished Tomb at Petra, while another unfinished tomb at Hremat near Madain Saleh in Saudi Arabia has only the crow-stepping completed.[12]

Having dressed the rock face in preparation to receive a monument, the Nabatean intention was clearly to animate the surface in the creation of the bas-relief facade. This led to an exaggeration of shape and form that is inconsistent with classical work of the period. For example, capitals which appear at first glance to be Ionic, turn out on closer inspection to be nothing of the kind. Some of those "Ionic" volutes are more like bulls' horns, the whole capital suggesting the form of a horned altar, while others resemble an animal's ears that have been cupped forward. Between the extremities of the cap there is a third protuberance, a blunt member resembling the lugs left on stonework to facilitate lifting. Thus, the overall appearance of these capitals is reminiscent of some giant, winged insect, often imparting to the facades the fanciful appearance of a stage set for an occult opera. It is a strikingly original poetic image that could only be read as being truly "classical" by a myopic rationalist.

To emphasize the vertical framework of their compositions, the Nabateans developed an ingenious compound pilaster form seen only at Petra. In the earlier facades of the double cornice variety, these pilasters are employed only to flank the compositions; in other words, only at the extremities where they literally serve to reinforce the frame of the facade. In its simplest form the pilaster is divided vertically so that the outer portion, to left and right, has a flat, rectilinear section, while the inner portion is approximately a quarter circle (or quadrant) in plan. Where the pilaster is of normal width, that is, the same as the central ones in the composition, the divided outer pilaster has exactly the same capital as the other pilasters. But in some cases these outer pilasters are wider, consisting of a normal pilaster with the quadrant segment as an addition. This not only gives greater width, and therefore importance, to these outer pilasters, but it also reduces the interval between them and adjacent pilasters. These truly composite features also had composite capitals, and their most developed form occurs in those additional, flanking pilasters of ed Deir (plate 12).

Interestingly these composite pilasters remain an essential characteristic of the Nabatean Classical period. In fact, rather than copying the guidelines provided by the Khasneh, the Nabateans' continued use of this pilaster device ensured not only the continuation of their own distinctive architectural expression, but also allowed them to effectively dismantle the entire classical system of rhythm and emphasis within a facade. This process may be observed in the Sextus Florentinus Tomb, for example, where the composite one-and-a-half pilasters occur only in the lower portion of the facade, yet their articulations extend up through the frieze, effectively taking on the role of supporting the segmental pediment that spans between the two central pilasters. In the Broken Pediment Tomb we find two pairs of split pilasters which are mirrored about the outer panels of the composition: this has the effect of making the central, doorway space, located beneath the gap between the broken halves of the pediment, into an apparently minor function of the facade; while the outer, flanking portions are each centralized beneath half a pediment by the framing effect of the mirrored, split pilasters. By applying this principle of creating conflicting centers of interest within a composition, as evidenced by the Broken Pediment Tomb, the Nabateans went on to achieve a complete dismantling of classical rhythm and harmony in the facade of the Palace Tomb (pl. 15, left).

In the first place, unlike any other monument at Petra, the Palace Tomb facade is designed not as an axial composition but as a duality (pl. 15, left). It therefore has no central doorway. Instead, there are four entrances, reading in terms of their pediment form (from left to right):

A (segmental pediment)—*B* (triangular pediment)—*B*—*A*

In other words, the pairs of entrances are mirrored about a central blank panel or negative space. Then, moving from the center out-i wards, to left and right, the composition turns its back on this central panel, thus further negating the center. This is achieved by having the pediments supported by split pilasters, so that the two central openings (*B:* triangular) have the quadrant (or quarter-circle) portion toward the opening. But this is only the beginning of the game, because the two outer, segmental pedimented entrances (*A*), which are narrower than the inner ones, are given greater importance by framing each of them with a further pair of split pilasters. This has the effect of setting up a further duality between the two larger, visually heavier, triangular pedimented central doorways and the two smaller, but more emphatically framed, segmental pedimented outer doorways.

There is a further complication and visual conflict, for, whereas the two central doorways have their split pilasters oriented toward their axes (i.e., with the quadrant portion of the pilaster toward the opening) the outer doorways have the reverse treatment. This results from the addition of the split pilasters that frame the outer, segmental pedimented openings, with the consequence that the rhythm of flat and quadrant surfaces in the pairing of the pilasters focuses the quadrant contours on the flanking spaces between pilasters rather than onto the doorway itself. Thus, in accordance with the working out of a duality in the composition, we have the negative space or blank panel in the center of the facade; but the outer doorways, having been increased in importance by the additional "framing" pilasters, are then made into negative elements by the resulting split pilaster rhythm, while the blank spaces flanking them are "framed" by the quadrant sections.

As if this were not complex enough, the second story of the facade reverts to a symmetrical composition, having pairs of normal pilasters supporting projecting sections of the cornice with the following rhythm:

a—b—b—b—c—b—b—b—a

This results in a wide central section (*c*), flanked on either side by three less wide sections (*b*), with an even narrower terminal section (*a*) at either end of the facade. At first glance there is no apparent relationship between the upper and lower stories. However, there is a relationship, in fact; one that, in the rhythm and positioning of elements in the upper story, cancels out the structural form and cadence established by that in the lower.

This sophisticated game with the elements of classical design does not amount to "instability in the sphere of architecture" as Browning suggests. Rather, it is that complex stuff which distinguishes an authentic architecture, based on an enduring memory and variations of its themes, from one that is merely copied from pattern books or misunderstood sources. Clearly, the Nabateans had the wit to understand classical models, but equally clearly, they chose to reject them in favor of their own "particular inclination."

Memory offered Nabatean architects not a program of copying but of adaptation to the needs of their own particular culture and environment. Located astride the trans-Arabian trade routes, a strategic position which gave the Nabateans their wealth, Petra certainly offers evidence of many external influences of architectural style; but, more importantly, many of its monuments reveal the confident emergence of a truly unique architectural expression. The Nabatean architectural evolution is therefore to be seen not simply as a pattern of eclectic exercises, a sort of Postclassicism, but rather as an early example of contextural regionalism. By marrying imported influences of style and technique with the character of the site and their own cultural nature, the Nabateans have left quite magical marks on the stones of the desert, carving and shaping a unique poetry of architecture and landscape.

EIGHT

▲

MEMORY OF THE UPPER ROOM, IMAGE OF COURT, TEMPLE, AND HEAVENLY MANSION

The early Christians devised a new temporal way of life to represent their spiritual conversion, but equivalent innovations in architecture did not manifest themselves overnight. That the process of transformation was slow was due in part to the Jewish background of many of the converts. The fact that Christianity was a suppressed and, consequently, underground movement resulted in an even slower process of representing the new faith in distinctive architectural forms. As Richard Krautheimer confirms, Christian congregations developed even a loose organization only gradually, while ritual was also loosely interpreted at the beginning of the second century. On Sundays congregations would assemble to pray at sunrise, gathering again in the early evening for a meal (agape) that recalled the Jewish meal on the Eve of the Sabbath.[1]

The believers in the New Covenant found themselves dogged by the practices of the Old Covenant, which they now regarded as outmoded and inappropriate. Those early believers also had neither the means and organization nor the interest in evolving an ecclesiastical architecture. They simply met in whatever place suited the occasion. To win converts a group might assemble in a Jewish place of worship—in Jerusalem the Temple precinct, elsewhere a synagogue, and so on. This meant that until about 200 A.D. a Christian architecture did not and could not come into being. Only the state religion of the Roman empire erected temples in the tradition and style of Greek and Roman architecture. The savior religions, depending upon the specific ritual form and financial status of a congregation, built oratories above or below ground but always on a small, essentially domestic scale.[2]

At the heart of the ritual was the communal meal, so the most common place of meeting was the dining room, which was frequently the uppermost room of inexpensive lower- and middle-class houses. This room would have been the only large room of the house and customarily opened onto a terrace. It would have been simply furnished with a table and three surrounding couches from which the dining room takes its Latinized Greek name, *triclinium.* This would have been the only room essential for the celebration of this memorial of the Last Supper. These typical, cheap one-family houses of not more than four stories thus became the model for the earliest oratories or community houses, all known examples of which owe their plan and form to the domestic architecture of the Eastern provinces.

By the beginning of the third century the basis for our present-day liturgy had evolved, with the communal meal confined to charitable meals for the poor (*agapai*) or funeral and memorial feasts held in cemeteries on or near the site of a martyrdom. The normal Christian celebration was divided into two distinct parts. Catechumens as well as the faithful could attend the first part (Mass of the Catechumens) which included readings from scripture, a homily and prayers. Only full members of the church who were baptized and in good standing could participate in the second part, the Mass of the Faithful, which had three ritual components: a procession of the faithful bearing offerings for the sacrifice and gifts for the church and distribution to the poor; the symbolic sacrifice in memory of Christ's crucifixion, the Eucharist; and the communion, the distribution of the bread and wine offered as the symbolic sacrifice, which replaced the original communal meal. The triclinium or dining room no longer sufficed as the rapidly expanding congregations required a large assembly room with a division between those who officiated at the ceremonies and the ordinary or lay members of the church. The bishop sat in an armchair, like a Roman magistrate, flanked by his presbyters, presiding over the assembly from a raised platform (the *tribunal*); while the congregation was seated outside this presbytery and arranged in strict order. The pattern of congregational seating varied in the different churches, probably influenced by preestablished local customs, with the men, women and children allocated to specific areas within the room.[3]

Furniture would have been simple and had to be portable so as not to provide permanent evidence of Christian assembly. It included the bishop's chair, a table (*mensa*) for the Eucharist and a second one to receive the offerings, with a railing to enclose the mensa and separate clergy from laymen. Adjoining the assembly room there had to be a *vestibulum* to which the catechumens withdrew to hear, but not see, the Mass of the Faithful. An elaborate liturgy had also evolved about the baptismal rite, involving anointment before and confirmation after baptism. This meant that both a baptistery and confirmation room (*consignatorium*) had to be provided. In addition, a number of ancillary rooms had to be provided for instruction of the catechumens, storage of altar vessels, celebration of agapai, even a library. The work of the church required offices and living accommodation for the clergy as well as storage for food and clothing to be distributed as charity to the poor. All these complex requirements generated a network of rooms that varied greatly in size, with those connected with the liturgy and associated rituals demanding a pattern of close intercommunication. Clearly, no temporary accommodation could serve these diverse ends, and an unconverted house would be equally inadequate. Consequently, any structure purchased by or on behalf of a Christian congregation would have to be modified to serve its needs.[4]

Such a building conversion is represented by the meeting house at Dura-Europos, which was acquired by a Christian congregation in 231 A.D., when it was substantially modified. Two rooms were merged to create a place of assembly that would have seated fifty or sixty people. Adjoining this is a room in which some thirty catechumens could have heard the Mass of the Faithful and be instructed; and this in turn leads into a small, rectangular baptistery complete with a tub under a canopy.[5]

In the earliest architecture of Christianity we therefore find the congregation exercising prudence by providing for its evolving needs behind the inconspicuous facade of a middle-class house. In addition to expunging its environmental memory, anxious to eradicate images and associations of alien religious practices, they had also to be cautious and avoid attracting attention and persecution. Temples of the Jews and of the Roman gods were equally anathema to those early

Christians, whose requirements, although increasingly complex, still reflected the domesticity of the mystical drama they reenacted, the Last Supper in the *anageion,* that "upper room, open to the light" of which Tertullian spoke. In any case as a sect that was still largely forbidden, the architectural representation of those early Christians by necessity had to be self-effacing.

A dramatic change in the pattern of Christian life, and therefore in architectural expression, emanated from Constantine's Edict of Milan in 313 A.D., which granted open recognition and official standing to Christianity throughout the Roman Empire. First of all this new status affected the liturgy of the Church, which now grew far more solemn and formal. This change of character in Christian worship was a direct consequence of the Emperor's active involvement in the Church. Constantine initiated the concept of Christ's "Vicar on Earth," a role he appropriated for himself. Because of the Emperor's participation, the perception of Christ's relationship to his followers was also modified. Instead of being the humble, miracle-working savior, the God of the Christians was now seen as the Emperor of Heaven. As a result Christian liturgy became a ceremonial performed before God, or before the bishop as his representative. The ritual form of this new liturgy borrowed its solemnity and dignity from those ceremonials performed before the Emperor or his magistrate. Over time there was a gradual blurring of the distinctions between imperial officialdom and that of the Church. For example, minor clergy in solemn procession would carry the bishop's insignia of rank, the missal and candles into the church. Following them would come the bishop, wearing the robes of a high magistrate. To preside over the Mass, the bishop would then take his place on a throne, looking every bit like a Roman official seated on his *sella curulis.*

With this increase in the pomp and circumstance of the ritual, the role and participation of the laity was bound to diminish. Under Constantine, the portable wooden table that had formerly only been brought in for the Mass of the Faithful was replaced by a permanent altar that was frequently decorated and adorned with precious materials. Sometimes a canopy, similar to the *fastigium* under which the Emperor sat when presiding at court, was constructed on columns and arches over the altar, as for example in the *heroon* or "Baptistery" of Diocletian's Palace at Split.

Clearly, this increasing emphasis of ceremony in Christian worship demanded a new ground plan to give architectural expression to the distinction between the area required by the clergy for celebration of the Mass and the place designated for the lay congregation. It was now a case of hearing rather than witnessing the Mass, because the sanctuary created to accommodate the permanent altar and seating for the clergy was now raised above the level allocated to the laity and further segregated from them by a screen.

A second-century Christian would have had quite a shock, had he returned to earth in the fourth century and attended Mass. Gone was the domestic image of the Last Supper that would have been part of his environmental memory. That recollection of the upper room, with the table that was carried in after the catechumens had gone out to the vestibulum, had been replaced by a scene that would have appeared to him as being suspended somewhere between pagan ritual and imperial ceremony. He would have been stunned by the size of the congregation, for the thousands of converts pouring into the new official religion had increased attendance from tens to hundreds. Under Constantine, Christian worship soon gave up its domestic intimacy. The sense of privacy and discretion associated with the upper room, still found at SS. Giovanni e Paolo in Rome in the fourth century,[6] was soon abandoned. Instead, Christian worship emerged to fulfill a major and colorful role in imperial public life. What the very early Christian would have found on his return was an elaborate performance that required a more splendid stage than the simple Last Supper of his own memory. This ceremony demanded an architectural character of matching spaciousness, ritual order, and symbolic representation.

Christianity had readily embraced the formalism of Roman officialdom, but there was still no question of its subsuming the religious imagery of pagan antiquity. In fact, pagan temples were not appropriate models since they were basically designed to house a passive graven image, not an active clergy and a congregation of hundreds. Denied the resource of pagan religious forms, the Church therefore sought its own identity in the adaptation and transformation of Roman public and official architecture. The building prototype eventually selected for transformation into the congregational expression of Christian worship was the Roman basilica. Our modern understanding of this form—a long, high nave that is flanked on either side by one or two lower aisles, with clerestory lighting of the nave through windows above the aisle roofs—is a somewhat simplified and standardized version of the extremely varied antique columned halls from which the Roman basilica derived.

The simplest Roman basilica was an aisleless hall that may have been spatially subdivided by supporting columns or piers. More elaborate forms enveloped the central hall, or nave, with either single or double aisles and galleries. Entrances were placed either at the end or along a long side; while the tribunal, or seat of the magistrate, had an equally varied location. Always raised upon a dais, this seat of the presiding official was sometimes located within the nave itself; but more usually it was withdrawn from the main body of the building into an apse of rectangular or semicircular plan. This apse might be located as the terminal and focal point of the nave, but it was more likely to be found on a long wall or even at the head of a side aisle. The common feature of this multicellular audience halls was an open timber roof, which was later converted into a flat or coffered ceiling by filling in between the bottom members of the trusses.

What made the Roman basilica particularly attractive as a model were its generalized characteristics as a building type: (1) its established function as an audience hall, accommodating a simple ritual and creating a quasi-formal ambience; and (2) its variable form which, unlike that of the pagan temples, was a flexible response to a nonspecific orientation. By accepting these generalized characteristics of building volume (principal and subsidiary spaces distinguished by different heights), building elements (opaque enclosing walls, transparent subdivisions of columns, clerestory lighting, and the ceremonial dais in the apse), and overlaying these with the stricter rubric of post-Constantinian ritual, it was possible to gather the generously loose framework of the Roman basilica into an appropriate expression of religious formalism.

The Roman basilica may therefore be classified as a variable performance in response to a standardized need. As such it was the public and official equivalent of the private and personal expression of the house. In its public form the house emphasizes its "guest room" the audience chamber, which projects an institutional image towards the visitor; while behind the scenes the private life of the "family" remains secret and discreet, an ancient way that has survived to this day in Mediterranean cultures.

The model provided by the basilica offered a perfect substitute for the domestic types that had been embodied in first- and second-century Christian structures. Domestic models had extended the informality of private life into the informality of semiprivate worship, reflecting Christ's emphasis on the merger of existential and spiritual needs. Becoming public, Christianity necessarily abandoned its discreet private image. Formalizing its pattern of worship, the Church

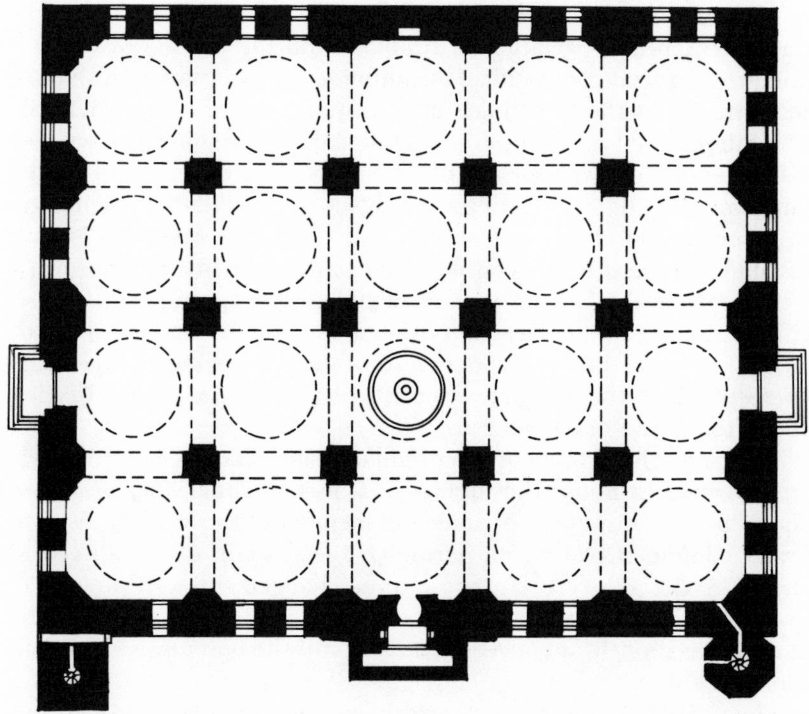

Figure 7. Bursa, Turkey: Great Mosque, late fourteenth century

simultaneously absorbed aspects of Roman public ritual. Thus, the columned hall, which entered the Roman architectural repertoire as early as the sixth century B.C. at Magna Ginaeia, passed on from Roman officialdom into the Christian consciousness.

While the elements of the Last Supper remained, this was no longer the shared feast of the upper room. The raised and frequently concealed dais of the sanctuary represented something of an intermediate stage between earth and heaven. Within the exclusive realm of this sanctuary, the priest celebrated Mass, reenacting a symbolic form of the Last Supper on behalf of the congregation. Of course, sheer numbers had militated against the continued intimacy and informality of the very early Church. Nevertheless, in isolating the celebrant and his assistants from the rest of the congregation, worship in a Christian basilica had by the fourth century mimicked the pagan idea of offering sacrifices within a mysterious inner room.

This Early Christian exercise in transformation still speaks to us today on the reinterpretation of tradition and the process of cultural and architectural continuity. The adoption and adaptation of the Roman basilica by the fourth-century Christian was, of course, not only to influence the future development of Christian architecture but also subsequently to have a profound effect upon the evolution of the Islamic mosque (fig. 7). Given the much stricter problem of orientation involved in aligning the axial *qibla* like a compass needle to Mecca, Muslim architects have been indebted to the Romans for the formal framework of the basilica, with its flexibility of planning and nonspecific orientation. The variable positioning of the *mihrab* on a long or short wall (according to the demands of the controlling qibla) exactly corresponds to the alternative models offered by the variety of plan forms found in Roman basilicas.

The generalized form of the original basilica that was so effectively transformed to house the dignity of Christian ritual, therefore also found its way into the environmental memory of the Muslim. A rectilinear columned hall which permitted the position of the apse, and therefore the axis of orientation, to be changed through ninety degrees, provided a natural framework of flexibility to accommodate the variable relationships between the qibla and site boundaries in urban mosque design.

The more rigid Christian development of the basilican model confined the orientation of the nave to that of its long axis. On the other hand, the orientation of Christian churches towards the east has not always been as exact as that of the magnetic relationship of the qibla to Mecca. Most churches were built to face east regardless of their locational relationship to Jerusalem, the rising and setting of the sun being more important than orientation to place. In this regard, therefore, Christians followed the older organizational pattern of building orientation as dictated by sunrise (day) and sunset (night), in emulation of the Egyptian temple. Traditionally, Christians have always allowed site boundary conditions to modify the west-east orientation of the nave and apse. This may also be seen as a consequence of Christian ritual, which demanded a direct expression in the plan form, making the biaxial choice offered by the Roman basilica inappropriate to church design.

Islam, by contrast, seeks an external reference point for its worship, the magnetic pull of faith towards Mecca. Within Christianity, on the other hand, the marriage of basilican form with Christian ritual may have allowed the congregation to expand many times over, but the memory of the Last Supper nevertheless persists. It is still reenacted within the room and not, as in Islam, by remote-control from some far-away external center. An essential distinction, therefore, between the architectural representation of Christianity and that of Islam is this: the former honors a presence while the latter remembers an absence.

This distinction is further developed in the iconographic, imagic character of Christian architecture, and the more purely geometric abstraction of Islamic forms and decoration. Such a contrast between readily memorable image and intellectually speculative abstraction may be valuable when we come to judge the intensity of a building's presence. The hidden dimension beyond surface appearance constitutes the substance or essence of that presence. When we find that our awareness is stimulated not by mere surface imagery but by a more profound and total sense of a building's space and form, when our perception of the physical nature of walls and roof fuses with a revelation of some unmeasurable quality of architectural presence, then our experience is heightened and our memory of it correspondingly deepened. This is surely Louis Kahn's meaning when he says, "only a work of architecture has presence."[7] It is necessary to feel the architecture "at work," actually *working* in space, in compressed time. If this presence is to emanate from a work, then those who create and build it must imbue it with an energy that can be released again to those who come later to visit the building and encounter its latent energy.

Basilican churches built after 313 A.D., in the remaining years of Constantine's reign, confirm the characteristics we have observed. The Lateran Basilica in Rome, for example, begun in 313 A.D., of which the foundations for both nave and apse have survived, had double aisles and transepts by 320 A.D. As Krautheimer notes, San Lorenzo fuori le mura in Rome, circa 330, had single aisles and no transepts.[8] Another basilica of the Constantinian period, San Sebastiano in Rome (ca. 313–15) had an ambulatory which continued its single aisle around the apse, with a number of apsidal-ended chapels off the aisle. The original basilica of St. Peter in Rome had double aisles with a transept at the very end of the nave, creating a separate sanctuary area for the clergy with the apse as a further extension of that area. It was common for the nave and aisles to represent the emerging church, since these parts were often built as a cover to the cemetery, that is, the catacombs beneath. In the case of St. Peter's, the transept and apse arrangement had a parallel but different origin.

Pagan antiquity had evolved an elaborate cult initiated by according divine status to its dead heroes, who might have been great kings, rulers, tribal chieftains, members of Roman patrician families, or even mythical heroes. The memory of these heroes was given an architectural representation by the construction of *heroa,* buildings that combined the functions of temple or sanctuary with that of a mausoleum. By 200 A.D. a *heroon* or *tropaion* erected to celebrate St. Peter's victory over death and paganism was the object of veneration on what is now Vatican Hill, and an *aedicula* believed to be this monument has been excavated by archaeologists. Apparently, the site of this heroon occasioned the construction and form of the transept and apse arrangement in the old St. Peter's basilica, representing the emergence of the martyr, risen from the catacomb beneath. As Krautheimer explains: "Fused with the chancel part into the transept, it had been rendered both visible and accessible to the crowds assembled in the nave and aisles."[9]

Both St. Peter's and the later Church of the Nativity at Bethlehem had the characteristic entry court of the catechumens, which at Bethlehem was originally surrounded by a roofed colonnade. The colonnaded court had other religious uses in the Constantinian period. For example, prosperous families developed the practice of acquiring for themselves a piece of eternal real estate, as it were, located in close proximity to the burial place of blessed martyrs of the Church. The architectural representation of this cult took the form of a *memoriam* precinct. Like the atrium of a large house or the court of the catechumens, it was surrounded by a colonnaded ambulatory that gave access to the family tomb chapels (*exedrae*). The cemetery of Manastirine at Salona is one example.[10] These structures might also be associated with a perpetuation of the pre-Constantinian funeral hall, or *triclinium,* where, as at Petra, memorial banquets for the dead were held. This practice of building private funerary estates on the sites of *martyria* ceased for two reasons. In the first place there was a dearth of land within immediate proximity to these sacred spots, but a further contributory factor was the revelry of "drunkenness and dancing, brawls, bawdy songs and gobbling" that came to be associated with them.[11] As we know from the Middle Ages, the pagan spirit of remembering the dead with merry-making was not easily put down by Christian solemnity.

The Church of the Nativity at Bethlehem has another significant feature in the octagonal tower that replaces the conventional apsidal termination of the basilican nave and aisles. The intent of the octagon, rather like the intent "made apparent" in the heroon of the original St. Peter's, is a visible manifestation of the event, Christ's birth, which is *remembered* in the crypt below. Like the original St. Peter's, too, the Church of the Nativity represents a solution to a complex problem. These two composite plans merged within a single building the meeting hall for the congregation and a monumental structure over a martyrium. But the different forms of these monumental "memories" represent the distinct differences of what is remembered. St. Peter's, like the covered cemeteries of Rome, was principally a graveyard and funerary banquet hall, while the shrine of St. Peter embodied in its transept represented his own tomb. For this reason St. Peter's was built outside the city, on the actual graveyard; it had no permanent clergy and Mass, when celebrated, would have been primarily for pilgrims, as the graveyard housed no earthly congregation. In contrast, there were no burials at the Palestinian sanctuaries, which were built within the cities to serve as cathedrals for resident congregations on a day-to-day basis. The Palestinian sanctuaries were therefore shrines in the true sense. These two different functions derived from different traditions and practices, and they were represented in distinctly different plan forms. In particular, the centralized planning of these memorial components—the octagonal structure at Bethlehem and the circular memorial in the basilica on Golgotha in Jerusalem—may be traced back to large imperial mausolea of late antiquity, such as Diocletian's mausoleum at Split.

Although the sources of the different components of these composite church plans are as clear as the ritual origins of elements, we cannot speak of norms in Constantinian church planning. The most remarkable characteristic of Christian church architecture during Constantine's reign is its great variety. Indeed, there was no concept of a church type that served a particular need or responded to place or region, only a sort of exploratory problem solving that links ritual functions with the remembrance of the history of the Church. The form of what we might think of as the typical Early Christian basilica does not evolve until the end of the fourth and the beginning of the fifth century. During Constantine's reign congregations and architects were therefore still experimenting with a variety of plan forms and their combinations. We find aisleless halls; basilicas; centralized structures; basilicas with and without apses; basilicas with projecting wings, with ambulatories or attached to centralized forms; as well as basilicas with and without atria; and structures completely enclosed by a precinct wall. These many variations were, as we have seen, generated by such variety in function as cathedrals, martyrium basilicas, and covered cemeteries. Even within these distinct functions we find variety of form, with Constantinian cathedrals including such different structures as the Lateran basilica and the cathedral at Trier.

The mausoleum built in memory of Constantine's daughter, Constantina, is placed against the narthex of the great covered cemetery of Sant'Agnese in Rome, and takes the form of a domed central space of circular shape that is lit by sixteen large clerestory windows in a drum carried upon an arcade, the archivaults of which are supported by twelve pairs of Roman composite columns. We know Constantina's mausoleum as the church of Santa Costanza. This example, together with those of San Lorenzo in Milan (ca. 375) (fig. 8), the Lateran Baptistery (ca. 315–440), and San Stefano Rotundo (ca. 468–83), celebrates the revival of the Roman temple form in Christian architecture. The elliptical plan of St. Gereon in Cologne is also of particular interest in relation to the centralized *templum* plan, because it takes what is essentially a centralized form and transforms it into a space that is at once ambiguously centralized and axial, introducing a mode that was to become a basic preoccupation with Baroque architects. St. Gereon was almost certainly built as a martyrium around 380 A.D., which would make it contemporaneous with the removal of the Emperor's official residence to Trier by Gratian. Its long sides are flanked by four semicircular, vaulted niches that thrust out of the elliptical form; while the east end is terminated by a larger, semicircular vaulted apse, and the west end has a colonnaded narthex with its own apses to north and south. Our interest in St. Gereon is the way in which an apparently centralized plan form is transformed to allow the particularization of both the east and west ends of what becomes an essentially axial church. For this reason it might be seen to plant in German soil one of the seeds of the so-called Carolingian Renaissance.

While the directional basilican plan, with or without its elaborations, predominated in the west, in the eastern or Byzantine empire the emphasis quickly moved towards a polarization within a centralized, domed space. This polarization was important not only for the evolution of the Eastern Orthodox or Greek Cross church plan, but also in the metamorphosis of the mosque. In fundamental, constructional terms it meant that the Eastern Church, with its perfect logic of centralized church planning, could build upon the more advanced struc-

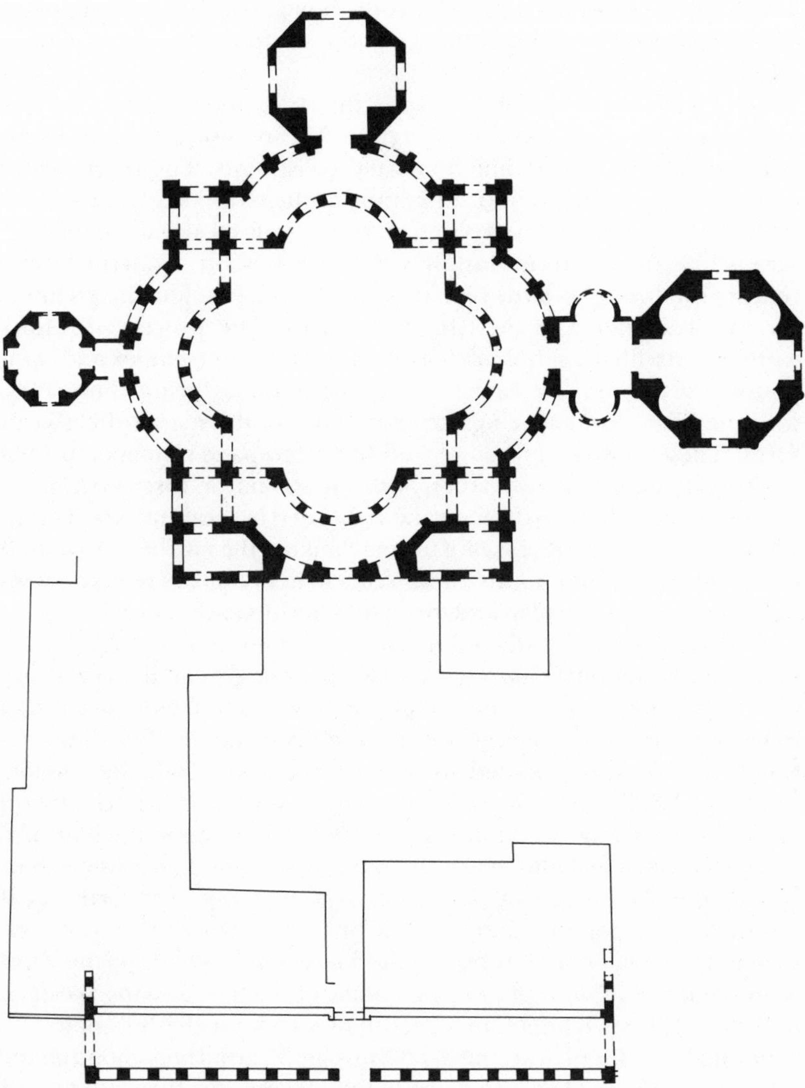

Figure 8. MILAN, ITALY: Plan of the Church of San Lorenzo, late fourth century

tural techniques of Roman architecture. The Western Church was held back, however, by a sense of confusion about the planning *intent* in response to the Christian liturgy and therefore about its structural solution.

The freedom to concentrate upon the structural solution that was enjoyed by the architects of the Eastern or Byzantine Church also, ironically, contained its own limitations and constraints. The result, as we know, is that the liturgy and expression of the Orthodox Church have remained frozen in the perfection of the centralized, domed structure. Meanwhile, the Western Church searched ceaselessly, from the fourth century on throughout the next thousand years, to refine the architectural representation of the Christian liturgy. This process of refinement began with the simplification of plan forms, the complex and composite plans of the Constantinian period gradually being eliminated, with the fifth century seeing the emergence of the standard basilican form. These new designs employed but a few basic elements, principally nave, apse and two aisles, with an atrium or forecourt and a narthex being added to the west end if dictated by local custom. A crypt was a very rare feature, as were towers flanking the narthex. Although there were later elaborations, these basic elements were to remain essential to western church plan and form until the fifteenth century.

Accepting the most advanced structural innovations of its Roman heritage, the Eastern Church set about resolving its architectural image of itself immediately, perfecting the forms and techniques it had inherited, specifically the centralized and divine dome. By its very nature, the centralized domed structure summarizes both the equable resolution of all mechanical forces and the inward-seeking orientation of the contemplative life. There is no sense of progress in the plan and three-dimensional geometry of the centralized church, because it represents not the pursuit of perfection as a progression toward a goal but the contemplation of the idea of that perfection. These two constructs of Christian architecture—the Eastern acceptance of the "limits of the possible" in representing cosmic perfection, and the Western defiance of "known limits" in a persistent search for the "unknown"—generated some of the most daring and inspiring monuments achieved by man. They also provided the models for the evolution of the Islamic mosque. For their part, Arab architects invented the pointed arch that gave the *energy* necessary to power the great Gothic cathedrals of Europe.

The Carolingian Renaissance, effected under the dynasty of Frankish emperors of a western "holy" Roman Empire—holy, that is, since Constantine—and the bonding together under the Franks of Italy, Germany, and France, lasted some two hundred years, from approximately the middle of the eighth century until the middle of the tenth. During that period, an entirely new internal arrangement, and therefore ground plan and external form, were evolved by those who generated this Renaissance and given to the monastery church and the cathedral.

This innovation and the entire concept of a distinctive Carolingian period in architectural evolution, is a relatively recent discovery. Not one piece of Carolingian architecture has come down to us intact—not even its most celebrated example, Charlemagne's Palatine Chapel at Aachen—and it is only in the past half-century that the efforts of such scholars as Kenneth Conant and Jean Hubert have succeeded in making coherent wholes of the much-modified fragments that remain from this period. The identification of the Carolingian contribution is of great significance, because the development of church architecture between antiquity and the Middle Ages passed through only three main metamorphic stages: (1) the wooden-roofed basilica of the classical and Early Christian Roman world; (2) the late antique and early Byzantine domed church; and then (3) the Carolingian church, with its superbly constructed and skillfully vaulted east *and* west ends.[12] This Carolingian metamorphosis therefore provided both the planning and the structural strategies necessary to transform the late antique conglomerate of stone post, timber truss, and stone dome into the comprehensive vaulting systems of first the Romanesque and then the Gothic church.

The principal contribution of the Frankish architects in the Carolingian Renaissance lies in their reconsideration of the "architectural entity." After Constantine, in the late antique church, we have seen that this entity evolved from the basilican typology of a high central hall flanked by lower aisles, through the addition of an east end in the shape of a domed martyrium or sanctuary. Because it derived from the earlier Roman temple form, this particularization of the east end is expressively indicative of a self-contained entity rather than a mere terminal feature to the processional "tube" of the basilican plan. As we have already noted, the addition of these centralized, domed spaces to one end of the highly directional extrusion of the basilican hall and the spatial compositions that resulted from these agglutinative assemblies of disparate, preexistent pieces of other architectures were both experimental and expedient. Christianity, having no immediate architectural heritage of its own invented new relationships of existing parts in reconstructing appropriate memories to represent the New Covenant.

All the elements we find in the Carolingian church had been inherited from Roman and Early Christian architecture, but it is their new and distinctive use that allows us to identify the unique Carolingian contribution. It is as recently as 1948 that Louis Blondel first published the results of his excavations at Saint-Maurice d'Agaune in the canton of Valais, Switzerland, which revealed that the original basilica, founded in 515 A.D. by King Sigismund, had been substantially rebuilt during the reign of Charlemagne (771–814 A.D.). The builders of the new structure had apparently left the original wooden-roofed nave and aisles in place, but in order to do this they had added a two-story apse at each end of the church. Significantly, Blondel also discovered that the apse at the west end was the larger of the two, while the plans of both conformed to what we know as the *confessio* type.

The confessio plan had originated in Rome, where it occurred by the end of the seventh century. By that time Rome was under continual attack from the barbarians, and the bodies of those Christian martyrs who had been interred outside the city walls were therefore in danger of desecration. To keep alive the memory and veneration of these holy men and women, their remains were exhumed and transferred to churches located within the city walls. To receive these precious relics, a confessio was dug beneath the floor of the sanctuary: this was a room only slightly larger than the martyr's sarcophagus. The faithful would descend from the floor of the sanctuary by two flights of steps that led into a narrow semicircular corridor, permitting them access to the saint's tomb located directly beneath the altar, where there would be just room enough for a few to kneel and say their prayers.

At least five Roman churches originally contained this confessio feature, notably San Crisogono, and all were built in the reign of Pope Gregory III (731–741 A.D.). In the case of the Carolingian use of the confessio plan arrangement, as found at Saint-Maurice d'Agaune by Blondel, in both apses this feature and its connecting semicircular corridor were on the same level as the nave—that is, at ground or entry level. The reason for bringing the confessio up to the nave level is significant and must be considered, as it stems directly from the continuing pattern of threats to the existence of the Church in the West.

The eighth century was a particularly violent and dangerous one for western Christians, and the faithful increasingly pinned their hopes for safety and survival upon the intercession of the saints, to whom they prayed, and the efficacy of holy relics in averting danger and misfortune. It was in response to this increased veneration of holy relics that Pope Paul I caused a large number of catacomb tombs to be opened up in 765 A.D. and the remains of the exhumed bodies distributed among the churches of Rome. By the end of the eighth century the exodus of some of those remains had begun, either secretly or with special papal permits; and the rest of Europe, but especially Gaul, came to receive these precious bones, beginning the practice of building into every Christian altar some fragment of a holy skeleton.

In this way the use of the Roman type of confessio spread northwards at the end of the eighth century and throughout the ninth. There is a confessio in both the great basilicas at Ravenna, Sant'Apollinare in Classe and Sant'Apollinare Nuovo; in Switzerland, as we have observed, at Saint-Maurice d'Agaune; in the celebrated St. Gall plan; in Germany at Seligenstadt; in Belgium at Nivelles; and in Gaul at the great basilica of St. Denis, which was consecrated by Pope Stephen II in 754 A.D. Yet, although the two "crypts" of the basilica at Saint-Maurice d'Agaune retained the plan form of the Roman confessio, they were built *not* underground but at nave level. Furthermore, the double-apse plan of Saint-Maurice occurs only once in Rome, appropriately in the ninth century church of the Schola Francorum that was erected by Charlemagne. Its form did not spread to Italy until the Romanesque period, and there are very few examples. The incidence of the crypt located at the nave level seems to be a feature inherited from the basilicas of Merovingian Gaul, according to Jean Hubert, where the saint's tomb normally rested on the floor of the sanctuary in the space between the altar and the apse.[13] The Carolingian "crypt" came to be built over these ground level tombs as a monument to commemorate the saint's triumph over the grave.

The double-apse form appears twice in the St. Gall plan, as well as at Fulda and in Cologne Cathedral; and it was eventually widely adopted in various transformations throughout the Rhineland and central Germania. As Hubert has noted,[14] this Carolingian use of the double apse might indicate possible references to the double apses found in the basilicas of Spain and North Africa, which occur as early as the fifth century, if it were not for one very significant functional difference. In the Spanish and North African examples the counter-apse constructed at the west end was specifically designed to receive a tomb; while in Carolingian churches the western sanctuary actually contained the main altar. Not only Saint-Maurice, but also Fulda, Centula, and Rheims cathedral attest to this fact, which means that these churches were, as Hubert puts it, "not oriented but 'occidented.' "[15]

The successive designs of the Fulda church play an important role in the evolution of this arrangement. But to understand this process it is first of all necessary to review the genesis and ensuing principles of liturgical orientation. The Temple of Solomon, in emulation of Egyptian temples, and then subsequently the great early Christian basilicas founded in Rome—St. John Lateran and St. Peter's—and the Church of the Holy Sepulchre at Jerusalem, all had entrances facing toward the east. It was the custom, based upon ancient Egyptian ritual, for the priest to greet the rising sun with prayer. Importantly, then, the obligatory daily prayers offered by the officiating priests in those early churches were so *oriented,* while those offered by the congregation were not. It was in all probability for this reason that, from the end of the fourth century, the organization of the church's interior functions were reversed, the sanctuary and the altar then moved from the west to the east end. The Constantinian basilicas remained, however, as models of this earlier, somewhat short-lived *memory* of the primeval pattern. It was these early churches, and in particular St. John Lateran, the first cathedral of Rome, that were to provide the inspiration for the churches of Gaul in the surge of new constructions that began at the end of the eighth century.[16]

The contribution of the church at Fulda, through its successive transformations, was rooted in the liturgy and its significant reform as an integral part of the Carolingian Renaissance. This reform, which was initiated in Gaul by Pepin the Short (715–768), who preceded Charlemagne as King of the Franks from 751 to 768, had its basis in the adoption of Roman liturgical practices that were then current in St. John Lateran and at St. Peter's. Its general use was then enforced by Charlemagne. Already in 742, King Carloman had called upon St. Boniface, one of the most persuasive advocates of the Roman liturgy, to reform the Frankish clergy.[17] In 744 a follower of St. Boniface founded the monastery at Fulda. Lying in one of the regions of Germania which the Franks had opened up to Christianity, Fulda therefore became an important new center of both monastic life and liturgical debate.

Fulda church soon proved too small for its rapidly growing community of monks, and was therefore rebuilt in 794 A.D. by the Abbot Ratgar. The enlarged church reproduced the plan of St. Peter's, Rome, with the principal altar in an apse at the west end, but adding a second apse at the east end that also housed an altar. This second

Fulda church, which also has the distinction of being the largest erected during the period, was only slightly smaller than St. Peter's basilica and had a large atrium, too, that recalled the one attached to its Roman model. But neither St. Peter's nor St. John Lateran's had an apse at the east end, and this liturgical counterapse (as opposed to the memorial apse or apsidal martyrium of fifth-century Spanish and North African examples) seems to have been invented at Fulda. Hubert is therefore inclined to see in it a sort of intermediate stage in the process of liturgical reform, a halfway house between local tradition and an emerging spirit within the Church. The Fulda example in the Carolingian period may be compared with the incidence of secondary oratories at the east end of *occidented* churches in southern France during the Romanesque period, such as that at Arles-sur-Tech.[18]

The Carolingian nave-level "crypt" was something entirely revolutionary in Christian architecture. In a sense it was like having a church within a church; the second, interior structure recalled the emergence from the catacomb of the martyrium in old St. Peter's, and housed a saint's tomb at the end of the nave with which it was approximately on a level. The crypt's vaulting then supported the sanctuary itself, thus creating the precedent for a raised sanctuary such as we find at San Miniato al Monte, Florence. Examples of this Carolingian crypt are to be found at Saint-Medard at Soissons, and Saint-Germain at Auxerre. Although responding to the same program, both these examples differ in plan. Both, however, abandon the narrow semicircular corridor of the original Roman confessio, and accommodate the praying supplicants instead in a broad, angled ambulatory, giving them room to move about as well as kneel at their devotions.[19]

The Carolingian crypt can therefore be seen to group together within the focal point of the church all the memoria—those family tombs and associated oratories—that had been scattered around the early Christian basilica. This is achieved by creating large rooms with recessed niches to act as burial chambers, like the antique mausoleums (as at Soissons). The result is the gathering together of separate representations of Christian memory and ritual into one complex and cohesive whole. In effect it is the creation of the Christian *permanence,* the House of God as the City of God in which there are many mansions. The complexity of this idea is in turn expressed in Carolingian architecture by erecting on the east side of the crypt an oratory of circular plan, which rises up several stories. This is a further aspect of the invention which we see in Saint-Germain at Auxerre, which became fairly common throughout the rest of Burgundy (for example, Flavigny, Saulieu, and Dijon) and existed too in Germany as at Hildesheim. Its origins may be traced back to the fourth-century martyrium form, as for example at the Church of the Nativity in Bethlehem, and it is similar to the Palatine Chapel at Aachen (ca. 798–815) which remains its most complete and perfect representation. The Palatine Chapel also witnesses most clearly the counter-influence of eastern church designs in the Carolingian Renaissance: if we did not know it was firmly anchored in Aachen we might well imagine it lying no further north or west than Venice.

The Carolingian reconsideration of the architectural entity of the early Christian sanctuary, in a sense splitting it so that there was an equal emphasis on worship and the liturgy at both ends of the church, is only part of the achievement of the Frankish architects. Facing the raised sanctuary over the vast crypt they also often erected at the west end of the nave a towerlike structure with vaulted stories, that we call the "westwork." Indeed, the Carolingian westwork was truly an architectural marvel. It has a seemingly infinite capacity to accommodate the growing demands of the Christian community that had been stimulated by the reforms of the Frankish kings, notably Carloman and Pepin, so that under Charlemagne and his successors the Christian communities could truly represent their emergence from the catacombs in their architecture. For example, the ground level of the westwork could serve as a vestibule or narthex as at Auxerre and Lorsch; or it could embrace a secondary crypt for additional precious relics, as at Centula. At Centula, the abbey of Fontenello, and Rheims cathedral, the first floor accommodated the west choir and the main altar. At Centula and Rheims, also, the westwork provided an entire parish church complete with baptistery. A tribune, where extremely important dignitaries would sit to hear Mass, and recalling the idea of the *fastigium* in the early Roman basilica, was a feature of the westwork at Seligenstadt-am-Main (begun 831 A.D.); and the Palatine Chapel at Aachen is known to have had one, also. Although only a fraction of the westwork at Auxerre can be reconstructed with any certainty, scholars believe it to have been somewhat similar to the great westwork at Corvey, which has survived (figs. 9 and 10).

The Corvey westwork was built between 873 and 885 A.D., and the entrance through a badly lit passage, with its square pillars supporting the groined vaulting, was apparently characteristic of both Rheims and Auxerre. Corvey's reputation, however, rests on the westwork's magnificent two-storied tribune, sitting astride the entrance and

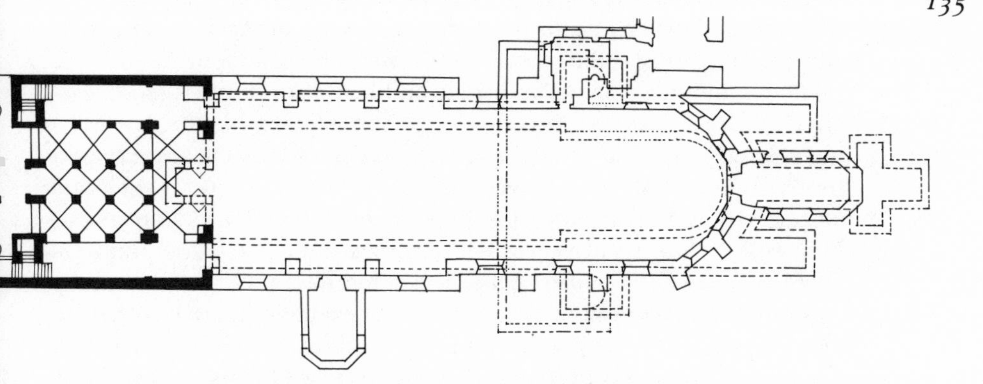

Figure 9. Corvey, Germany: Plan of the Abbey Church, begun 822

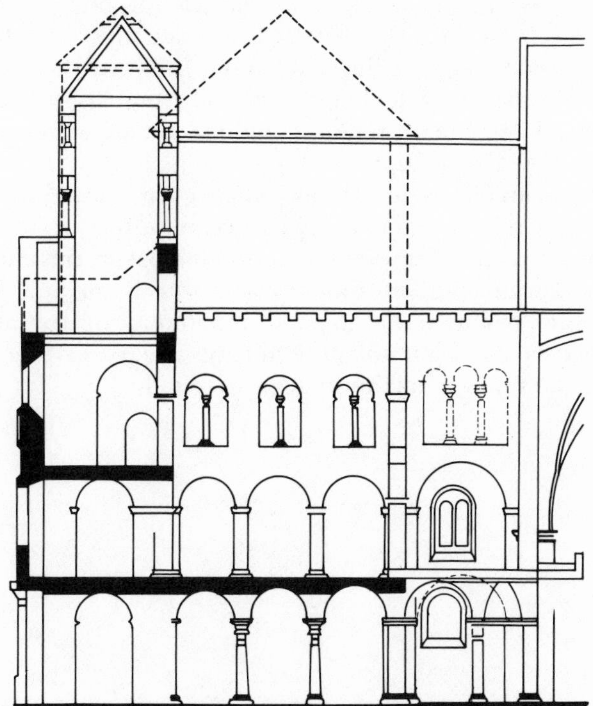

Figure 10. Corvey, Germany: Longitudinal section of the west end of the Abbey Church, showing the celebrated westwork, 873–885

flooded with light from its many windows. Sadly, there are few remains to demonstrate the ingenuity and scale of Carolingian architecture, but at Corvey and in the Palatine Chapel at Aachen we can at least begin to sense some of its inventiveness and grandeur.

The Carolingian monks and their builders distinguished the Christian church from the architectural forms of pagan antiquity. In "splitting the architectural entity" the Carolingian architects also created the framework for the achievements of the Romanesque and Gothic masters. By polarizing the ritual elements of the liturgy and giving these full architectural representation they anticipated such masterpieces as the twelfth-century cathedral at Mainz.

Today the practitioners of so-called Postmodernism are busily reassembling the pieces of previous architectures without the benefit of a ritual basis for their tired eclecticism. Meanwhile the problems of church design, like so many other design problems, have in a sense become oversimplified. The complex liturgy that evolved over the first thousand years of Christianity is now largely forgotten in favor of a vastly simplistic view of what early Christianity must have been like. Lacking true complexity in the ritual of our lives, and therefore in the building program, the tendency is to invent a complex veil of imagery and unrelated detail to represent intentions that are either misunderstood or do not exist at all.

Carolingian architects faced truly complex problems of liturgical ritual, problems that demanded substantial resources of both energy and ingenuity. In the Carolingian period important ritual intentions were being formulated and fought for: it was the natural energy of this process of evolution that gave the architecture of the Carolingian Renaissance its own vigor and authenticity. The work of the Carolingian architects remembers this struggle heroically.

NINE

ST. PETERSBURG: MEMORY OF A GARDEN, IMAGE OF AN EMPIRE

> [T]he Commission will be susceptible to such proposals as would bestow upon the city of St. Petersburg a state of dignity and grandeur, commensurate with its position as the capital of a large country . . . for the purpose of which it has been resolved to call upon all architects, Russian and foreign, and also including all interested amateurs, to apply their labors to the composition of a plan for the said city of St. Petersburg, together with a written dissertation.[1]

This announcement formed part of the rules for an international competition published on November 14, 1763, in the *St. Petersburg News* by the Commission for the Masonry Construction of St. Petersburg and Moscow that had been appointed a year earlier. Thus, sixty years after the city was founded by Peter the Great, a second attempt was made to devise a comprehensive development plan for the city that had replaced Moscow as Russia's capital during Peter's reign. The history of these attempts exemplifies the impossibility of realizing a city on such a rational and idealized basis; and its evolution between the beginning of the eighteenth and the middle of the nineteenth centuries demonstrates lucidly how the memory of succeeding generations shapes the plan and form of the preautomobile city. St. Petersburg mirrors in its development the erratic progress of Russia as it emerged from medieval serfdom into a great world power of the modern age.

The idea of the plan, the footprint of the city, is central to the formation of urban memory, and the peculiarities of the site must always play their part in shaping that idea. Most cities relate to a river, and its course does not often permit conformity to an overall gridiron plan. Many cities take advantage of hilltops for strategic or climatic reasons, and axial plans cannot readily be impressed upon hilly terrain. Nature thus plays her part in determining a city's outline, its compositional axes, its character and skyline, and therefore its presence in the landscape.

St. Petersburg is located within the delta of the River Neva, and close to the Baltic Sea. Thus its site shares certain common characteristics with those of Venice, Amsterdam, and Copenhagen. It was founded in 1703 after the armies of Peter I successfully stormed the nearby Swedish fortress of Nienschanz following a long siege. This action ended Russia's lengthy struggle to gain access to the Baltic; Peter's first action, three days after the final battle, was to go downstream along the Neva, measuring the depth of the river for future navigation. These measurements established that seagoing vessels could proceed upstream only along the wider branch of the Neva, known as the Bolshaia Neva, as the Malaia Neva was too shallow for large ships. This information was critical in the selection of the site for fortifications necessary to protect the newly conquered territory. The Swedish fortress of Nienschanz was located further upstream but, with the knowledge that the lesser branch of the Neva was not navigable, Peter's military council decided to abandon the old Swedish site and establish the new Peter and Paul Fortress close to the fork in the river and adjacent to the Vasilevski Island (see fig. 11). This decision was important in that it projected the outline of a future city which would include not only both banks of the Neva proper but also embrace Vasilevski Island together with the north bank of the Bolshaia Neva and the south bank of the Malaia Neva downstream. The city was thus to have three distinct districts, each separated from the other by the river. These constraints created considerable obstacles to both the planning process and the creation of a poetic urbanity.

Figure 11. St. Petersburg, Russia: Plan showing the relationship of the original Peter and Paul Fortress to the original Admiralty Fortress, c. 1705

With the building of the Peter and Paul Fortress on an island close to the north or right bank of the Neva, immediate military and defense needs were secured. More than that, the proximity of this fortress to Vasilevski Island meant that the land mass available for development inevitably encompassed large expanses of open water. This factor was to establish the character and, ultimately, the scale relationships of the central area of St. Petersburg in the eighteenth century. Already in 1704 the decision had been made to move the Admiralty to St. Petersburg. The Russian Admiralty at that time was not simply a Ministry of Naval Affairs. Where the Admiralty was, there keels were laid and ships built. Now that Russia had access to the Baltic it wanted to launch its newly built vessels into the Gulf of Finland as quickly as possible, and the location of the old Admiralty on Lake

Ladoga impeded that process. The new Admiralty, therefore, had to both adjoin navigable waters and also serve as a second fortress for the defense of the Neva estuaries. A site was selected opposite the eastern cape of Vasilevski Island. This highly strategic location ensured that the Neva could now be covered by cannons from both sides, making it virtually impossible for enemy ships to penetrate upstream beyond the island. Thus the siting of the Admiralty, like that of the Peter and Paul Fortress, had a strategic rationale: With the positioning of these two elements, the basic decisions concerning the growth of the city had been made, and the stage was set for planning the new capital.

As the delta of the River Neva is basically flat and marshy (Neva means "swamp" in Finnish), there were no physical obstacles, either from land formation or vegetation, to the planning of St. Petersburg. Features to take into account were the river, the bay, the configurations of land masses that form the shorelines of the delta, and the network of streams and rivulets that make up the delta. Although its location suggests comparison with Amsterdam and Venice, the dominance of the River Neva as it cuts St. Petersburg into three distinct districts rules out any real similarity with those Dutch and Italian models. Nevertheless, Peter had been very impressed by Amsterdam. As the setting for his exhilarating apprenticeship in the naval arts, it had entered his environmental memory, and he continually exhorted his architects to follow the manner of the Dutch in building his new capital.

On a trip to the west in 1716, Czar Peter met the French architect Jean Baptiste Alexandre Leblond at Pyrmont spa. By August of the same year Leblond had arrived in St. Petersburg to take up his duties as chief architect of the city. Leblond was a talented pupil of LeNôtre, who designed the gardens for Louis XIV's Versailles. In his plan for St. Petersburg prepared in the first week of January, 1717 (see fig. 12), Leblond did not follow the canal model of either Amsterdam or Venice. Anecdotes say that an even earlier plan that Leblond had rushed into execution in 1716 called for a grid of intersecting canals on Vasilevski Island for drainage and transportation, but that Peter the Great's trusted advisor Menshikov, who owned most of the island, sabotaged Leblond's efforts to please the Czar. In any case, nothing of that scheme survives in Leblond's extant plan of 1717.[2]

As a protégé of LeNôtre, Leblond was a rationalist, who believed in regular and orderly planning principles. If we seek the sources of Leblond's design for St. Petersburg, therefore, we should look to: (1) French seventeenth-century fortified towns, particularly those by

Figure 12. JEAN BAPTISTE ALEXANDRE LEBLOND: Plan for the city of St. Petersburg, 1717

Vauban;[3] (2) the proposal by Erik Dahlberg for the Swedish city of Karlskrone of 1683; (3) the new plan for Copenhagen published in 1690; and, possibly, (4) LeNôtre's layout of the Versailles gardens.

We are accustomed today to speak of the Palais de Versailles as being more "city" than "house." Certainly the axial organization of LeNôtre's garden design influenced a number of city planning proposals. This radial feature of planning, which first occurs at the Piazza del Popolo in Rome in the second half of the sixteenth century, was the essence of unity and conceptual clarity in Leblond's proposal for the new Russian capital. Leblond based the geometrical logic of his design on the implied natural axes of the site, namely those suggested by the meeting of the River Neva with Vasilevski Island and already supported by the positioning of the Peter and Paul Fortress. A map of St. Petersburg dating from 1725, incorporating two radials in the layout of the Admiralty District on the south bank of the Neva, suggests Peter's support of Leblond's ideas and the implementation of some of his principles. However, three major factors obstructed the realization of Leblond's grand plan, which was centered on Vasilevski Island. The first of these was the physical separation of this proposed "heart of the city" from the mainland. Also, the island was low-lying and therefore subject to frequent and disastrous flooding. In addition, the earlier selection of the Admiralty site had already generated development along the south bank of the Neva in what became the Admiralty District. Soon after the completion of the original Admiralty Building a number of palaces were built to the east of it as the residences of various members of the royal family, the nobility, and courtiers, most of whom had some connection with the Admiralty. Thus, it was the establishment of the Admiralty and the supporting development along the south bank of the Neva to house members of Peter's retinue and civil servants that confirmed the Admiralty District as the real center of the future city.

The nature of Leblond's plan—a network of squares located within a gridiron or on intersecting radials—required a physically spacious center for St. Petersburg that made Vasilevski Island an obvious choice as the site. Indeed, from a theoretical point of view the south bank of the river could not be imagined as the site for this center because of its peripheral position in the configuration of land masses. Geometrically, the Vasilevski Island seemed to be the true center, although Leblond's plan reveals the physical difficulty of making the center of the island into the actual focus of a water-based city. Indeed, had Leblond adopted Venice as his model, the siting of the Palazzo Ducale and the Piazza di San Marco might have suggested a more direct relationship of public open space to the river—a full celebration of civic ritual at the water's edge. However, Leblond's combination of gridiron and radials had the effect of corsetting all civic space so it could not have a connection with the water. In fact, although the geometry of Leblond's plan for St. Petersburg recalls that of the Versailles gardens, the spatial implications of the two designs are quite different. At Versailles it is the palace that acts as the focus of the design: all radials lead either to it or emanate from it. Since Leblond's design anticipates a city and not a garden, however, the intersections of the radials offer the focal intentions of his plan.

Whatever the conceptual strengths of the radial plan form, Leblond's results are less emphatic and successful than the model. An intersection in a garden layout, allowing one to approach down one avenue and depart along another, has a completely different meaning and effect from that of arriving in a ritual space within the city. In the

Plate 1. Pompeii, Italy: Villa of the Mysteries, Second-Style painting showing realistically painted but paradoxical architecture, second half of the first century B.C.

Plate 2. Pompeii, Italy: House of Lucretius Fronto, Third-Style painting showing scene that combines family life with allegory, mid-first century

Plate 3. ANDREA PALLADIO: Villa Barbaro (now Maser), near Vienza, Italy, 1555–60, the main facade

Plate 4. Andrea Palladio: Villa Barbaro (now Maser), near Vienza, Italy, 1555–60, central pavilion of main facade, showing the salon balcony that looks down to the farm: the room with a view

Plate 5. ANDREA PALLADIO: Villa Barbaro (now Maser), near Vienza, Italy, 1555–60, the cruciform salon on the *piano nobile,* with Paolo Veronese's murals 1560–62, showing *trompe l'oeil* representations of mythology, idealized landscapes, and everyday life in the villa: a view of the room

Plate 6. Michael Graves: Portland Building, Portland, Oregon, 1982

Plate 7. PETRA, JORDAN: Khasneh or Treasury adjacent to the Siq, c. 120

Plate 8. PETRA, JORDAN: steps cut into the rock on the ascent to the High Place

Plate 9. PETRA, JORDAN: jinn blocks near the Bab el Siq, c. 150 B.C.

Plate 10. PETRA, JORDAN: Obelisk Tomb above the Triclinium in the Bab el Siq, c. first century B.C.–first century A.D.

Plate 11. PETRA, JORDAN: Palace Tomb (left) and the Corinthian Tomb (right), c. first century B.C.–first century A.D.

Plate 12. PETRA, JORDAN: ed Deir or the Monastery, showing a detail of the upper portion of the facade, with the broken pediment and isolated piers, c. first century B.C.– first century A.D.

Plate 13. PETRA, JORDAN: Street of Facades, clearly showing the different uses of the crow-stepping motif, c. first century B.C.–first century A.D.

Plate 14. PETRA, JORDAN: *betyl* monolithic shrine to the stone god Dushara, in niche framed by pilasters, c. 200 B.C.

Plate 15. PETRA, JORDAN: Palace Tomb, detail showing the right-hand end bay and the complex rhythms generated by the use of framing pilasters, c. first century B.C.–first century A.D.

Plate 16. ALVAR AALTO: Atrium of the Academic Bookshop, Helsinki, Finland, 1966–69: an urban fragment

palace garden the raison d'être is to generate vistas: in the garden landscape it is better to travel than to arrive.

To have applied the lessons of Versailles, which he certainly knew by heart, Leblond would therefore have had to adapt them to the distinctive expectations of the city. What is much more likely, however, is that he took the plans of French fortified towns of Sebastien Le Plestre (Vauban)[4] as his model and, in planning the new fortress of St. Petersburg, combined their introspective and unfestive character with his ideas about the axes of great park design.

Leblond's plan suggests a closed system which offered an overall pattern, dominated by uniformity of effect and so introverted as to provide little sense of grandeur or climax in the urban composition. Le Nôtre's design for the Versailles gardens and park combines a rational layout with poetic effects. As evidence of Leblond's apparently quite different intentions, however, we have only his geometric planning diagram. It may seem curious that Peter, whose image for his new capital was represented by the picturesque Dutch style, should have chosen the French rationalist as his architect. However, Leblond's planning rationalism was at least partially vindicated in the St. Petersburg eventually completed as Russia's westernmost military bastion. Peter's focus on military strategy points to French fortified city design rather than garden layout as the probable primary source of Leblond's inspiration (although we must admit that Peter's rationalism is more formal than strategic in the plan of 1704).

Given the circumstances, there was little chance that Leblond's grand and comprehensive design for St. Petersburg would survive the vicissitudes of history. Attenuating Leblond's effectiveness were such factors as the island's tendency to flooding, the transfer of the Admiralty to the city, and Peter's failure to support his good intentions with personal supervision of the plans and works. (Peter tried to compensate for his continual absence by draconian measures against those who disobeyed his instructions.) If the anecdotes cited above are even partly true, Menshikov's enmity may have been a factor, as well. Yet Leblond's concept of radiating streets was to provide the essential planning strategy of the Admiralty district on the South Bank, the one place where he had made no provision for this treatment.

The authenticity of the 1725 map, with its representation of the two radials that focus upon the Admiralty, is verified by a directive signed by Peter I and dated ten years earlier, in May, 1715. The directive requires the incorporation of those radial streets into the planning process. It is indicative of Peter's persistent absences from his new capital that, although his nobles and courtiers built themselves palaces to the east of the Admiralty, the Czar himself did not have an adequate court residence in St. Petersburg. While Leblond's plan placed Peter's future palace in the center of Vasilevski Island, various Russian nobles acquired prime sites and built their palaces on the south bank of the Neva. Peter himself used the palace of the powerful Count Menshikov for his official receptions and audiences. Count Apraksin, who died without an heir, left his palace to Peter II (1727–30). The former Apraksin Palace was on the waterfront adjacent to the Admiralty, and it is on the site of this property that Bartolomeo Francesco di Rastrelli later built the celebrated Winter Palace for Peter II's successor, the Empress Anna Ivanovna (1730–40). To allow the creation of the Winter Palace adjacent properties were either bought up or confiscated.

The remodeling of the old Apraksin Palace and its conversion into the new Winter Palace began in 1736 (see fig. 3). Although there were many other noble residences in the immediate vicinity on the banks of the Neva, the area also contained many much less elegant wooden structures that housed local tradesmen, shipbuilders, and artisans. These poorer neighborhoods were clearly not desirable in the center of the expanding capital but, as many of the citizens who owned property in those areas had been forcibly settled in the new capital and were far from happy with their lot, confiscation of Peter's only legacy to them might have resulted in rioting. The problem was mysteriously but effectively solved by two fires. The first spread south and the second east from the Winter Palace, both leaving the royal residence unscathed. Following the second conflagration the blacksmiths, candlemakers, and other hazardous trades were banned from the Admiralty District, while only stone structures with proper masonry foundations were allowed to replace the old wooden houses. This had the effect of forcing out all those former owners who could not afford such expensive construction. At the same time, the Empress Anna withdrew the right of her courtiers to live within the palace. This generated a flurry of building activity to fill the vacant lots of the now expanded Admiralty District with well-constructed stone residences for the remainder of the royal household.

The elitist character of the Admiralty District was farther extended by regulations forbidding any wooden structures to adjoin stone ones. Thus, with the whole area cleared of tradesmen and the lower middle

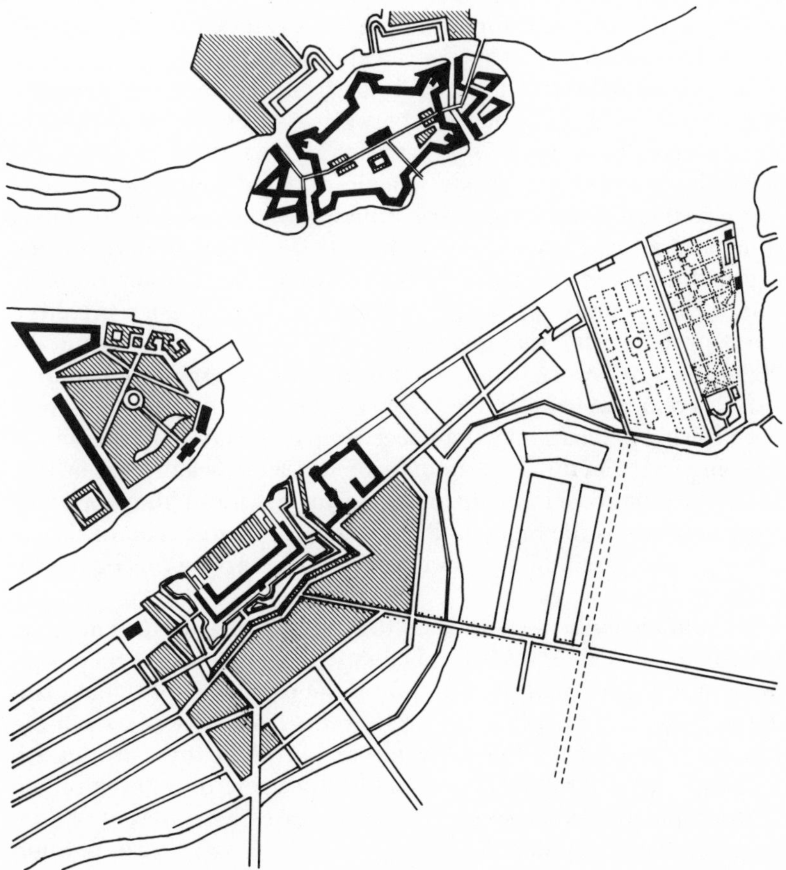

Figure 13. The central area of St. Petersburg, showing the Admiralty in relation to the Strelka of Vasilevski Island and to the Peter and Paul Fortress, 1736

class, the Admiralty District became an enclave for the court and aristocracy. The displaced owners, having been forced off the land given them by Peter I as an enticement to settle in the new capital, had to be content with rebuilding on the less salubrious Vasilevski Island to the west and the Petersburg District on the north bank of the river. The development of the remainder of the city finally received a boost, therefore, not from the projected royal palace and the courtly traffic of Leblond's grand axes but from the unplanned evolution of the Admiralty District and the forced migration of those citizens who had built and sustained Peter I's western experiment.

The first radial street to be laid out from the Admiralty was the Nevski Prospect, already planned between 1712 and 1718, and one of those referred to in Peter I's directive of May 20, 1715. However, the completion of the present-day scheme of three converging radials, known as the "three prongs," was achieved as the result of the establishment of a Commission for the Orderly Development of St. Petersburg in June 1737 (see fig. 14). A Russian architect, Peter Eropkin, headed this commission, and it included another Russian architect, Ivan Korobov, who was engaged in building the new Admiralty (1732–38). Their work brought the beginning of systematic planning to the development of St. Petersburg. Many of the proposals produced during Peter I's reign had been prepared without the benefit of surveying instruments. The commission therefore began their task by ordering a topographical map of the city to be made. This map, which became known as the Sigheim Plan, was thus the first map of St. Petersburg to be based on a proper survey of the territory using instruments.

The commission's work appears to have proceeded efficiently, because six months later, by December 1737, not only was the map complete but it already had drawn upon it the commission's initial planning proposals. By April 1738 the Empress Anna received from the commission a detailed scheme for the creation of the three prongs. Although the eastern radial, the Nevski Prospect, owed its development to Peter's initiative in the second decade of the eighteenth century, the western radial, which was also the subject of Peter's 1715 directive and known as the Voznesenski Prospect, and the central radial, Gorokhovaia Street ("Street of Nuts"), were still in a rather incomplete state twenty years later. The Nevski Prospect had a historical role in the structure of the new city because it served to connect the old Novgorod Road with the center of St. Petersburg: it also had a symbolic function in that, already in Peter's time, it visually reinforced the view from the Admiralty toward the "ecclesiastic city" represented by the Alexander Nevski Monastery.[5]

In considering the proposal contained in the 1738 scheme for the three prongs it is important to understand that the land mass south of

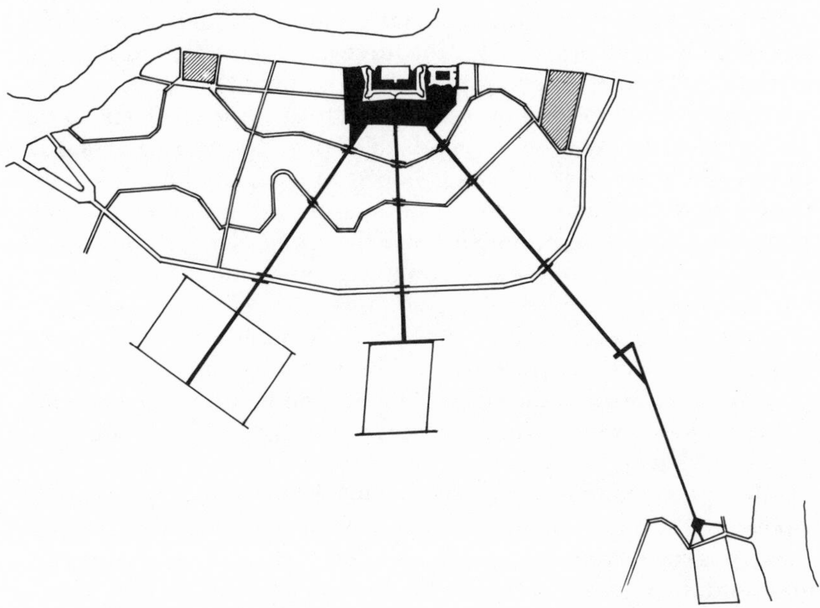

Figure 14. The "three prongs" of St. Petersburg, centered on the Admiralty, with the system of canals and waterways developed in the city center. 1737

the Admiralty is traversed by two smaller rivers, the Moika and the Fontanka, which have the effect of creating two islands (one nestling within the other) and contribute substantially to the idea of St. Petersburg as "the Venice of the North." When the three prongs proposal was presented to the Empress Anna, the Gorokhovaia Street stretched from the Admiralty Field only as far as the Moika. The commission's proposal was to extend this street south, through properties that had belonged to Count Apraksin, to the Fontanka, and then on to link up with the emerging Zagorodnaia Street beyond that. In addition, the route of Voznesenski Prospect was to be straightened and extended to form the western radial.

The development of the Gorokhovaia Street and the Voznesenski Prospect was to have not only planning significance but also a rational and strategic importance. For its chief military support the Russian monarchy depended upon two regiments of Guards, the Ismailovski and the Semenovski, and their effective location and housing had therefore to be given particular attention in the planning of St. Petersburg. Following its proposal for the three prongs the Commission for the Orderly Development of St. Petersburg drafted a resolution to locate these two regiments beyond the Fontanka at the terminals of the two new avenues. By August 1739 detailed plans for the regimental areas were in existence, and it was hoped to complete them by 1740. Bridges were built across the Moika to facilitate the shortest path between the military encampments and the Admiralty Field in case of emergency. Because of the decision to accommodate the soldiers and their families in conventional houses rather than barracks, more land was needed than originally planned. Thus, work was delayed and these military suburbs, based on a gridiron that had no relation to the city plan, were not completed until the second half of the eighteenth century. These awkward excrescences are already present, however, in Makhaev's plan of 1753.

Unlike their Roman counterparts that lead from the Piazza del Popolo to (1) the Spanish Steps and the Quirinale; (2) the Campodoglio, Colosseum and the ancient *fora;* and (3) to the Pantheon and the Piazza Navona, the St. Petersburg radials have no satisfactory terminals on the periphery of the city. The three prongs nevertheless remain as an outstanding feature. Their focus is the Admiralty tower, and the effectiveness of this center in the planning composition is heightened by the development of concentric links between these main arteries. These links, suggested by the natural paths of the Moika and the Fontanka, and now embodied in the city in the form of canals and cross streets, allow one to digress to east or west while walking through the city, but always returning, whenever any of the three prongs is crossed, to the magnetic presence of the Admiralty spire.

This "magnetic field" has, of course, an enormous impact on the overall spatial ordering of St. Petersburg, which is consequently limited by the basic geometry generated by its three prongs. At the same time, those radials confirm the civic importance of the Admiralty as the main progenitor of the city's final plan form, as well as underlining the significance of the River Neva and its quays, and stressing the contrast of the Admiralty's "other side"—the near-Venetian ideal suggested by the proximity of Rastrelli's Winter Palace to the water. Thus, in progressing from the river by way of the Admiralty and Admiralty Square, then moving out along one of the radials, one is repeatedly drawn back to the Admiralty Tower. As one weaves back and forth, the memory of the River Neva is ever present in the canals that in turn reflect their images of the city. St. Petersburg is one of those rare urban flora that, springing from neoclassical seeds, has produced both monumental blooms and a profusion of delicate blossoms in a close, near-Romantic proximity. The main difference between St. Petersburg and Helsinki is that the former, through its skillful harnessing of the Moika and the Fontanka into a system of canals, achieves a complex interaction of architecture and water, of reality and reflective memory; while the latter offers no introspective relief for the patterns of cold northern light on remembered but alien southern surfaces.

Makhaev's plan of 1753, published by the Academy of Science, confirms the development of the three independent and disparate parts of the city, with the Admiralty District offering the only evidence of an identifiable planning concept.[6] Fifty years after the founding of the city, however, those three prongs were still badly defined and appeared to be further blurred by irregular building masses on all sides. The idea of the center of the city only really becomes clear in the context of those essential concentric routes based on the Neva and formed by the Moika, the Fontanka, and the future Ekaterinski Canal (fig. 15). At this time Rastrelli's Winter Palace was being completed and its extravagant Baroque detail would have contrasted sharply with the modest old Admiralty designed by Ivan Korobov in the provincial early Renaissance style. The Makhaev map also records the planning of the Vasilevski Island that was begun in Peter I's time, with its repetitive gridiron pattern that more or less follows Leblond's east–west axis but is without any major focus or feature of architecture and space. The layout of the Petersburg District behind the Peter and Paul Fortress, on the north bank of the Neva, is seen to be even more random and inconsequential. Indeed, the construction of stone buildings within the vicinity of the Fortress was forbidden in the interests of defense, a prohibition that was not lifted until 1809 when Finland was absorbed into the Russian Empire and the border with the old Swedish enemy was moved west to the Tornio River. This lack of substantial building in the Petersburg District made it the first candidate for replanning. Although Makhaev's map reveals these deficiencies quite clearly, Egorov[7] asserts that what is represented is still an idealization of St. Petersburg and that the actual state of the city was much more chaotic than this record suggests.

The Peter and Paul Fortress, with the prominent tower and spire of the Peter and Paul Cathedral, provides a distinct focus to the north

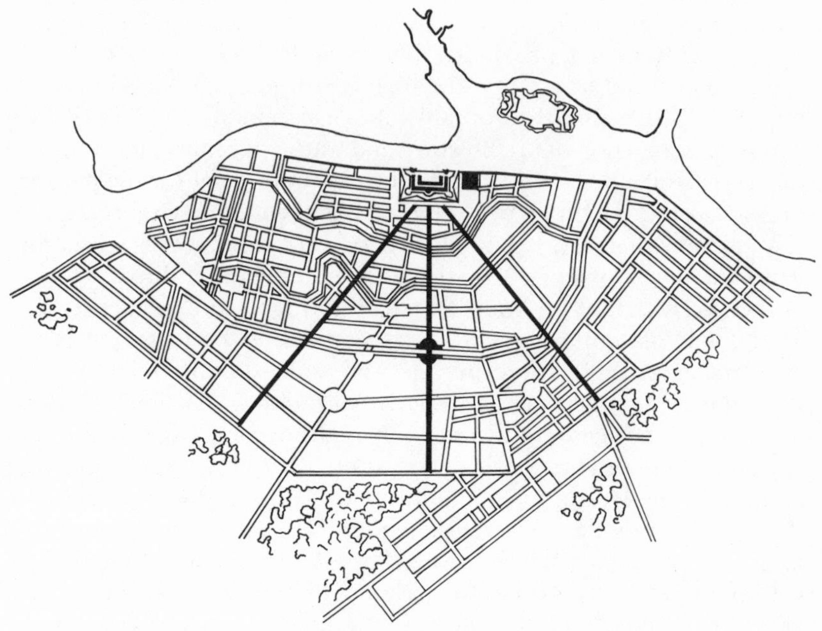

Figure 15. Plan for the unification of the Admiralty District of St. Petersburg, after 1753, showing the "three prongs." Developments in the second half of the eighteenth century and the first half of the nineteenth neglected the central prong and concentrated on the right-hand one, the Nevski Prospect

from the Angliiskaia (English) Quay in front of the Admiralty and also from the Winter Palace. Nevertheless, the flat land on which the Petersburg District is situated to the north of the fortress island, combined with its distance from the center of the Admiralty District, presented insuperable problems. There was little possibility for the Petersburg District in the background to compete successfully for attention with the dramatic skyline of the Peter and Paul Cathedral in the foreground of the view to the north bank of the Neva. Thus, the two parts of the city that could become unified visually were the Admiralty District on the south bank of the Neva and the Vasilevski Island opposite. The various projects proposed to effect this visual unity left the existing geometry of both districts undisturbed.

In the case of the Petersburg District, however, it was decided to make the Peter and Paul Fortress the central focus of the north bank in the way that this role was already fulfilled by the Admiralty on the south bank of the river. This was to be achieved by creating a semicircular canal at the northern extremity of the outer defenses and earthworks of the Fortress, which would in turn receive the axes of a further three prongs: the two outer radials would stop at the canal, while the central avenue would lead into a large square that looked onto the fortifications. Although this restructuring of the Petersburg District would have achieved a balanced plan composition of the north and south banks of the Neva in a way that Leblond's design had not, it failed to offer a system of spatial coherence to the city as a whole. Indeed, the vast distances across the city, the width of the Neva itself, and the lack of topographical variety in the delta marshland had made this an insoluble problem from the outset. The planning of the Petersburg District thus became a separate issue from the organization of the city center, and therefore also from our concern here.

We return, then, to the problems of effecting visual cohesion between the Admiralty District and the eastern cape of Vasilevski Island, known as the Strelka (see fig. 13). Leblond's plan had treated each of the three districts as separate entities, with its center located on Vasilevski Island. It could be said that Leblond recognized the difficulty of coordinating the whole ensemble by ignoring it. In particular, he made no provision for any compositional link between the Strelka and the Admiralty which lay immediately opposite. An examination of the Admiralty District as it had developed in the first half of the eighteenth century reveals two interesting facts. First the Admiralty itself determines the visual center of the entire district, with the Dvortsovaia Quay to the right and the Angliiskaia Quay to the left seemingly of equal importance in the waterfront composition. Within the composition as a whole, however, the more central position of the Dvortsovaia Quay suggested a more emphatic architectural treatment, which indeed it began to receive with the construction of Rastrelli's Winter Palace. Second, this concentration of development to the east of the Admiralty was accompanied by a discrepancy in the realization of the three prongs, whereby the development of the central prong was neglected in favor of Nevski Prospect, which lies closest to the

Dvortsovaia Quay (see fig. 16). Although in practical terms this violation of the symmetry of the radials focused on the Admiralty tower was both logical and necessary, it made no contribution to overcoming the fragmentation of the plan as a whole. These two facts, however, served to stress the importance of the part now to be played in the overall composition by the development of the Strelka on Vasilevski Island.

As we have seen, the Admiralty, the Winter Palace, and the other buildings along the Dvortsovaia Quay had become the most important elements in the center of the composition, while the quay itself was immediately opposite the Peter and Paul Fortress. The Dvortsovaia Quay also had great functional importance in the developing life of Russia's new capital, as it provided the vector between the Winter Palace as the center of court life and the Summer Garden as the principal recreation area of the aristocracy. Its significance was recognized when, beginning in 1764, this entire stretch of the waterfront was faced in granite.

A uniform slope toward the Neva, the density of granite, and a monumental simplicity of detail brought to the waterfront a flawless sense of unity and continuity. Such a base required a similar monumentality in the buildings that sat on it, a quality not possessed by the structures then existent. The Commission for Masonry Construction sent a report to Empress Catherine the Great (1762–96) in 1765, in which an increased height of buildings along the Neva was proposed together with a general control on cornice lines and architectural character. This report received the Empress's approval and the reconstruction of the Dvortsovaia Quay began with the aim of achieving "a single facade" along the waterfront.[8] Vallin de la Mothe's design for the Old Hermitage adjacent to the Winter Palace continued the base and cornice lines of Rastrelli's building, and maintained the general proportions and pattern of fenestration of the Palace, retaining his own individuality while bringing the theory of a unified facade into architectural reality. Georg Feldten, a German architect who had begun the granite facing of the waterfront, was then commissioned to design the Second Hermitage or Reserve Palace in 1771. He followed de la Mothe's example, repeating certain features from the Old Hermitage such as the rustication and cornice lines, but more importantly emulating the Frenchman's example in attention to massing, scale, and the articulation of parts in the overall composition. Finally, the last building to conform to the concept of the unified facade on the Dvortsovaia Quay was Giacomo Quarenghi's Hermitage Theater, in

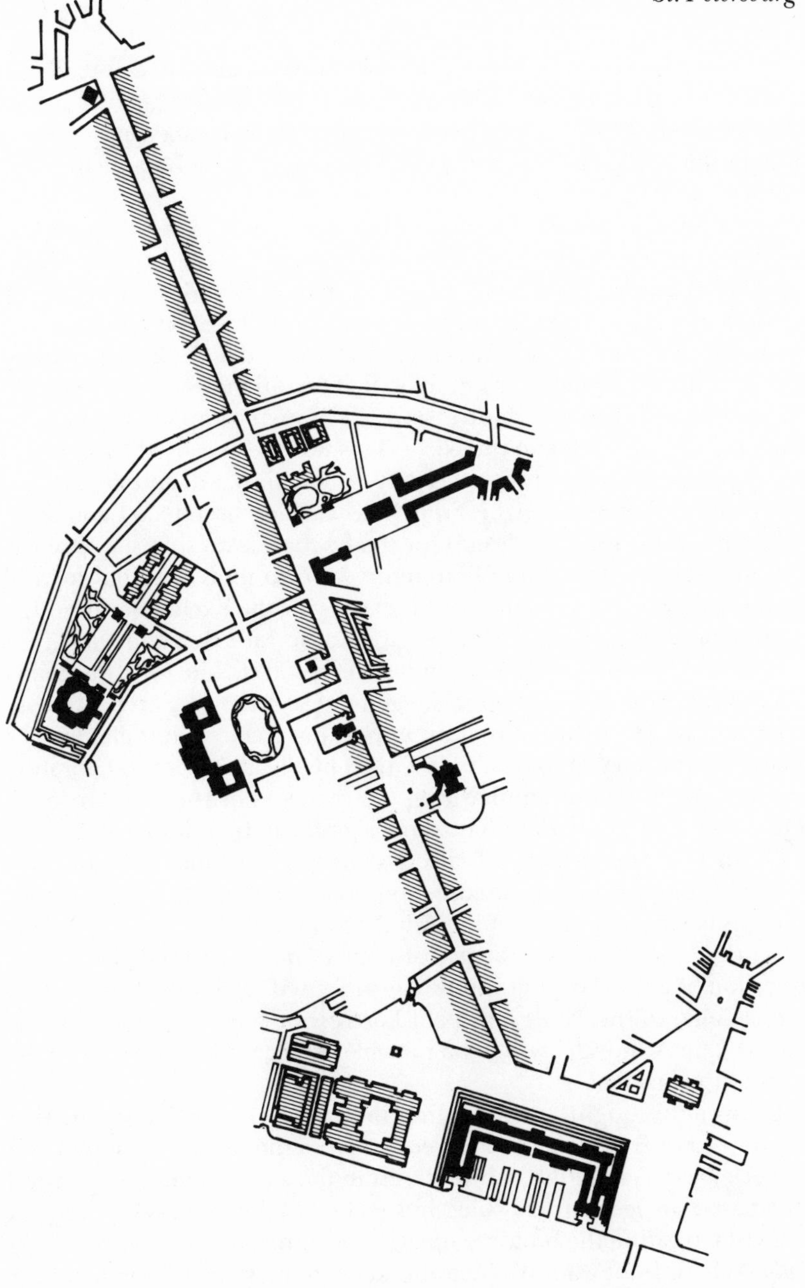

Figure 16. St. Petersburg, Russia: Development of the Nevski Prospect

which the Italian architect combined his command of mature eighteenth century classicism with references to Rastrelli's fanciful use of the Baroque. With the completion of the Dvortsovaia Quay project the design of the Strelka, or cape of Vasilevski Island, became the next architectural task.

Leblond's proposal, as revealed in his original plan of 1717, had avoided the use of axes to determine the center of the city as a whole. He had centralized the planning of Vasilevski Island but treated the Strelka as a separate entity, outside his axial grid. As far as we can tell from his plan, his intention for the cape was to define the contours of the shoreline by building right up to it. The rational alternative would have been to follow the natural axis of symmetry implied by the relationship of the Strelka to the Neva. This was the axis used by Leblond in his proposed layout for the rest of Vasilevski Island, and the one pedantically adhered to by the French neoclassical architect Thomas de Thomon in his realized design for the Exchange on that site. But the Italian architect Giacomo Quarenghi was of a more original turn of mind, and it is unfortunate that his design for the Exchange, although commenced, was abandoned following Catherine's death in 1796.

Quarenghi took over the planning of the Strelka in 1782 but made no radical proposals to change the general layout of the area. His contribution was to propose that an important architectural element be placed at the very tip of the island, thus finally abandoning Leblond's more modest idea of emphasizing the contours of the cape. Instead, Quarenghi sought to dominate the insignificant buildings in the vicinity with one major piece of civic architecture, at once a monument within a composition of monuments and a landmark that would place the Strelka in the context of the Admiralty and the Peter and Paul Fortress (fig. 17). By this strategy, of course, he also raised the vexing question of axes. To what should his proposed Exchange Building relate axially, to the Peter and Paul Fortress or the natural axis of the Neva? The Admiralty was not a possible choice since its axis lay to the west of the Strelka.

Quarenghi sought a visual rather than a new rational axis, one that stemmed not from the site as given but from the site as developed and experienced. As an Italian his interest in the axis was not a theoretical one based on geometrical rules, but related to the more poetic idea of the vista, treating the building not as a coordinated object but as a *revelation.* He did not want his building to be in the right position "on the plan." It was more important for him that it should reveal itself effec-

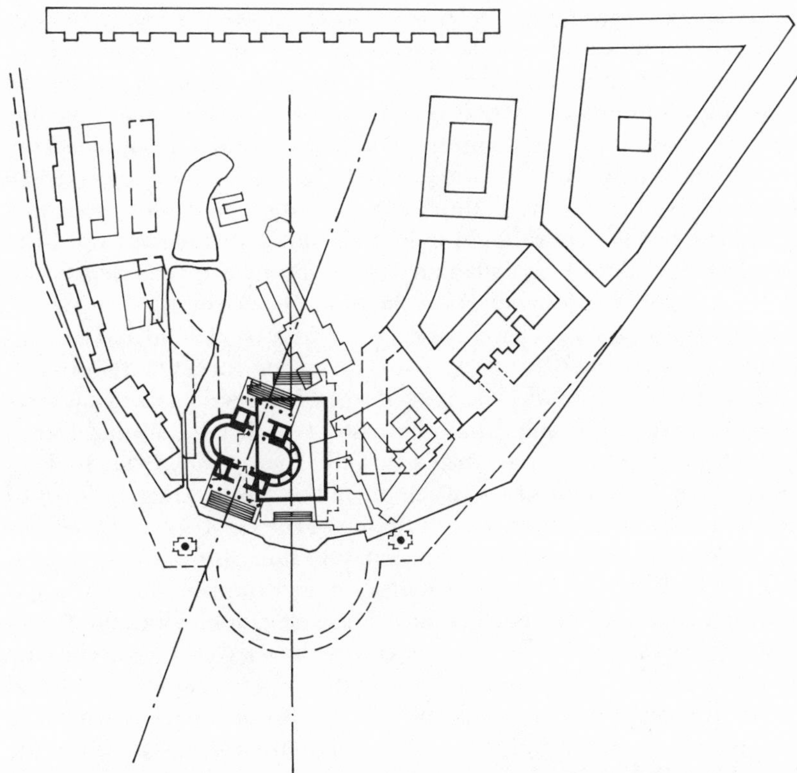

Figure 17. St. Petersburg, Russia: Plan of the Strelka on Vasilevski Island, showing the form and position of Quarenghi's design for the Exchange with apses (1782–85), in relation to de Thomon's completed building (begun 1805)

tively in the cityscape, and the principal artery from which the Exchange would be seen was, of course, the Dvortsovaia Quay. Quarenghi's concept of the planning axis for the terminal building on the Strelka thus contrasted strongly with that of the French rationalists—Leblond who prepared the original city plan and de Thomon whose design for the Exchange was eventually adopted. An understanding of these different sensibilities, based on the respective Italian and French planning models, is important in assessing the significance of Quarenghi's design and the reasons why his intentions were misrepresented and his unfinished Exchange allowed to decay.

We have observed that the Dvortsovaia Quay was the principal thoroughfare used by St. Petersburg aristocracy, passing in their carriages between the Winter Palace and the Summer Garden. It was clearly Quarenghi's intention that, as they traveled west along the quay, the capital's most important citizens and their visitors would be confronted across the Neva by the entrance facade of the Exchange. To achieve this objective he laid out the Exchange on a visual axis that linked the Strelka with the Summer Garden. Thus, the splendid Roman Doric portico of his Palladian design would have been clearly visible for most of the journey from the Summer Garden to the Winter Palace, reinforcing the civic link between Vasilevski Island and the Admiralty District. In creating this visual axis, therefore, Quarenghi recognized the transfer of civic power from Vasilevski Island (as proposed by Leblond) to the Admiralty District (as dictated by naval strategy). Furthermore, he recognized that the Dvortsovaia Quay had become the major vector of social activity in the capital, the real focus of city life for the aristocracy. The midpoint of the Dvortsovaia Quay corresponds more or less with the visual axis to the spirit of the Peter and Paul Cathedral, and from this midpoint also the portico of the Exchange would have presented almost a true elevation. Thus, the St. Petersburg aristocracy would have perceived themselves to be in the true center of the city—a center defined by the intersection of the visual axes that connected them with the focal points of the city's other two districts, the St. Peter and Paul Cathedral on the fortress island of the Petersburg District, and the Exchange on Vasilevski Island. The center of the Quay literally represented God and Mammon! Quarenghi's axis for the Exchange modified the "natural" one of the Strelka, emphasizing its poetic imagery rather than the rational order embraced by Leblond and de Thomon.

The construction of Quarenghi's Exchange, begun in October 1782, was frequently interrupted by suspension of the building funds, so that ten years later it remained incomplete. Then, in 1793, the wooden roof was torn off in a storm. Although basic repairs were effected, the building began to deteriorate from that time on. Czar Paul, who succeeded his mother, Catherine the Great, in 1796, abandoned the work, and by the end of the eighteenth century a commission recommended that it was impractical to proceed further with construction. It was therefore demolished and replaced, during the reign of

Czar Alexander I (1801–25), by the new Exchange designed by Thomas de Thomon.

Criticism of Quarenghi's ill-fated building centers on the fact that he chose to ignore the element of natural symmetry suggested by the almost equal branching of the River Neva at the Strelka. He has been accused of placing his Exchange Building at an arbitrary angle to the natural compositional axis created by the junction of the river with the island.[9] As we have observed, this was no arbitrary decision but a very deliberate one. In fact the variation between the so-called natural axis and the one used by Quarenghi is approximately 22.5 degrees, which is hardly an accidental discrepancy. Egorov is right to castigate present-day critics who judge the design "on the basis of the planning theories of the first half of the 19th century, comparing the situation of the unfinished Exchange with the design of Thomas de Thomon." He goes on to say: "To judge Quarenghi's solution on the basis of its failure to subordinate the siting of the building to the direction of the natural axis of the landscape is to declare this axis the eternal and unchangeable measure of all aesthetic evaluation."[10] Yet Egorov is equivocal in his defense of Quarenghi's perspicuous logic against de Thomon's abstract rationalism, for he tells us that:

> With the design of the Exchange Quarenghi achieved *in one bold stroke* the balance of all other elements of the central ensemble. The slight inclination of the axis of the building from the axis of the island toward the southeast provided additional emphasis to the left bank of the Neva. . . . thus underlining the spatial importance of the mainland waterfront as a major element of the central ensemble.[11]

In the very next chapter we are informed, in almost identical words, of de Thomon's equal success based on the quite contrary principle of that "eternal and unchangeable" axis.

> The new project by de Thomon succeeded in completing the ensemble around the Neva basin *in a single bold stroke.* In architectural terms the problem was solved by a single new building and by reshaping the cape of Vasilevski Island. The organization of the Strelka was achieved by two means. First, de Thomon placed the Exchange on the natural axis of the water basin, thus subordinating all the other elements of the ensemble to the formal and spatial importance of the Strelka and making the relative imper-

> fection of the Dvortsovaia waterfront less apparent. Second, architectural monumentality was used to reinforce the spatial importance of the building. . . . By making the Exchange visually important, Thomas de Thomon directed the view away from the Dvortsovaia Quay, guiding the eye in the direction of the Strelka.[12]

In the first place, it was Quarenghi, not de Thomon, who originally thought of emphasizing the Strelka "by a single new building" and he should have full credit for this invention. It is difficult to imagine what Egorov means by "the relative imperfection of the Dvortsovaia waterfront," an achievement he had earlier accorded "a definite architectural primacy" on the left bank—the only developed one, after all. And what had been Quarenghi's intention if it was not to make his Exchange visually important?

The only clues would appear to exist in the relative positions from which one may view the composition of the ensemble. Surely the sole position from which the natural axis of the Strelka, and de Thomon's Exchange upon it, takes preeminence is a downstream craft in midstream. From such a point of view admittedly, de Thomon's Exchange would come to the front stage position with both St. Peter and Paul and the Dvortsovaia Quay assuming background roles. Peter the Great's main concern for the image of his new capital had been to impress visitors approaching the harbor from the Gulf of Finland, hence his decision to locate his original Winter Palace to the east of the Admiralty, which dictated the positioning of the Summer Garden and so on. Thus, it was Peter's vision that had established the ultimate importance of the Dvortsovaia Quay, and Quarenghi had recognized the wisdom of this vision in relating his Exchange to that vector. Indeed, all the qualities with which Egorov credits de Thomon's design had been carefully considered by Quarenghi—all, that is, save one. The subtlety of Quarenghi's design made the reshaping of the Strelka shoreline unnecessary, and even undesirable. Finally, although even Leblond's rational plan for the Strelka had employed the "natural axis" of symmetry, this device was entirely used for the internal order of Vasilevski Island and not for its external relationship with other parts of the city. Indeed, the reason Leblond probably abandoned this axis in the planning of the Strelka becomes apparent when we examine de Thomon's design; the use of the natural axis through the point of the Strelka can generate no visual axes with either the St. Peter and Paul Fortress or the left bank of the Neva.

The attribute that indisputably belongs to de Thomon's design is that of "monumentality." In this sense his design did alter the architectural balance of the constituent parts of the central ensemble, as Egorov says, but in my view this was to the detriment of the whole. Of course the completion of the Strelka took the development of the city center a stage further. Finally, in the nineteenth century, the earlier dreams of the Commission for Masonry Construction to lay out, as in Western Europe, large squares surrounded by beautiful buildings were finally realized. There had been no social purpose for such squares in the city structure of the eighteenth century, but the reorganization of government departments under Alexander I (1801–25) called for a building program to house the new ministries. It was this bureaucratic reorganization that ultimately led to the reconstruction of the residential area to the south of the Winter Palace, with the reconstruction of the Dvortsovaia Square between them, and the creation of Senate Square and St. Isaac's Square to the west of the Admiralty, with the Admiralty Boulevard linking the two areas. Here once again is the evidence of institutions as generators of urban forms.

By the time the Russians defeated the French in 1812 a new dimension had entered the planning of St. Petersburg. In the organization of the complex of squares between the Winter Palace and St. Isaac's Cathedral and the Senate House, the niceties of axial planning still had their ritual place. In reality, however, the military machine had taken over from the civic ideal, and the prime function of this system of squares was that of a giant parade ground. There are vestiges of Leblond's garden plan of squares and radials in the completed city but these seem diagrammatic amidst the cliff faces of the many monumental edifices. Quarenghi's Hermitage Theater and his gentle play with the axis of the Exchange were the last subtle gestures in the realization of Peter's western capital.

Peter the Great had wanted to create an elegant city along European lines, but his idea of elegance was modestly based on the provincial Renaissance model of Amsterdam. Although he might have appreciated the completion of the three prongs he had designated, and possibly Rastrelli's Winter Palace and Quarenghi's Hermitage Theater might have pleased him, his memory of a European capital would not have corresponded with St. Petersburg as it was completed under Alexander I (1801–25) and Nicolai I (1825–55). Nevertheless, Peter sought power as well as charm in the creation of his new capital, and the effect of both is to be found today in its legacies from the planners and architects of the eighteenth and nineteenth centuries.

TEN

▲

AALTO'S USE OF MEMORY: THE URBAN FRAGMENTS

Alvar Aalto was born in 1898 at Kuortane, a small village in the Finnish province of Ostro-Bothnia. By the time his mother died in 1903 the family had been living for some time in the small town of Aläjärvi. Between 1903 and 1907, the Aaltos moved again, this time to the provincial seat of Jyväskylä. The young Alvar therefore came to spend his formative years in a city which, although of relative importance in the then Russian Grand Duchy, was small in scale and had none of the significant architectural monuments Rossi calls *permanences,*[1] that characterize similar centers of local government in northern, central, or southern Europe. Even today, the distinction between city and country is blurred in Jyväskylä, especially if one strays far from the main thoroughfare—the Kauppakatu, or "Shopping Street"—with its small cluster of civic and commercial buildings. The University, located on the hills of the northern outskirts less than a mile from the center of downtown, has the image of a "forest town" rather than that of an urban campus.

When Alvar Aalto was a teenager, growing up in Jyväskylä, the confusion of town elements with those of the country was much greater. In a very real sense we might view the forest itself as the *permanence* of Jyväskylä,[2] with the fragmented representations of urban life-style merely suggesting the sketchy outlines of a civilization that is yet to be. Apart from the ideas of locus conveyed by church, market square, cafés, and restaurants, the pattern of the town was more one of open space than the tight knot of buildings which characterize the urban fabric of older European cities. The image of the city which we conjure up when we focus our memory on the evolution of urban history would not have been part of Aalto's consciousness as he grew up in Jyväskylä, never more than a few steps from the forest that stakes out every Finn's memory of space and distance. Even Carl Ludwig Engel's official and somewhat artificial Neoclassical delineation of the Grand Duchy's new capital of Helsinki was still outside the young Alvar's experience and therefore his conscious memory.

Aalto himself emphasized his childhood and upbringing in the countryside of provincial Finland with his anecdote of some Helsinki citizens, who while the young lad was still attending school in Jyväskylä, were talking of a young genius who would come from the north to study architecture at the Polytechnic Institute.[3] This story is an excellent example of what Gaston Bachelard calls our "dreaming consciousness," in which its *subject*—in this case an ambitious country boy—presents his own dream of success as an imaginary folklore created by his imagined admirers and prospective clients. It is, perhaps, also a demonstration of the French concept of *l'esprit de l'escalier.* It is highly likely that Aalto invented this scenario long after he had arrived in the capital and sensed his real achievement; namely, to translate himself from the loose architectural but constricting social framework of Jyväskylä to the bustling ambience of Engel's new capital, where neoclassical formality was jostled by vigorously idiosyncratic buildings which housed the ferment of nationalism and revolution. Indeed, Aalto's somewhat ironic representation of his own aspirations reflects a common idealized expression of the new romance of nationalism that characterized Finnish optimism in the period immediately following Finland's release from Russian bondage in 1917. A similar "horoscope" appears in Reima Pietilä's autobiographical notes, concerning the revelation to his mother of the architectural fortunes of the son she would bear.[4] Such ideas of young men being "called" out of the forest and other remote regions—in Pietilä's case it involved his parents' return from Seattle to Turku—to become the heroes of the new republic, corresponds to Finnish tribal memories as recorded in the *Kalevala* and other folk epics.

Whatever his aspiration, however, Aalto was not to practice his profession in Helsinki until 1933, that is ten years after he opened his first office. He graduated from the Polytechnic Institute in 1921 and did some work in Seinajoki and Tampere before opening his original office in Jyväskylä in 1923. Thus, he returned at the age of twenty-five to the forest town of his childhood dreams, where he soon built the town's Workers' Club (1923–24). This early work of neo-Palladian inspiration has become something close to Rossi's concept of a *permanence* in the town because of its unique form and changing patterns of use. It is also one of the few examples in Aalto's entire oeuvre of a detached monument within a city. Our interest here, however, centers rather on his proclivity for the *non-monument,* either responding to patterns in an existing urban fabric, or miniaturizing other urban memories in the creation of new contexts.

In my original critique of Aalto's complete work I wrote that, early in his career, he demonstrated that one generator of his design gestalt was classicism, but that "this was very much associated with the requirements of particular sites."[5] I went on to identify Aalto's complementary design strategy as having its origins in the organic informality of building groups found in (1) Finnish vernacular architecture—for example, the farms of central Finland such as the one at Pienmäki near Jyväskylä; (2) the freedom of planning and expression found in designs of the National Romantic Movement; and (3) the irregularity of the spaces that make up so many Italian *piazze.*[6] In collecting material for my first Aalto book, I came to realize what had been going on, behind the scenes as it were, in Aalto's architectural process. This understanding of Aalto's creative use of environmental memory led in turn to these present explorations and my speculation that Aalto's truly unique contribution to modern architecture was his ability to avoid direct "catalog" reference to the traditional sources of style and form by resorting instead to his "dreaming consciousness" of remembered environments. This highly developed flexibility of approach accounts for much of the elusiveness and conflict in his later work, because it is frankly difficult to identify the sources of his inspiration and therefore the vectors of his creative leaps.

My thesis concerning the origins and uses of what I have called Aalto's *urban fragments* is, however, well supported by examples throughout Aalto's career. We may begin with his entry in the competition for the Finnish Parliament Building (1923), executed only a few months after he opened his Jyväskylä office. In this competition the question of the most appropriate location was left to the competitors in the initial stage, and Aalto chose a site adjoining the Helsinki harbor. The significance of Aalto's original proposal on the harbor site is that he saw the Parliament Building as the "missing link" in Engel's neoclassical framework for the center of the new Finnish capital. In Engel's plan it was the "Great Church," now the cathedral, that dominated the grouping of civic and university buildings. Aalto quite rightly viewed the Parliament Building competition as the means of completing Engel's design by the addition of this missing piece, the main political symbol of the newly created Finnish nation.

His design, appropriately entered under the motto "Piazza del Popolo," maintained Engel's scale and simple massing in a single building with a giant classical order, offering in its associated harborfront piazza a focus for the new national spirit of democracy. Aalto's design would have closed the harbor frontage at its east end, framing Engel's City Hall and creating a potential focus for civic activity that, sixty years later, is still missing from Helsinki. By extending the spirit of Engel's composition right down to the harbor front and increasing the complexity of this public space, Aalto's design offered the possibility of linking the functions of City Hall, National Parliament, and the Presidential Palace. In short, it would have provided that essential ingredient of all major cities—a sense of downtown. The decision not to use the harbor site was a major factor in the irrevocable process of neutralizing the magnetism of central Helsinki. Although Aalto subsequently built the Enso-Gutzeit *palazzo* on this original Parliament Building site, neither the scale nor the significance of this office building could achieve the civic grandeur of his very first urban idea.

Aalto's entry for the Töölö (Helsinki) Church Competition (1927) created a grouping of four separate architectural elements—church, campanile, and associated buildings—around a piazza, a composition that recalls his second-stage Parliament Building Competition entry. The historical reference, the urban fragment that is remembered here is, of course, the Italian hilltown. Both the Töölö and Viinikka Church (also 1927) competition designs represent further developments in Aalto's idea of an urban composition as first expressed in his entry for the second stage of the Parliament Building Competition. Thus, the idea of the small Italian piazza whose space is made complex and dynamic by the disposition of church, campanile, or baptistery within a tight urban framework—an idea outside Aalto's immediate urban experience—was firmly established in his mind and work before he was thirty; and it was to remain an important image in his environmental memory for the next four decades.

In fact he was not to use the idea of the urban fragment again for more than twenty years. Although Aalto's original entry in the competition for Viipuri City Library of 1927 and his revised design of 1928 both embraced the concept of a piazza, it was a requirement of the architectural program for the competition. Uno Ullberg, who was the Viipuri city architect at the time of the competition, had a clear recollection of a previous competition for the original Aleksanderinkatu site in which the winners had included a ceremonial public space in their design.[7] When the library competition was written, therefore, Ullberg provided for a future cultural center in the conditions, together with the implication that both the library and the center should front onto a *Monumentalplatz.* Thus, the idea of the piazza in Aalto's designs for the Alexander Street site was in Ullberg's environmental memory rather than Aalto's. No trace of the piazza idea, however, remained in the executed design on the new site adjacent to the cathedral. The cathedral site had been substituted for the original one as a result of popular demand that the city's magnificent tree belt should not be eroded by a monument. With that change of site, Ullberg's dream of a *Monumentalplatz* became a historical footnote.

Significantly, none of Aalto's planning projects for the 1930s and 1940s refer to the idea of a remembered urban fragment. These projects included the redevelopment of Norrmalm, Stockholm (1933), the housing area at Sunila (1938–39), the village plan for Säynätsalo (1942–44), the town center competition for Oulu (1943), and the town center competition for Avesta, Sweden (1944). But in 1948, with his original winning design for the National Pension Bank, Helsinki, and again in 1949, with his successful project for the Säynätsalo Town Hall competition, we see clear evidence of Italian urban space remembered in the creation of new urban fragments.

Immediately following the end of the Second World War, in 1946, Aalto was reappointed as a visiting professor at MIT. Early in this renewed attachment to the Cambridge campus, he was commissioned to design a new graduate residential facility which was to become the Baker Dormitory. As I have already noted,[8] this building marked a watershed in Aalto's mature work because its construction ushered in the rich collection of red brick designs that were to dominate his architecture of the 1950s. Although I will not argue that the Baker Dormitory is also the first instance of Aalto's developed use of the urban fragment after those early precursors of 1927, the dormitory's complex form is extraordinary and cannot be entirely explained in terms of the building's relationship to two such strikingly different contextural features as the Charles River and Massachusetts Avenue. Indeed, I do want to propose that its elusive and complex geometry could be seen as a response to the fact that, although an urban framework is suggested by the meandering line of the river and the axiality of the campus thoroughfare, *no urban fabric as such actually exists.*

Aalto was particularly insistent that the Baker Dormitory is a completely functional solution, reflecting the need for the students' rooms to relate to the river, and for the staircases on the campus side of the building to meet the requirements of the fire marshal.[9] The plan continues Aalto's preoccupation with the serpentine wall—a *memory* of contours found in the Finnish landscape which can be traced back to the ceiling of the Viipuri Library lecture room (1935), and the vases designed for the Scandinavian Glass Competition (1936), becoming fully developed in the main display wall of the Finnish Pavilion for the New York World's Fair of 1939. The dormitory plan resembles a Constructivist representation of space, such as an architectonic *proun* by El Lissitsky, while the form of the building is highly expressionist. From all these points of view the Baker Dormitory is of particular interest and repays study.

Although its plan form is determinedly modern, the actual appearance of the Baker Dormitory is not. Those expressionist brick masses—which even in his early sketches Aalto showed as softened by creeping vines—recall a material tradition that goes back five thousand years and which dominated the Baltic region in the Middle Ages. We have only to remember the great city walls of the Hanseatic ports of Lübeck, Gdansk, and Viborg (Finnish Viipuri) itself to discover one source. It is important to understand that Aalto's interest in red brick has a complex history of sources. Although the material was not exactly common in south and central Finland this had more to do with cost than nonavailability, and its use is always significant, therefore, from the Middle Ages onwards. As he grew up in central Finland Aalto was certainly familiar, for example, with the parish church of Hattula, a truly great monument of Finnish medieval architecture whose fine brick external walls are justly renowned. Irma Savolainen rightly emphasizes that, at Hattula: "The use of brick, and the horizontal friezes and ornamentation on the outside walls shows that the builder was influenced by the architecture of the southern Baltic."[10]

When Aalto went to study in Helsinki, and particularly after he had moved his office from Jyväskylä to Turku in 1927, he would have come to know this southern Baltic tradition more closely. On the island of Suomenlinna are the massive brick fortifications of the eighteenth century which the British shelled during the Crimean War. To the west is the fine medieval church of Porvoo with its celebrated elaborate brick gable and even more splendid brickwork on its detached bell tower. In Turku itself is the medieval brick cathedral which demonstrates, more than any other structure in Finland, the broad range of possible brick expression, from the monumentality of its walls to the delicacy of its arches, pier ribbings, and a host of other fine details. Furthermore, in 1927 Aalto entered and won the competition for the city library of Viipuri. By 1928, then, when he went for the first time to Holland, he would have been familiar with the great defensive walls of the easternmost bastion of the Hanseatic League.

The Dutch brick tradition is notable, of course, because of the many fine monuments in that material found in Holland and also because of its profound influence upon English architecture and, therefore, that of the United States. On his first visit to Holland in 1928 Aalto saw not only the superlative urban fabric of burghers' houses in Amsterdam but also Wilhelm Dudok's almost unequaled modern use of brick in the Rembrandtlaan (1919) and Minchelers (1925) schools, and his recently completed Town Hall, all in the garden city of Hilversum. Thus, having had considerable exposure to the Baltic brick tradition in his own country, Aalto would have realized that this tradition was still alive and well in modern architecture. There is, however, no evidence of this realization for two decades; that is, not until Aalto finds himself back in the United States after the Second World War. After several visits to the Boston area where the red brick tradition still survives, he would probably have begun to feel himself at home. In that part of America he would have been able to identify with the many examples of his own Baltic tradition that had been transformed through Dutch and English use and transplanted to the New World.

All of this perhaps helps to explain Aalto's choice of brick as the cladding material for the Baker Dormitory and its dominant position in his architecture of the 1950s. It also suggests a link between the urban fragment and the Constructivist/expressionist character of the Baker Dormitory—a link that exemplifies a bridge between history and modernism in Aalto's work. For it seems to me that Aalto's *urban fragment* performs two basic tasks in the environmental framework: first, it remembers another time and another place; then, with its contemporaneous adaptation of that *memory*, it offers to the suburbs that complex scenario of space and function which speaks of *permanence*.

If we look at Aalto's original design for the National Pensions Bank in Helsinki, the *Forum Redivivum* project, we can readily see the operation of this idea of providing a synthetic memory of a universal concept of space and form as a means of structuring the present. Aalto's new building, or, more importantly the new building group, does not at all represent modernism in appearance. Conceptually, however, Aalto's urban fragment is truly modern precisely because it denies the finite character of the urban artifact as a monument, and offers instead that essential complexity and coherence which dissolves the object per se in order to create a sort of built-in context to which the urban fragment then responds. Indeed, the *piazze* and buildings which made up the *Forum Redivivum* design are made more monolithic in the executed building than in the design, showing Aalto's developed ability to replace the elemental compositions of 1927 with fragments that represent more complete pieces of the urban fabric. Gone are the individual bits which characterize the Töölö and Viinikka church projects. In their place is a coherent whole, an urban fiction, the creation of an entirely new yet recognizable *place*, which brings to the suburban *non-place* the permanence we can recognize at Hattula or Turku. And the social significance of according to this new building type those aspects of permanence we associate with the great medieval market halls and churches must play its part in our appreciation of Aalto's concept of such a building complex.

Recognizing Aalto's buildings of the 1950s as urban fragments rather than isolated architectural monuments is essential if we are to understand his true contribution to modern architecture. After the fact we may come to appreciate how such a holistic methodology is more valuable to architects, planners, and city-dwellers than the image-laden stage sets of Venturi, Graves, and Moore. In the 1980s, we welcome Peter Eisenman's parallel strategy of the urban fragment, the "missing piece," the spatial matrix of the non-building. That vision makes Eisenman's design for the Arts Center at Ohio State University refreshing and far more vital than other projects full of pedantic reference to the encyclopedia of architectural models. For Eisenman's proposal speaks directly of organic integration, a process which goes beyond mere contextualism in seeking to build those coherent wholes we find in the medieval city.

It is important also to distinguish here between Rossi's concept of the *typology* and my definition of Aalto's *urban fragments.* I have previously described Aalto's design strategy in such building complexes as being modeled upon generic examples of urban space, particularly the Italian piazza. Such a description is, however, not sufficiently precise, for, as we have seen in chapter 4, to take something as a model implies: (1) that it can actually be copied, and (2) that the intention is to copy it. Recently I heard a music critic say: "Originality often consists of copying something in such an original way that the original becomes entirely concealed in the new work." As that critic was describing the innovative technique of no less a master than George Frederick Handel his definition was clearly not intended as a slight. Perhaps we can say, therefore, that Aalto copied his "models" not like students of neoclassicism or the Beaux Arts, but more in the spirit of Handel. For it seems quite clear that Aalto set out to use *themes* that were recorded in his environmental memory, but it is equally clear that his intention was to invent broad variations on those themes.

In music, of course, variations on someone else's theme, whether undertaken by Handel, Beethoven, or Stravinsky, necessarily involve representing the original not in Bergson's "ready-made clothes" but in an innovative form. This was also Aalto's intention in his variations on memorable themes. In the first place the memories that Aalto drew upon, although fairly specific in his early church designs, became increasingly generic or thematic as his work matured. Thus, neither the *Forum Redivivum* design nor that for the Town Hall at Säynätsalo has any specific identity with an original model. Both projects as built operate on a number of different levels, as well. Conceptually, both are indebted to the use of the piazza and the atrium in the context of the historic city. In both projects, the idea of the piazza is especially strong in the plans as compared to the visitor's experience. But there are also a number of other concepts operating in the built forms.[11]

At Säynätsalo, for instance, the "piazza" or "atrium" around which the elements are grouped is, in reality, *neither.* Any sense of public or formal space is neutralized by what is nothing more or less than a domestic garden. At the National Pensions Institute, this same dominance of the garden idea also disarms any spatial formality that is suggested by the plan. What is more, at Säynätsalo, whereas the exterior masses announce a substantial and impressive building, the architectural character of the interior court is decidedly small scale and domestic. Once we have climbed the monumental staircase at Säynätsalo the monument itself disappears. Having made the architectural representation of dignity and significance, so that we may step out of the forest and climb into the "palace" of local government, Aalto then allows us to find ourselves back in a world of recognizable intimacy of house and farmyard. The Säynätsalo building is at once both a small office and a large house.

Of course, as we have observed, Aalto's continuation of the Baltic brick tradition is significant in that it also imparts a certain familiarity to the material being of these compositions. But, lest we should be in any doubt concerning the relationship of historical memory to this modern period, Aalto activates his historical theme material with determinedly modern variations of form and detailed expression.

When I described the Säynätsalo Town Hall in my earlier study,[12] I remarked on: (1) the recurrence of the disjointed unity that characterizes the grouping of buildings on traditional farms in central Finland; and (2) a more than casual reference to the form and composition of Wilhem Dudok's Hilversum Town Hall. But what I had failed to notice, until my return visit to Säynätsalo in 1983, was the presence of strong Constructivist themes which—"played on a different instrument"—have become muted and barely recognizable variations of the original notation. Previously, I had seen those interpenetrating volumes that are rendered in brick, and rightly thought of Dudok's Dutch brick schools of the 1920s. But Aalto's masses are more dynamic and less tame than Dudok's response to the already watered-down precepts of Frank Lloyd Wright and De Stijl: in fact, they have a more direct connection with the revolutionary forces at play in Russian Constructivism. While plan and material at Säynätsalo speak of the Middle Ages in Italy and the Baltic tradition of brickwork, those turbulent masses also confirm the building's roots in the twentieth century. It could not possibly have been conceived before those experiments of the 1920s.

This revelation led me to look again at a number of Aalto's other urban fragments, to see if this obvious debt to Constructivist spatial dislocation had further echoes. The project that followed the Baker Dormitory and preceded the Säynätsalo Town Hall, that is the National Pensions Institute, seemed a natural object for such scrutiny. For some time—at least since the late 1960s—I had thought of Aalto's curious detail at the intersection of internal corners on the Institute's exterior as but further evidence of the sense of incompleteness celebrated in so much farm construction in central Finland. These joints suggested continuity with some future extension—the implication of those "open-ended" farmhouse details. Upon reexamination, these same disjunctive connections proclaimed a disruption of the formal and material cohesion of the status quo. And this break with conventional form and construction is undeniably the hallmark of the Russian Constructivist experiment.

We have traced the origin of Aalto's interest in the urban fragment back to his earliest urban design project, the Finnish Parliament competition, in the second stage of which the architect adopted the idea of a public space contained by a group of buildings. And we have suggested how the Baker Dormitory for MIT became the catalytic design in the process of transforming Aalto's early enthusiasm for the Italian urban fragment into a unified whole, and his ability to integrate modern architecture into the city. Then we have examined how this newfound coherence was worked out in the National Pensions Institute and Säynätsalo Town Hall. Both those projects followed closely on the design of Baker House, dating from 1948 and 1949 respectively. Although there are other examples of his use of the urban fragment in the 1950s, the total period in which it is found is confined to the decade 1948–58. By 1959, when he won the competition for the design of the town center at Seinajoki, Aalto had apparently abandoned the dense coherence that characterizes his urban fragments. This was unfortunate because the town center of Seinajoki, and subsequently that of Roveniemi, would have benefited enormously from such condensed complexity. After thirty years of producing outstanding work, the late 1950s marked the beginning of the decline in Aalto's performance which, with some notable exceptions, we witnessed in the 60s. Of all his projects and buildings in the last eighteen years of his life, only one, the winning Altstetten Church and Parish Center project of 1967, attempted to recapture the idea of the urban fragment, and that design was unexecuted.[13]

Of the 1950s works that interest us here, therefore, we must first mention the former Pedagogical Institute, now University of Jyväskylä, the relevant part of which dates from 1952. It was conceived while the Säynätsalo Town Hall was under construction and entered in the competition with the motto "urbs"! As we remarked earlier, the true permanence of Jyväskylä is the forest itself: how appropriate, therefore, that Aalto should have planted his own candidate for the city's built permanence in that very forest. For the central auditoria building was, at the time of its completion in 1957, the one building in Jyväskylä which had to accommodate not only the Institute's pedagogic functions but also its concerts, its theater, and indeed all its cultural and civic life as a community. Thus, the building program of this complex of functions provided Aalto with an ideal framework of "urban events" upon which to shape his urban fragment for Jyväskylä. In the first place this piece centers on an indoor piazza, a "public" open space which, just like the town square, receives the main flow of pedestrian traffic brought into it by the arteries that pass through it, linking the city with the campus in the process. Aalto seized on this internalized image of urban functions and developed a main street that connects the internal piazza with the forest clearing on the city side and the campo of the campus itself. Then, within this interior "street" he embodied the complete image of the Italian hilltown, with a subsidiary "street" in the form of a great flight of steps that climbs the "hill" and gives access to smaller auditoria at intermediate landings on its way. Along the edge of the "piazza" there are hints of a framing colonnade, while in the corner a café hugs the boundary of this space. Every detail of the generic urban fragment is remembered in this interior construction of Jyväskylä's missing "downtown."

Some of these ideas of the "street" and the "square" had indeed already been embodied in Aalto's winning entry for the plan of the Helsinki Technical University at Otaniemi, submitted in the previous year (1949). But this project, like the remainder of the Jyväskylä campus, lacks the density necessary to capture the spirit of an urban fragment and, in consequence, one feels too much of the perimeter condition and not enough penetration into the "heart" of this academic town. At Jyväskylä, in fact, we see the campus, as developed, reaching into the forest and merging with it, so much so that Kirmo Mikkola has described its image as that of "forest town."[14] Whenever the idea and spirit of the city falls into disrepair, we are aware of nature's readiness to reinhabit its old domain and reassert its own permanence.

The remaining examples of Aalto's urban fragments are less completely worked out, and therefore less significant. My contention, however, is that they are of particular relevance to the central problem of today's suburbs since they offer valuable clues about the non-monumental celebration of place. Some particular building types or functions, of course, lend themselves more to the creation of urban fragments than do others. We have reviewed a town hall (Säynätsalo); a government center (Pensions Institute), and a university (Jyväskylä). Significantly for the suburbs, the remaining examples are a cultural center, a museum, and a parish center.

The Cultural Center for Wolfsburg (1958–63) has a number of symbolic roles in the context of the post-World War Two Germany which produced it. On the one hand, of course, it reasserts the old Germanic passion for *Kultur*; while on the other it represents the survival of the

Protestant work ethic and its contribution to economic recovery. But above all it signifies an attempt to respond to the suburban desert—the result of increased automobile ownership—of which Wolfsburg, as the headquarters of the Volkswagen company, is itself a representation. In other hands the temptation to erect a monument to Volkswagen might have been irresistible, but Aalto's solution has nothing of monumentality in its form. While it is true that the external walls of the auditorium and lecture room corner do engage in some civic gesturing, this has to be read against the seemingly endless car park with its hundreds of VW beetles rather than in the context of a *Monumentalplatz.* Instead, the building "looks into itself" instinctively, for it is the instinct of the true urban fragment to look into its own heart and soul, just as it is the instinct of the monument to make a great show of its sense of fashion, and the instinct of the suburb (with its "underground skyline") to deny any idea of locus.

In Aalto's plan for the Art Museum for Aalborg, Denmark (originally designed in 1958, but not constructed until 1972–73), the central court, although displaced in fact by a lecture theatre, remains as an idea in the plan, which gathers itself inward in the characteristic way of the urban fragment. Although this museum is built in a park, it offers no monumental presentation on the exterior. Instead, it is cut into the site as if to emphasize its internalization. Similarly, Aalto's unbuilt project for the Parish Church and Center at Altstetten, Zurich, takes its inspiration from the "street" which literally connects the heart of the center with the outside world. In spirit, the Altstetten project seems close to Säynätsalo, although less complex and somewhat incomplete even for an urban fragment. I have already suggested also how some of Aalto's domestic architecture responds to Alberti's metaphor of the house representing a city in miniature. That idea connects in turn with the evidence that there is a certain modularity in Aalto's work that, at least conceptually, links one use of his fragment strategy with another.[15]

One important aspect of that modularity is the persistence of the idea of the open-air, public space as an enclosed atrium in Aalto's buildings. Indeed, although Aalto did not succeed through his work at MIT in having any influence on modern American architecture, still it is arguable that the garden-paved Ford Foundation Building in New York by Kevin Roche and John Dinkeloo in 1967, and the subsequent rash of atrium buildings that occurred in the United States during the 1970s, owed at least some debt to Aalto's pioneering work with this fragment of internalized urban space in the decade between 1952 and 1962. Even the original Pensions Institute design of 1948 had a central atrium with massive skylights—derived possibly from Aalto's original use of an internal top-lit space in the Viipuri Library (in 1933). It was just as likely, however, to have been prompted by his memory of frequent visits to the bar in the Adlon Hotel, Helsinki, which has a fine top-lit atrium. Although the nineteenth-century example at Cleveland, Ohio, and Frank Lloyd Wright's Larkin Building in Buffalo, New York of 1904 are equally admissable as American precursors, the fact is that Aalto was alone during the 1950s in adapting the nineteenth-century top-lit atrium for new uses.

That the Pensions Institute of 1952 represents a late watershed in Aalto's career is due in no small measure to his development of the top-lit atrium in that building. He went on to further refine the idea of the enclosed atrium, or piazza in this case, in his Rautatalo ("Iron House") design of 1952. Here the framing of the central court on the upper level is achieved by shops and a café, making the source of his environmental memory indisputable. In the neighboring Academic Bookshop, designed in 1962, Aalto modified the piazza idea so that the shop becomes the microcosm of the city (see pl. 16). Like a covered book "market" the Academic Bookshop protects Finnish bibliophiles from the severities of Helsinki's winter climate, while harnessing the energy of their browsing into layers of activity that are revealed to each customer as a fragment of urban complexity. This is the complexity hinted at in Roche and Dinkeloo's Ford Foundation Building, although its realization is inhibited by the fact that, while the general public has access to the garden path through the building, the upper floors are institutional rather than public.

The urban fragment, at once one and many things, is free of the dictatorship of style: it seeks a repose in its own modest accommodation of complex and contradictory programs. When those complex and contradictory programs are expressed stylistically, as Venturi suggests,[16] the result is a monument. Placed in a suburban context the principal effect of the monument is to remind the suburbs of what they are not and cannot be, namely urban. Through its innate principle of accommodation, the urban fragment offers an urban density at a pedestrian scale. Its true contribution, therefore, is to bypass the fossilized knowledge of form and to connect us directly with the deep well of experience—our environmental memory.

E L E V E N

▲

L'ESPRIT DE L'ESCALIER

Let us consider two images. The first of these is the serpentine wall Alvar Aalto designed for the Finnish Pavilion at the New York World's Fair of 1939. The second is Marcel Duchamp's *Nude Descending a Staircase* of 1912. In bringing these two images together I wish to suggest that the significance of Aalto's serpentine wall in the history of modern architecture was comparable to that of Duchamp's picture within modern painting. Aalto's bold statement in that wall was startling, and its effect upon the shape of things to come should have been enormous. But in 1939 another more shocking phenomenon of history gripped modern man as we slipped into the Second World War.

The peace resulting from the armistice of 1918 had been unbearably brief, a mere couple of decades. In the first of those peaceful decades, Finland finally emerged as an independent nation—after almost six centuries of foreign domination by the Swedes from 1342 until 1809, followed by more than a century of Russian Czarist rule. During that first decade Aalto had been preparing to become a master of modern architecture, a task which he completed brilliantly in the period from 1927 to 1933 with the design of three internationally recognized masterpieces: the premises for the Turku newspaper *Turun*

Sanomat (1927), the tuberculosis sanitarium at Paimio (1929–33), and the City Library for Viipuri (1927–33). During the second decade of peace between the world wars, Aalto transformed himself and the prospects for modernism. The ground rules for what Aalto sometimes referred to as "an autonomous architecture" were never really formulated explicitly. Aalto hinted at them in his occasional and very fragmentary texts; but he was no polemicist. As Reima Pietilä has observed, he "left others to guess what he was up to."[1]

Let us look more closely at both the *Nude Descending a Staircase* and Duchamp's other painting in the same mode, *The Passage from Virgin to Bride* of 1912 (also known as *The Bride Stripped Bare by Her Bachelors, Even*—both titles apply to our purpose). They seem to me equally relevant in explaining both a central thesis and a persistent dilemma of modernism, for Duchamp's images encapsulate the restless energy of modern man in a representation of perpetual motion. In *Nude Descending a Staircase* this motion is essentially the vertical one of a stair progressing through space, while *The Passage from Virgin to Bride* celebrates the more usual case of a horizontal rite of passage. But—and this is a far-reaching reservation—although we are caught up in patterns of motion in the construction of both compositions, this motion is merely simulated. The elements of the paintings are determinedly abstract and make only fleeting references to recognizable forms. In other words, the motion simulated in Duchamp's paintings has to do with the *idea* of motion rather than motion represented per se. This seems to me an important breakthrough because it indicates that abstract imagery, rather like symbolic imagery, can circumvent the limitations imposed by Plato upon the relationship of the image to the idea.

This Platonic obstacle in the idea–image cycle, and the modern artist's struggle to overcome that obstacle, is poignantly described by the Belgian surrealist painter, René Magritte, in a letter to the French philosopher, Michel Foucault.

> The words *resemblance* and *similitude* permit you forcefully to suggest the presence—utterly foreign—of the world and ourselves. Yet, I believe these two words are scarcely ever differentiated, dictionaries are hardly enlightening as to what distinguishes them.
>
> It seems to me that, for example, green peas have between them relations of similitude, at once visible (their color, form, size) and invisible (their nature, taste, weight). It is the same for the false and the real, etc. Things *do not* have resemblances, they *do* or *do not* have similitudes.[2]

Magritte goes on to stress the core of the Platonic dilemma concerning ideas and their pictorial or imagic representation, thus:

> Only thought resembles. It resembles by being what it sees, hears, or knows; it becomes what the world offers it. It is as completely invisible as pleasure or pain.
>
> But painting interposes a problem: There is the thought that sees and can be visibly described. *Las Meninas—The Servants* is the visible image of Velasquez's invisible thought. Is the invisible, therefore, sometimes visible? Only on condition that thought be constituted exclusively of visual images.[3]

And the artist concludes by forcefully describing the relationship between the idea, the image, and the object: "[I]t is evident that a painted *image* —intangible by its very nature—hides nothing, while the tangibly visible *object* hides *another visible thing* —if we are to trust our experience."[4]

With these thoughts in mind concerning idea and image, subject and object, we will return to Alvar Aalto (our subject) and in particular his representation of the staircase (our object). But before we can discuss this image of the staircase, we must first consider the idea of the staircase, the very nature of man's desire to represent in architectural terms the action of vertical motion through space.

When I was teaching in the Middle East I quickly came to appreciate a difficulty in approaching with my Arab students the problems of vertical circulation in buildings. This may seem hardly surprising since many of them came from desert environments where the single-story dwelling is the dominant representation of family and community life. The same could be said for many of my American students, who also hail from vast deserts of seemingly endless surburban bungalows. Yet every Arab community has a mosque, and each mosque has its minaret. In American architecture, on the other hand, ever since the safety elevator was invented in 1853 there has been a pitched battle between horizontal nature and vertical ambition. As we have already noted, the elevator represents time and motion rather than space. Of course, in a typical Portman hotel building we can see the space we are passing through in those glass boxes, but such disembodied experience is not to be compared to the effort of progressing through vertical space as we mount or descend a staircase. Similarly, although the minaret is symbolic of the muezzin's progression to a high place from which he summons the faithful to worship, in fact the reverend gentleman no longer climbs the stairs to sing his plaintive chants. Instead, everything is now done by loudspeakers hooked up to a central recording of the muezzin's disembodied voice.

To reflect this symbolic shift of imagery in contemporary Islamic architecture, I persuaded one of my students in Amman to design an open steelwork tower with two loudspeakers that normally repose on the ground, but are hoisted *symbolically* to the top of the tower to broadcast the call to prayer at the appropriate hours. The thesis was that, since the means of calling the faithful to prayer had been modernized, its architectural expression should also be modern. The traditional idea of *ascent* by the muezzin to a "high place" (as in chapters 2 and 7) has been displaced by a mechanical representation of this ritual. The idea of the tower that is embodied in the traditional minaret, therefore, has also been transcended. Consequently the high place itself has become an abstract point in space, because there is no longer any progression toward it in the sense that we understand such progression through space, as an actual physical and experiential movement from one level to another. This displacement of the aspiration to move from one plane to another and loss of the actual experience of such progression is symptomatic and characteristic of Functionalist modernism, which seeks to substitute mechanical representation of an event for the evolution of the real thing. The point of the student's minaret exercise, which substituted a sort of loudspeaker elevator for the traditional enclosed stair, was to underline the abstraction of mechanical representation and the disconnectedness of that abstract gesture regardless of its ingenuity or appropriateness.

My example of this very modern minaret negates, of course, the fundamental nature of the staircase. In contrast, the Functionalist modern architect's concept of the stairway has been very much concerned with the assertion of its role as a progressive element. The modern staircase must literally advance the idea of spatial progression by demonstrating its functional activity anatomically, in other words *as a nude staircase ascending.* Now, traditional history of architecture is essentially a history of spatial ordering and formal expression that depends upon constructional ingenuity and the geometrical ratios we call proportion. In this history the idea of progression, and therefore the idea of the staircase or the corridor, has almost no part. Architectural history, criticism, and theory has centered upon points of arrival: the room, the atrium, the piazza. Meanwhile the means of getting there—the street, the alley, the stairs—in some cases the very anatomy of the house or the city, is often ignored both in the planning process and in the discussion of spatial and formal order. Indeed, the history of architecture tends to deny the maxim that "it is better to travel than to arrive." Instead, theory suggests the contrary, that "it is better to arrive than to travel"!

Interestingly, Vitruvius does not even mention the staircase, although he does speak of the temple steps: "The steps in front must be arranged so that there shall always be an odd number of them; for thus the right foot, with which one mounts the first step, will also be the first to reach the level of the temple itself."[5] In this briefest of references there is a direct connection between number and experience: that connection is the ritual procedure for negotiating those steps—first the right foot, then the left, then the right, and so on. To Vitruvius, therefore, the process of traveling was clearly important, indeed it constitutes an integral part of the architectural object—the temple—and its formal representation.

In Baroque space, of course, the staircase is very often the vehicle for exploiting movement through plastic volumes and their interpenetration. The transition from plastic and volumetric themes of sixteenth-century architecture to the full spatial experimentation of the Italian Baroque is a central theme in Bruno Zevi's *Architecture As Space*. Zevi describes Michelangelo's work, for example, as "an agitation of the contents of the sixteenth-century walled-box,"[6] referring specifically to the entrance of the Biblioteca Laurentiana in Florence as the archetype of that architect's work. He describes Michelangelo's use of the giant orders as no longer fitting quietly within the walls or volume, but providing a "plastic symbol" of the need to open up the walls, enlarging, disrupting, and bursting them in the process. And he says: "The mounting steps break into and dominate the small space as though calling for revolt against its static stereometry."[7]

Zevi proposes that Michelangelo could not break entirely with the "walled box" idea of *cinquecento* space, but instead altered its walls and volumes, giving them new emphasis in one of the most dramatic moments in the history of architecture. That moment truly opened the way for the creation of Baroque space. All that Zevi says is true, of course, but much more as well. While Zevi gives particular emphasis to the role of the staircase in the composition, he seems to completely miss the point of the way in which the staircase bursts out of its conventional box and generates the dominant movement in the constricted little anteroom to the Biblioteca Laurentiana. As in Vitruvius' description of the ritual steps of the temple, the staircase offers the connection between the delineation of space and form and the actual experience of its true dynamic.

The evolution of human consciousness reveals an interdependence between the symbolic and the functional roles of the staircase. As far as we know, the Garden of Eden, for all its virtues, was a more or less flat plane surface upon which Adam and Eve stood and across which they fled from God's wrath. The idea of verticality, the sense of above and below, is already established in the Garden, however, by the presence of trees. By their very nature and form trees represent growth and the achievement of a vertical scale. Thus, early in human consciousness of the world the tree came to represent aspiration, an ambition to transcend the lowly, horizontal plane of existence. In order to reach the fruit on the Tree of Knowledge, that succulent morsel which Eve so passionately desired, in all probability Adam had to shin up the trunk and actually climb the forbidden tree. Part of the knowledge he would have gained is the dramatic sense of an overview of his world. An overview, after all, is always listed as one of God's attributes. Perhaps it was this overview, indeed, which God was unwilling to share, and therefore put the forbidden fruit out of reach so that it would become accessible only if man had the arrogance to climb the tree. In the process he would gain knowledge of the divine dimension of the vertical scale which links the earth with the heavens. He would have lost his humility—but what a gain!

Certainly, having been drummed out of the Garden Club, man soon began to erect his sacrificial altars in a "high place," of which Petra in Jordan provides a stunning example. And there can be little doubt that, up there closer to the heavens, the priests must have sensed themselves closer to their gods, a memory shared even now by those who ascend to the High Place in Petra. Yet Yahweh specifically forbade such a transcendent experience, for we read in the Book of Exodus his commandment that "You shall not go up steps to my Altar."[8] And we recall the Lord God's reaction when the Babylonians created the first constructed high place by building the Tower of Babel. He is recorded as saying: "This is the beginning of what they will do. Hereafter they will not be restrained from anything which they determine to do." And so saying He "scattered them from that place all over the earth; and they stopped building the city."[9] This was clearly an early warning issued from God to the architects and planners, informing them that he suffered extreme displeasure when they usurped his vertical dimension.

In Islam there is no altar, and the followers of the Prophet Muhammad worship their true god Allah by prostrating themselves, that is, by staying as close to the horizontal plane as possible. Although it is from a "high place," at the top of the minaret that the faithful are called six times a day to prayer—as though, symbolically, Allah is calling them from on high—yet it is in the garden of the prayer rug, the figure and ground of the *kelim*, that the faithful pay their respects to their Creator. Significantly, also, the Islamic pulpit—the *mimbar*—is simply a flight of steps which the *sheikh* ascends in order to give his homily, to explain the word of God from the top step. Thus the *mimbar* is a further architectural representation of a "high place," although in this case one *from* which God speaks through the clergyman to his people.

The contrast of our horizontal plane of existence—garden, prayer rug, bed, or board—with the vertical thrust of aspiration, whether this manifests itself in a "thirst for knowledge" or more worldly ambitions, is a persistent theme in human consciousness of the world and, by implication, in its architectural representation. Returning to the anatomy of a building and our analogy of traveling and arriving, we should remind ourselves that in medieval architecture the staircase is aptly described by the German word for it, *Treppenhaus*; it is literally a separate room, another house, through which one passes on one's way.

Alvar Aalto was particularly fond of reverting to this completely enclosed form of staircase, a propensity he inherited from his immediate precursors, the architects of the Finnish National Romantic movement. In fact, Aalto never really used the liberated staircase established by Italian Renaissance models; although, in the top-lit atrium of the National Pensions Institute, he exposes one side of the access staircase as though in an anatomical sectional view cut through the volume. Indeed, in all Aalto's work, the staircase preserves its sense of mystery and otherness. These qualities may be observed in Aalto's staircase designs for buildings as functionally disparate as the Villa Mairea, Säynätsalo Town Hall, the University of Jyväskylä and the Enso-Gutzeit headquarters in Helsinki. Aalto seemed not at all interested in stripping off its foundation garment, as it were, and revealing its naked function.

At much the same time as Constructivists were revamping the Tower of Babel as the Tatlin Tower and reviving the Islamic *mimbar* as a *tribune* from which Lenin could preach the Marxist alternative to theology, the Functionalists liberated the staircase in a revolutionary spirit. The treads, unfurled, fly through space. The stairs expose shapely spine and ribs; some of them flaunt elegant curves. No longer constrained within the spatial sequence of order from room to room, the Functionalist staircase openly becomes a sex symbol. Gone is the chastely closeted box of the *Treppenhaus*.

In *The Poetics of Space,* Gaston Bachelard describes precisely the vested symbolism of the *Treppenhaus* as a link in our spatial consciousness. He tells us that: "A house is imagined as a vertical being. It rises upward. It differentiates itself in terms of its verticality. It is one of the appeals to our consciousness of verticality. A house is imagined as a concentrated being. It appeals to our consciousness of centrality."[10]

With the liberated movement of the Functionalist staircase, this sense of concentration is dissipated. The bachelors of Functionalism have stripped bare the architectural bride. No longer hidden in her chamber, concealed by her camisole, she flaunts the articulation of her strictly modern parts. If we can overcome the Functionalist canon of anatomical exposure and the Marxist critique of the object rather than the soul, perhaps we can also embrace the staircase once again with the affection she deserves, assuring the transformation of the brittle, highly socialized Mademoiselle de l'Escalier once more into a respectable *Treppen Hausfrau*.

TWELVE

THE BODY OF KNOWLEDGE AND THE BODY OF ARCHITECTURE

I began with the idea that individual buildings, and the configuration of urban form and space, offer us an essential framework of consciousness to which we refer in order to "talk to ourselves." Strømnes goes so far as to propose that civilization does not exist without the "cultural functions" fulfilled by architecture, asserting that its capacity to *remember* and *give order* to human action is quite unique. According to Strømnes, architecture achieves this remembering and ordering "by having a durable structure of suitable proportions."[1] His concept is poetic and rather elusive. Yet the idea of "suitable proportions" certainly speaks of familiar and recognizable relationships in our surroundings, relationships that remember for us and help give order and coherence to our spatial thinking. In the same way, the notion of a "durable structure" conjures up a framework of references that continuously provide a meaningful extension of our being and to which we are, therefore, connected.

Our environmental memory is not a fixed quantity, of course, but a growing, organic awareness of our surroundings. We bring both our knowledge and awareness to the environmental theater. Our ability to interact with our surroundings depends upon the way our senses have been cultivated, especially upon our faculty of perception. If our senses have been blunted by a monotonous repetition of limited references, as, for example, in the endless suburb, then our consciousness is also impaired. And the process of awareness, or consciousness, and production are inseparably linked in the creation of building forms and urban spaces. Thus, the framework of environmental memory (or consciousness) cannot depend upon separate entities or things viewed or considered in isolation; rather, it requires a collection of things that are related in kind or nature, or are capable of suggesting such a relationship. The process of environmental memory is therefore enhanced by—and also seeks to make—*connections.*

It is the importance of this sense of connection that I wish to stress in conclusion, because both spatial and formal perception represents our awareness of those external extensions and manifestations of our inner being. Bachelard underlines the significance of this connection: "Not only our memories, but the things we have forgotten are housed. Our soul is an abode. And remembering "houses" and "rooms" we learn to "abide" within ourselves. Now everything becomes clear, the house images move in both directions: they are in us as much as we are in them."[2]

What Bachelard describes is the very essence of environmental memory: the essential interdependence of humanity and the images that surround us, or with which we surround ourselves—for they "are in us as much as we are in them." When these external references become part of our consciousness they enter our inner being. In this way, continuity and interaction connect the images in our environmental memory with our thinking, particularly creative thinking.

Reporting on Huttenlocher's research, Strømnes confirms that the old idea that thinking is "speaking in one's head" has been displaced by the realization that people think in part by using images in their heads.[3] From this realization we understand how imagery, as the raw material of thought, is also at the very core of creativity. Of course, the distinction between a literary dialogue of "speaking in one's head" and the visual dialogue implied by "using images in one's head" is a fine one. Indeed, the difference between the focal concentration on imagic material and a broader scan of narrative reference is often blurred, because thinking must involve "talking to ourselves" about images. The images we use in thinking are part of, and regroup to form, new narrative frameworks. Any attempt to separate one from another may be a convenient analytical device, but such technical shortcuts merely emphasize our contemporary sense of cultural dislocation and disconnectedness.[4] To reiterate Bachelard: the images are in us only as much as we are in them, and images can only be "in us" when they are truly part of a context within which we originally memorized them.

Remembering particular houses and rooms activates our consciousness of the continuity of the object with our subjective awareness of its existence as recalled. Our recollection will be particular and personal, unless someone has told us how we should evaluate such recollection so that our process of memory becomes "tutored" and our later recall of memory becomes educated. In this sense, all education is an intervention in the process of environmental memory. The cultivation of environmental memory must depend upon actual encounters with space and form, and upon the assimilation of images and symbols that recall and represent them. We might, therefore, refer to those experiences or *encounters* as being enacted within the *body of architecture,* while the images and symbols which recall and represent those encounters form part of our *body of knowledge* about architecture. There is, of course, no substitute for direct encounters with the body of architecture. These encounters lay the very foundations of our environmental memory long before we become aware that this fundamental process of construction is actually going on.

In contrast, the body of knowledge about architecture is descriptive and theoretical. Pragmatic description of materials, the elements of building, and the geometry of construction must all be considered in combination with a theoretical framework that concerns itself with established principles of order and relationship on the one hand, and on the other with more abstract and esoteric matters such as significance or meaning, intention, interpretation, transformation, and so on. It is possible to study the body of knowledge without the benefit of operating directly on the body of architecture. Indeed, this happens, regrettably, in much of our studio-based design education. Such an incomplete approach to learning might be compared with that of a medical student acquiring knowledge of anatomy and pathology without actually dissecting a corpse or examining cells under the microscope.

This does not discount the value of theory in approaching the body of architecture. On the contrary, without a firm theoretical basis it is not possible to have an overview and, therefore, to understand the relationship of the parts to the whole. To be sure, theory is not absolutely indispensable. If a genuine tradition flourishes within an art or craft, by which material limitations, techniques of assembly, and the ordering of the whole artifact can be conveyed reliably from generation to generation, then theory takes a back seat or transmits only what can be learned by direct experience.

Our present difficulty stems from severe cultural dislocation over the past two hundred years. In the process we have become disconnected from prior traditions of craft and art. Over the same period of time the body of knowledge has greatly increased in all fields. In architecture, we have forgotten that theory and practice are both intertwined inseparably with not only the science of material being but also the poetics of formal appearance. In consequence, we have succeeded in separating theory so that it is remote from other areas of study. This process of dislocation may be compared with that of children taught the theory of language—its grammar and syntax—but not given experience in applying this theory by writing essays, stories, and poems. While the children learn the elements of language and the structure into which these elements fit, educators may discourage or ignore the actual process of building language experience and exploring literary space. Consequently, the child's house of language will be incomplete, and his memory of its rooms will be disconnected and blurred.

Literary space has particular relevance to the range of environmental memory and the scope of theory in solving both problems of architecture and those of urban space and form. This relevance centers on the potential relationship of disparate and apparently unconnected parts—factors that are either known or can be located and studied—to the ordering and creation of new wholes. In projecting new ideas in design, architects often speak of the *parti,* or "the big idea," that provides the *Gestalt* or *raison d'être* of the structure, form, space, and appearance we have in mind.

Theoretically we could say that a *parti* arises from one of three basically different sources: (1) a known *architectural precedent,* that is, a particular building or group of buildings (what Rossi calls a typology);[5] (2) a *metaphor,* that is, an image from outside architecture, such as a shell or wing—something that will stand in for the architectural idea at the initial, conceptual stage (what Norberg-Schultz calls an "intermediary object");[6] and (3) a *narrative framework,* that is, a discursive literary description or scenario that, by elaboration of a theme or landscape, suggests relationships or provokes curiosity about such relationships.

References to *precedent, metaphor* or *narrative* necessarily require the presence of an environmental memory that has been developed by meaningful encounters not only with architecture, but also with poetry, the theater, the novel, nature, and so on. Theory, if it is to be the cultured, civilized alternative to the ideals of a craft tradition, must feed upon culture and civilization. For an Italian like Aldo Rossi, the genesis of environmental memory is immediately more apparent and complex than for Australians or Icelanders. Similarly, anyone living in a city senses—sees, feels and smells—the various stimuli of memory and, consequently, of narrative structure and poetic metaphor. As Louis Kahn put it: "A city is a place where a small boy, as he walks through it, can see something that will tell him what he wants to do his whole life."[7] Similarly, the student who studies at a university embedded in a great city will dissolve the walls of the classroom and the boundaries of the body of knowledge, because his curiosity is extended by that complex theater of encounters for which the city, the body of architecture, is the framework.

Extension of curiosity is, of course, of particular relevance to the student of art and architecture. How does the student fare, however, in a small town or a rural university? What happens to a student in the average American state university remote from a large city? For that student the body of knowledge is necessarily confined, because it cannot readily be extended by direct encounters with the body of architecture. A student who comes from the countryside or from a small town will tend to compound the limits of environmental memory if he or she then goes on to study at a small-town university.

Is that proposition then true or false? Frank Lloyd Wright believed that the city neither posed the questions nor offered the answers to questions architects should ask. For Wright, nature provided an alternative framework of reference which posited an organic architecture and a way of life that embodied principles of dispersal and individualism, rather than the concentration and collective responsibility that vivify the urban community. Wright's beliefs derived from his environmental memory of the farm and of life in scattered, rural communities. In his nonconformist view, the good, simple country life was always preferable to the complexity and evils of the city. Clearly, nature and the countryside, and images of the farm with its buildings clustered within the open landscape, are an essential part of environmental memory. Both the country and the city provide their own distinctive images towards the building of the whole structure of environmental memory. Wright's memory of farm and country was greatly expanded by his reference to other cultures as an alternative source to the forbidden city. Nevertheless, Wright argued for one kind of partial environmental memory, just as Rossi advances another.

Awareness of the total scope of environmental memory remains of value, however, not only for the theorist and philosopher but also for teachers at all levels of education: it should inform their teaching strategies. Meanwhile, individual teachers may stress country or city, poetics or technology. Sensitivity to the full range of potential encounters will increase the sense of excitement and adventure of education, the *frisson* one can best feel on Browning's "dangerous edge" of things. With a novel or a poem as his vehicle, the country boy can find his way into the labyrinth of the city, just as the city girl can clear her head with a breath of country air.

Where in architecture's past can the students of today learn how city and country may meet and tame each other? Andrea Palladio certainly teaches us through the design and images of his villas about the idea of the formal house as an urban intervention in the country. He tells us nothing, however, of the intervention of the country in the city. For such an image we must look at London or Cracow, or turn, for example, to such a description as Thomas Fuller's sixteenth-century account in the *Worthies of England:* NORWICH is (as you please) either a city in an orchard or an orchard in a city, so equally are the houses and trees blended in it; so that the pleasure of the country and the populousness of the city meet here together. Yet, in this mixture, the inhabitants participate nothing of the rusticalness of the one, but altogether of the urbanity and civility of the other."[8]

For many students the university itself may well be the nearest approximation they will experience to the scale and complexity of the city, if they return, after graduation, to the twilight of the suburbs or to some small town. There is little compensation for them in the American compulsion to label the smallest hamlet as a "city." This misnomer is not simply an error in the use of language but a fundamental cultural shift that confuses the concept of description with the nature of encounters.

It is possible to make substitutions at the notional stage of conceptual thought, considering a metaphoric or narrative reference to stand in place of a true precedent or model. But changing the label on something does not change the nature of that thing. Magritte plays a great deal with the tension, and indeed even a sense of the ridiculous, between the titles of his paintings and the subject matter of the pictures themselves. But this is his surreal intention, to underline discrepancies between visual images and verbal descriptions. Now, to call a place with a population of less than one hundred souls a city is truly surreal!

The problem is not simply that we run the risk of losing our second language of space and form; the danger is rather to language as a whole. Our kaleidoscopic juggling with images is as literary as it is visual. Our imagic resources of thought and expression have both visual and narrative components. At the heart of modernism, it appears, is the problem of expressing the present with reference to but in clear contradistinction to, the past. Before we can address this problem we need some sort of historical perspective, such as we find in literature, painting, and architecture. With such a view over the terrain of imagery that makes up this variegated landscape of ideas, we can see where our minds have traveled, and we can spot the oases and valleys yet to be explored.

There is no guarantee of arrival at any place of significance, yet we must travel. If we cannot distinguish between the knowledge we have and the knowledge we seek, we cannot ask the right questions along the road. In fact, we need a map: if the city is a labyrinth, a plan will ensure that we don't get lost in its exploration.

As a prosaic example, we may ask how helpful, for example, is the freshman course in English composition that focuses upon asking the student to complete "incomplete" sentences and paragraphs. Such a strategy presupposes that the student understands the concepts of "complete" and "incomplete." But to achieve this understanding it is necessary to comprehend both information and narrative as nonlinear and nonprogressive until unambiguous relationships are identified. For literature, unlike history, is not a matter of facts and figures, forms and dimensions: it is rather a poetic narrative that allows a free interchange between the real and the apparent.

The concept of environmental memory is not a conventional idea about the use of history. It is essentially modern because it is random in its sources—at least in its untutored experiential sources. The farmer's daughter receives intense impressions as truly as the city boy. Magritte asks, "Is the invisible sometimes visible?"[9] To which we may answer: *environmental memory allows us to make the invisible become visible.*

We have depended too much on extrapolation from science and art history in attempts to formulate current architectural theory.

Through his spatial poetics, Bachelard focuses our attention on actual experience linking our dreaming consciousness to physical encounters with architecture. "In the attic it is a pleasure to see the bare rafters of the strong framework. Here we participate in the carpenter's solid geometry."[10] Through such metaphors Bachelard lays bare the body of architecture.

These esprits de l'escalier are not simply "afterthoughts," realized at the turn of the landing on the way down to the front door. Rather, they afford an overview of the terrain that we gained by climbing to the roof of the house which "imagined as a vertical being . . . rises upward . . . (and) differentiates itself in terms of its verticality."[11]

In much the same way, when we climb to the top of the tower on a city's walls, the effort of climbing, the exhaustion and exhilaration combine to intensify our grasp of the landscape as far as the horizon.

NOTES

Preface

1. See Paul Frankl, *Principles of Architectural History,* 157.
2. See John McAndrew, *Venetian Architecture of the Early Renaissance,* x.

Introduction

1. See Paul Frankl, *Principles of Architectural History,* 157.
2. See Aldo Rossi, *A Scientific Autobiography,* part 1, especially 1 and 33.
3. See Frode Strømnes, "On the Architecture of Thought," *Abacus No. 2* (Museum of Finnish Architecture, Helsinki, 1980), 7–29.
4. Frances Yates, "Architecture and the Art of Memory," a paper delivered at the Architectural Association, London, in 1980.
5. The word *memory* is used here in Aldo Rossi's sense of adaptive reuse; see *The Architecture of the City,* chapters 1 and 3.
6. See Gaston Bachelard, *The Poetics of Space,* Introduction, xi–xvi.
7. Ibid., xiii, xi.
8. Ibid., xi. Note that Bachelard goes on to speak of "reverberation" from a poetic image: "It is as though the poem, through its exuberance, awakened new depths in us," xix.

PART I: ARCHITECTURE AS THE TOOL-KIT OF MEMORY

Chapter 1: The House of Memory

1. Frances A. Yates, *Giordano Bruno and the Hermetic Tradition,* 1. My concept of modern man is used here to represent our post-Renaissance consciousness, in which Platonic and other "pagan" aspects of awareness complement the more simplistic Christian position of the Scholastics.
2. The other two volumes are *The Art of Memory* (1966) and *Theatre of the World* (1969).
3. André Chastel, *The Myth of the Renaissance, 1420–1520,* 62–63.
4. Ibid., 62–63.
5. Ibid., 64.
6. Synesio, *De insomniis* (ca. 405–406 A.D., translated by Marsilio Ficino), see André Chastel, *Myth of the Renaissance,* 65. For more on Synesius' psychology of dreams, see Jay Bregman, *Synesius of Cyrene,* especially 145–154.
7. Chastel, *Myth of the Renaissance,* 65.
8. George of Trebizond, *Comparatio Aristotelis et Platonis,* in Chastel, *Myth of the Renaissance,* 65.
9. See chapter 4, "Image, Memory, and Spirit of Place."

10. Yates, *Giordano Bruno,* 24.
11. Frances Yates, *The Art of Memory,* 4.
12. The author of *Ad Herrenium,* as quoted and summarized by Yates, *Art of Memory,* 5.
13. Ibid., 6–7
14. Ibid., 7–8.
15. Yates, *Art of Memory,* 72–74, quoting Thomas Aquinas, *Summa theologiae,* II, II, quaestio XLIX, articulus I.
16. Aquinas, *Summa.* I, quaestio V, articulus 4 ad 1, in Erwin Panofsky, *Gothic Architecture and Scholasticism,* 38.
17. Erwin Panofsky, *Gothic Architecture and Scholasticism,* 45; in Yates, *Art of Memory,* 79.
18. See John Summerson, *The Classical Language of Architecture,* 9.
19. See unpublished manuscript of Sir Christopher Wren, *Discourse,* in the Library of All Souls College, Oxford. Discussed in Eduard F. Sekler, *Wren and His Place in European Architecture,* 51.
20. Letter from Christopher Wren in France to a colleague, in papers and reminiscences of Wren, *Parentalia,* by Stephen Wren, 1750, 261. In Sekler, *Wren,* 45.
21. See Frode Strømnes, "On the Architecture of Thought," *Abacus No* 2, 7–29, 9.
22. Ibid., 10–11.
23. Ibid., 10.
24. Ibid., 14.
25. Ibid., 17.
26. Ibid., 21.
27. Ibid., 21.
28. Ibid., 25.

Chapter 2: The City as a Mirror of Consciousness

1. See Book of Genesis, 3:21–24.
2. Gen. 2:8–9.
3. Gen. 6:13–16.
4. Gen. 4:8–12.
5. Gen. 4:16–17.
6. Gen. 4:18–22. The sons of Lamech are mentioned as part of the history of the art in the Regius manuscript purporting to be the constitution of the Art of Geometry, dating from just before 1400. See Joseph Rykwert, *AA Files,* No. 7 (Architectural Association, London, 1984), 22.
7. Gen. 4:13–14.
8. See Julian Jaynes, *The Origin of Consciousness in the Breakdown of the Bicameral Mind, 6–8.*
9. Ibid., 10.
10. Gen. 3:21.

11. Jaynes, *Origin of Consciousness*, 13.
12. Gen. 4:2.
13. Gen. 4:12.
14. Jaynes, *Origin of Consciousness*, 52–53.
15. See Jacques Ellul, *The Meaning of the City*, 6.
16. Ibid., 6–7.
17. Ibid., 7.
18. Gen. 11:1–4.
19. Gen. 11:6.
20. Gen. 11:7–9.
21. See Ellul, *Meaning of the City*, 15–16.
22. Exodus 20:24–26.
23. Ellul, *Meaning of the City*, 7.
24. See St. Augustine, *Sermons*, Book III, "De ascensione."
25. Jaynes, *Origin of Consciousness*, 55.
26. A.R. Luria and Karl Pribram, *Psychophysiology of the Frontal Lobes;* Ernest W. Kent, *The Brains of Men and Machines.* The following discussion of the evolution of mind and the relationship between mental and visual imagery is indebted to the insights of Bruce H. McCormick of Texas A&M University.
27. For further discussion of the ideas of the nucleation of the city, and the institutional subcenter within the whole, see chapters 3, 4, and 6.

Chapter 3: The Celebration of Place

1. Edmund Bacon, in *The Design of Cities*, 83, 95 et seq., sees regularity behind the diverse forms of medieval *piazze.* According to Bacon, a piazza typically links and fuses the civic with the religious life of a city, while a secondary axis breaks away to the main physical feature of the city—its river, or a view over its domain.
2. Aldo Rossi, *A Scientific Autobiography*, 18–19.
3. R.T. Rundle Clark, *Myth and Symbol in Ancient Egypt*, 29.
4. Ibid., 29.
5. Ibid., 32–33.
6. Genesis 1:6–7.
7. Clark, *Myth and Symbol*, 38.
8. Ibid., 38.
9. Ibid.

Chapter 4: Image, Memory, and Spirit of Place

1. See also Malcolm Quantrill, "Reima Pietilä—A Notional Appraisal," *Architectural Association Quarterly*, vol. 9, no. 1 (1977), 53–59.
2. For reviews of recent work in this area, see Stephen Kosslyn, *Image and Mind* (Cambridge, MA, 1980) and *Ghosts in the Mind's Machine* (New York, 1983).

3. See Christian Norberg-Schulz, *Genius Loci,* especially chapter 1.

4. See Aldo Rossi, *The Architecture of the City,* 40–41.

5. Norberg-Schulz, *Genius Loci.* 5–15.

6. For "topoanalysis" see Gaston Bachelard, *The Poetics of Space,* 8.

7. Ibid., xi–xvi.

8. Hendrick Petrus Berlage (1856–1934) believed that geometry is the ordering power of architecture, a concept akin to that of a building's "mystical" dimension or *energy,* and both J. J. P. Oud and Gerrit Rietveldt were influenced by his work and ideas. Oud, however, in his efforts to rationalize architectural thought, denied any such "mystical" component in Berlage's geometric systems, seeing them merely as mechanical means for creating order and clarity.

9. Aldo Rossi, *A Scientific Autobiography,* 1.

10. See John Ruskin, *The Seven Lamps of Arhitecture,* 167–169.

11. Ibid.

12. Ibid.

13. Rossi, *Scientific Autobiography,* 24.

Chapter 5: A View of the Room—A Room with a View

1. See Malcolm Quantrill, *Ritual and Response in Architecture,* 71–76.

2. Michael Graves, "Representation," in *Representation and Architecture,* Ömer Akin and Eleanor F. Weinel, eds., 27–89; 28–30.

3. Ibid., 33.

4. Ibid., 33.

5. Ibid., 33.

6. Ibid., 39.

7. Ibid., 39.

8. Ibid., 30.

9. Ibid., 42–45.

10. See Christopher Gray, *Cubist Aesthetic Theories,* 4.

11. Piet Mondrian, *De Stijl* exhibition catalog, 65.

12. Ibid., 41.

13. Ibid., 41.

14. There was one notable exception, however, in terms of a new building type. The emergence of the palm house, the railway station, and the exhibition pavilion celebrated, in glass and iron, the birth of the industrial shed.

15. See Stéphane Mallarmé, "Symphonie littéraire," *Oeuvres complètes,* 262.

16. Graves, "Representation," in Akin and Weinel, *Representation and Architecture,* 30–33.

17. For a more detailed discussion of Mallarmé's ideas in this context, see Christopher Gray's *Cubist Aesthetic Theories,* 13–20.

18. Ibid., 17–18.

19. Ibid., 18.

20. See note 11 above.

21. See Georges LeMaître, *From Cubism to Surrealism in French Literature,* 112–113.

22. Jean Royère, poet and friend of Apollinaire, in a letter to Ramon Gomez de la Serna, quoted by de la Serna in his preface to Guillaume Apollinaire's *Il y a.*

23. See Gray, *Cubist Aesthetic Theories,* 38.

24. See Malcolm Quantrill, *Reima Pietilä: Architecture, Context and Modernism,* chapter 1.

25. Juan Gris, recounted by Daniel-Henry Kahnweiler, in *Juan Gris: His Life and Work,* 145. Author's emphasis.

26. See Guillaume Apollinaire, *The Cubist Painters: Aesthetic Meditations,* 12–13.

27. Ibid.

28. Ibid.

29. See chapter 9.

30. See chapter 10.

31. See the U.S. television film "Beyond Utopia: Changing Attitudes in American Architecture," Blackwood Productions (Los Angeles), 1984.

32. Gaston Bachelard, *The Poetics of Space,* 12.

33. Ibid., 13.

34. See chapter 10.

Chapter 6: The City and Its Habitations: The Anatomy of Memory and the Labyrinth of the Soul

1. See Aldo Rossi, *A Scientific Autobiography,* 23.

2. Quoted in Frances Yates, *The Art of Memory,* 131–132.

3. Rossi, *A Scientific Autobiography,* 15–16.

4. Peter Eisenman, introduction to Aldo Rossi, *The Architecture of the City,* 5.

5. See Gaston Bachelard, *The Poetics of Space,* 8 (author's emphasis).

6. See Sandro Chierici, *La Lombardie romane,* 61. Author's translation.

7. Rossi, *Architecture of the City,* 40–41.

8. Ibid., introduction to the American edition, 18.

9. See Giulio C. Argan, *The Renaissance City* and Helen Rosenau, *The Ideal City.*

10. Rossi, *Architecture of the City,* 21.

11. Ibid., 21.

12. All discussed in Rossi, *Architecture of the City,* 27, 36, 38, 48, 53–54, et seq.

13. Ibid., 22.

14. Ibid., 24.

15. Ibid., 29.

16. Ibid., 59–60.

17. Ibid., 55.

18. Ibid., 32.
19. Ibid., 109.
20. Peter Eisenman's metaphor of spiral and labyrinth, in his introduction to the American edition of Rossi's *Architecture of the City,* 2–3.
21. Bachelard, *Poetics of Space,* 8.
22. Ibid., 4.
23. "Beyond Utopia," 1984.
24. Bachelard, *Poetics of Space,* 6–7.
25. Ibid., 17.
26. Ibid., 18.
27. Ibid., 18.
28. Ibid., 20.
29. Ibid., 25.
30. Ibid., 25.
31. See Michel Foucault, *This Is Not a Pipe,* 15–18.
32. Bachelard, *Poetics of Space,* 76.
33. Ibid., 76–77.

PART II: MORE A MATTER OF SUBSTANCE THAN OF STYLE

Chapter 7: Myth and Memory in the Landscape: The Nabatean Monuments at Petra

The author was Professor of Architecture at the University of Jordan from 1980–1983, when this study was initially prepared. It was originally presented as a lecture at the Department of Architecture, Massachusetts Institute of Technology in February 1982 and first published in *Art International,* vol. 26, no. 1 (March 1983), as "An Architecture of Particular Inclination."

1. Cited by Eduard F. Sekler in *Wren and His Place in European Architecture,* 54–55. Manuscript is in the Library of All Souls College, Oxford.
2. Significantly, Christian Norberg-Schulz makes several references to Petra in *Genius Loci.*
3. See John Ruskin, *The Seven Lamps of Architecture,* chapter 6, section 3, "The Lamp of Memory."
4. As one refers to the map of Petra, figure 6, the Bab-el-Siq approach is just off the map to the right, toward the east.
5. On Madain Saleh and other sites of Nabatean culture, see *An Introduction to Saudi Arabian Antiquities,* published by the Department of Antiquities and Museums, Ministry of Education, Kingdom of Saudi Arabia, Riyadh, 1975.
6. See Iain Browning, *Petra,* 93.
7. Ibid., 80–83.
8. Ibid., 93.
9. Ibid., 90.

10. Ibid., 97.
11. Ibid., 96.
12. *Saudi Arabian Antiquities,* 50–51.

Chapter 8: Memory of the Upper Room, Image of Court, Temple, and Heavenly Mansion

1. Richard Krautheimer, *Early Christian and Byzantine Architecture,* 2.
2. Ibid., 3.
3. Ibid., 4–5.
4. Ibid., 5.
5. Ibid., 6–7.
6. Ibid., 8.
7. John Lobell, *Between Silence and Light,* 48.
8. Krautheimer, *Early Christian Architecture,* 31.
9. Ibid., 35.
10. Ibid., 29.
11. Ibid., 30.
12. Jean Hubert, J. Porcher, and W.F. Volbach, *Carolingian Art,* 50.
13. Hubert, et al., *Carolingian Art,* 57.
14. Ibid., 57–58.
15. Ibid., 58.
16. Ibid., 58–61.
17. Ibid., 310.
18. Ibid., 62.
19. Ibid., 63.

Chapter 9: St. Petersburg: Memory of a Garden, Image of Empire

In 1969 the author began research on a study of Peter I's creation of St. Petersburg, which was to be published as *Western Windows for the Czar.* This study was undertaken with his Russian colleague George Simunek, who was then living in London. When Simunek died in 1971 the project was set aside. The present chapter reviews some of that work in the light of Iruii Alekseevich Egorov's book *The Architectural Planning of St. Petersburg,* which has regrettably been out of print for a number of years.

1. *St. Petersburg News, Supplement No. 91,* November 10, 1763. Quoted in I.A. Egorov, *The Architectural Planning of St. Petersburg,* 43.

2. Robert K. Massie, *Peter the Great: His Life and His World,* 606–608. The story is told that after consulting with Peter, Leblond designed a canal city on Vasilevski Island in the Amsterdam mode. However, Menshikov had no wish to see either his power usurped or his palace grounds cut up by canals. Therefore he defeated Leblond in a characteristically devious way, by seeing to it that the canals were built too shallow and too narrow for ships to pass. Chastized by Peter for this failure, Leblond did not dare to challenge

Menshikov directly. When Peter asked, "What can be done to carry out my plan?" Leblond replied, "Raze, sire, raze . . . and dig the canals anew." But that was too much even for Peter. It is said that Peter would visit the canals and stare moodily at what might have been.

3. Sebastien Le Plestre, Marquis de Vauban, French military engineer (1633–1707).

4. Marshal Vauban, see note 2 above.

5. The Alexander Nevski Monastery is a shrine of Russian nationalism. Grand Duke Alexander defeated the Swedish general, Birger Jarl, who led the Catholic army sent on the Pope's orders, at the Battle of Novgorod in 1240. Subsequently, Alexander took the name Nevski, from the River Neva on which this battle was fought. He became a legendary figure, an early hero of the Russian people, and was later canonized by the Russian Orthodox Church.

6. For Makhaev's map of 1753, see I.A. Egorov, *The Architectural Planning of St. Petersburg,* 46.

7. Egorov, *Architectural Planning,* 45–47.

8. Ibid., 57–59.

9. This argument was, for example, advanced under Stalin by A. Bunin and M. Kunglova in their article "Concerning the Architecture of a Capital City," which appeared in *Academy of Architecture,* No. 1 (1936) and is quoted by Egorov in *The Architectural Planning of St. Petersburg,* 70.

10. Ibid., 71.

11. Ibid., 67. (Author's emphasis.)

12. Ibid., 93. (Author's emphasis.)

Chapter 10: Aalto's Use of Memory: The Urban Fragments

1. See Aldo Rossi, *The Architecture of the City,* 57–61; also chapter 4.

2. Reima Pietilä's view is that: "The trees are the true inhabitants of the earth; we are only visitors." In conversation with the author, Tenhola, Finland, July 1985.

3. See Paul David Pearson, Alvar Aalto and the *International Style,* 10.

4. See Malcolm Quantrill, *Reima Pietilä: Architecture, Context and Modernism,* chapter 2.

5. See Malcolm Quantrill, *Alvar Aalto: A Critical Study,* 34.

6. Ibid., 34.

7. The author is indebted to Professor Otto Meurman, formerly Architect/Planner in Ullberg's office, Viipuri, for this information. He brought the connection between the 1912 competition and that for the Viipuri Library of 1927 to the author's attention, when they met in Helsinki on February 24, 1983. See *Arkkitekten,* March 1913, 40–46, for the original competition drawings of the *Monumentalplatz.*

8. Quantrill, *Alvar Aalto,* 109.

9. Ibid., 111.

10. See Irma Savolainen, *Mediaeval Stone Churches of Finland,* 94.

11. See also chapter 1, where Strømnes's discussion is cited concerning the contrast between the simple topological system of language rules used by Finnish-speaking people, and the simple vectoral system of the Swedish speaker.

12. Quantrill, *Alvar Aalto,* 128–136.

13. Ibid., 197, 203, 205, 208, 219, and 237.

14. See Kirmo Mikkola, ed., *Alvar Aalto vs. the Modern Movement,* Jyväskylä, Finland, 1981.

15. Quantrill, *Alvar Aalto,* 162.

16. Robert Venturi, *Complexity and Contradiction in Architecture.*

Chapter 11: L'Esprit de l'Escalier

Originally given on March 29, 1985, at Texas A&M University as the introductory paper in the 1985 Rowlett Lectures, of which the author was Chairman.

1. See Malcolm Quantrill, *Reima Pietilä: Architecture, Context and Modernism,* 189.

2. See Michel Foucault, *This Is Not a Pipe,* 57. Compare this view to that of Thomas Aquinas on similitude and images, chapter 1.

3. Foucault, *This Is Not a Pipe,* 57.

4. Ibid., 57.

5. Vitruvius, *Ten Books on Architecture,* Book IV, 4, 88.

6. See Bruno Zevi, *Architecture As Space,* 132–133.

7. Ibid., 133.

8. Exodus 20: 24–26.

9. Genesis 11:6–9.

10. See Gaston Bachelard, *The Poetics of Space,* 17.

Chapter 12: The Body of Knowledge and the Body of Architecture

1. Frode Strømnes, "On the Architecture of Thought," in *Abacus No.* 2, 9.

2. Gaston Bachelard, *The Poetics of Space,* xxxiii.

3. Strømnes, "On the Architecture of Thought," 14.

4. In fact, some current research suggests that *remembering* visual imagery and *creating* new visual images may take place in the same part of the brain. See, for example, Stephen Kosslyn, *Ghosts in the Mind's Machine.*

5. Aldo Rossi, Architecture of the City, 51–61.

6. Norberg-Schulz, *Intentions in Architecture,* 33; 179 et seq.

7. Louis Kahn, quoted in *Between Silence and Light* by John Lobell, 44.

8. Thomas Fuller, *The History of the Worthies of England,* vol. 2, 487.

9. René Magritte, letter to Michel Foucault in Foucault's *This Is Not a Pipe,* 57.

10. Bachelard, *The Poetics of Space,* 18.

11. Ibid., 17.

SELECTED BIBLIOGRAPHY

BOOKS, EXHIBITION CATALOGUES, VIDEOTAPES

Akin, Omer, and Eleanor F. Weinel, eds. *Representation and Architecture,* Silver Spring, MD, 1982.

Alexander, Christopher. *The Timeless Way of Building.* New York, 1979.

Allen, J.P., and Paul Bureu, ed. *Noam Chomsky: Selected Readings.* New York, 1971.

Andrews, Wayne. *Architecture, Ambition and Americans.* New York, 1964.

Apollinaire, Guillaume. *The Cubist Painters: Aesthetic Meditations.* New York, 1949.

Argan, Giulio C. *The Renaissance City.* New York, 1969.

Arnheim, Rudolf. *The Dynamics of Architectural Form.* Berkeley, CA, 1977.

Arslan, Edoardo. *Gothic Architecture in Venice.* London, 1971.

Bachelard, Gaston. *The Poetics of Space,* trans. Maria Jolas. Boston, MA, 1969.

Banham, Reyner. *Theory and Design in the First Machine Age.* New York, 1960.

Bazin, Germain. *The Baroque: Principles, Styles, Modes, Themes.* London, 1968.

"Beyond Utopia: Changing Attitudes in American Architecture." Television film, Blackwood Productions (Los Angeles), 1984.

Bialostoki, Jan. *The Art of the Renaissance in Eastern Europe.* Oxford, U.K., 1976.

Bloomer, Kent C., and Charles W. Moore. *Body, Memory, and Architecture.* London and New Haven, CT, 1977.

Bon, Antoine. *The Ancient Civilization of Byzantium.* London, 1972.

Bonta, Juan Pablo. *Architecture and Its Interpretation.* New York, 1979.

Borsi, Franco. *Leon Batista Alberti.* Florence, Italy, 1974.

Bregman, Jay. *Synesius of Cyrene.* Berkeley, CA, 1982.

Brown, Peter. *The World of Late Antiquity.* London, 1971.

Browning, Iain. *Petra.* Revised ed. London, 1980.

Capelli, Gianni. *I Mesi Antelamici nel battistero di Parma.* Parma, 1983.

Carlo, Giancarlo De. *Urbino.* Milano, 1966.

Chastel, André. *The Crises of the Renaissance 1520–1600.* Geneva, 1968.

———. *The Myth of the Renaissance 1420–1520.* Geneva, 1969.

Chierici, Sandro. *La Lombardie romane.* Geneva, 1978.

Cirlot, Juan-Eduardo. *The Genesis of Gaudian Architecture.* New York, 1967.

Clark, R.T. Rundle. *Myth and Symbol in Ancient Egypt.* London, 1978.

Comerio, Mary C., and Jeffrey M. Chusid. *Teaching Architecture: Proceedings of the 69th Annual Meeting of the Association of Collegiate Schools of Architecture—1981.* Washington, DC, 1982.

Conant, Kenneth John. *Carolingian and Romanesque Architecture 800 to 1200.* Harmondsworth, England, 1966.

Conrads, Ulrich. *Programs and Manifestoes on 20th-Century Architecture,* trans. Michael Bullock. Cambridge, MA, 1970.

Davey, Peter. *Architecture of the Arts and Crafts Movement.* New York, 1980.

Della Valle, Anna. *Palladio: La sua eredità nel mondo.* Vicenza, 1980.

Down to Earth. Exhibition of mud architecture at Centre Georges Pompidou. Paris, London, 1982.

Drexler, Arthur, and Thomas S. Hines. *The Architecture of Richard Neutra: From International Style to California Modern.* New York, 1982.

Durand, Jean-Nicolas-Louis, 1800. *Recueil et parallèle des édifices de tout genre, anciens et modernes.* Reprint. Princeton, NJ, 1981.

Egorov, Iruii Alekseevich. *The Architectural Planning of St. Petersburg,* trans. Eric Dlutrosch. Athens, OH, 1969.

Ellul, Jacques. *The Meaning of the City,* trans. Dennis Pardee. Grand Rapids, MI, 1970.

Foucault, Michel. *The Archaeology of Knowledge and the Discourse on Language.* New York, 1972.

———. *This Is Not a Pipe,* trans. James Harness. Berkeley, CA, 1982.

Frampton, Kenneth, ed. *Modern Architecture and the Critical Present.* London, 1982.

Frankl, Paul. *Principles of Architectural History: The Four Phases of Architectural Style, 1420–1900.* Trans. and ed. James F. O'Gorman. Cambridge, MA, 1968.

Fry, Edward P. *Cubism.* London, 1966.

Fuller, Thomas. *The History of the Worthies of England.* P. Austin Nuttall, ed., 4 vol. [London, 1840.] Facsimile ed., New York, 1965.

Gallet, Michel. *Claude-Nicolas Ledoux.* Paris, 1980.

Giedion, Siegfried. *Space, Time and Architecture.* Cambridge, MA, 1965.

Gilland, Wilmot G., and David Woodcock, eds. *Architectural Values and World Issues: Proceedings of the 71st Annual Meeting of the Association of Collegiate Schools of Architecture—1983.* Washington, DC, 1984.

Grabar, Oleg. *The Formation of Islamic Art.* New Haven and London, 1978.

Grabow, Stephen. *Christopher Alexander—The Search for a New Paradigm in Architecture.* Boston, 1983.

Gravagnuolo, Benedetto. *Adolf Loos: Theory and Works.* New York, 1982.

Gray, Camilla. *The Great Experiment: Russian Art 1863–1922.* New York, 1962.

Gray, Christopher. *Cubist Aesthetic Theories.* Baltimore, 1953.

Gropius, Walter. *The New Architecture and the Bauhaus.* London, 1935.

Hammacher, A.M. *Magritte.* New York, 1974.

Henderson, Linda Dalrymple. *The Fourth Dimension and Non-Euclidean Geometry in Modern Art.* Princeton, NJ, 1983.

Hines, Thomas S. *Richard Neutra and the Search for Modern Architecture.* New York, 1982.

Hitchcock, Henry-Russell. *In the Nature of Materials.* New York, 1942.

———. *Architecture: Nineteenth and Twentieth Centuries.* Harmondsworth, England, 1969.

Hopper, Vincent Foster. *Medieval Number Symbolism.* New York, 1938.

Hornung, Erik. *Conceptions of God in Ancient Egypt—The One and the Many.* London, 1983.

Hubert, J., J. Porcher, and W. F. Volbach. *Carolingian Art.* New York, 1970.

Introduction to Saudi Arabian Antiquities. Roger Wood, photographer. Kingdom of Saudi Arabia, Riyadh, 1975.

Irving, Robert Grant. *Indian Summer—Lutyens, Baker, and Imperial Delhi.* London, 1981.

Jaffe, Hans L. *The De Stijl Group: Dutch Plastic Art.* Amsterdam, 1963.

———. *De Stijl.* New York, 1971.

Janis, Harriet, and Rudi Blesh. *Collage: Personalities, Concepts, Techniques.* Philadelphia, 1967.

Jaynes, Julian. *The Origin of Consciousness in the Breakdown of the Bicameral Mind.* Boston, MA, 1976.

Johnson, Paul. *Civilizations of the Holy Land.* London, 1979.

Jordy, William H. *American Buildings and Their Architects.* New York, 1976.

Kahnweiler, Daniel-Henry. *Juan Gris: His Life and Work,* trans. Douglas Cooper. [New York, 1946.] Revised ed., New York, 1969.

———. *The Rise of Cubism.* New York, 1949.

Kent, Ernest W. *The Brains of Men and Machines.* Peterborough, NH, 1981.

Kivinen, P., P. Korvenmaa, and A. Salokorpi. *Lars Sonck (1870–1956): Architect.* Helsinki, 1981.

Kolehmainen, Alfred, and Veijo A. Laine. *Suomalainen Talonpoikaistalo.* Helsinki, 1980.

Koppelkamm, Stefan. *Glasshouses and Wintergardens of the Nineteenth Century.* New York, 1981.

Kosok, Paul. *Life, Land and Water in Ancient Peru.* Long Island, NY, 1965.

Kosslyn, Stephen. *Image and Mind.* Cambridge, MA, 1980.

———. *Ghosts in the Mind's Machine.* Cambridge, MA, 1983.

Krautheimer, Richard. *Early Christian and Byzantine Architecture.* Baltimore, MD, 1965.

Kristeller, Paul Oskar. *Renaissance Concepts of Man and Other Essays.* New York, 1972.

Kunstler, Gustav, ed. *Romanesque Art in Europe.* Greenwich, CT, 1968.

Le Corbusier. [*Vers une architecture.* 1923.] *Towards a New Architecture,* trans. Frederick Etchells. New York, 1946.

———. *The City of Tomorrow.* Cambridge, MA, 1971.

Ledoux, C.N. *L'Architecture considerée sous le rapport de l'art des moeurs et de la législation.* [Paris, 1804.] Facsimile reprint. Nordlingen, 1981.

LeMaître, Georges. *From Cubism to Surrealism in French Literature.* Cambridge, MA, 1947.

Lippard, Lucy. *Surrealists on Art.* Englewood Cliffs, NJ, 1970.

Lobell, John. *Between Silence and Light.* Boulder, CO, 1979.

Lucie-Smith, Edward. *Art Now: From Abstract Expressionism to Surrealism.* New York, 1981.

Luria, A.R., and Karl Pribram. *Psychophysiology of the Frontal Lobes.* New York, 1973.

Mallarmé, Stéphane. *Oeuvres complètes.* Paris, 1945.

Malraux, André, and Georges Salles, eds. *Byzantium—From the Death of Theodosius to the Rise of Islam.* London, 1966.

Markus, Thomas A., ed. *Order in Space and Society.* Edinburgh, Scotland, 1982.

Massie, Robert K. *Peter the Great: His Life and World.* New York, 1980.

McAndrew, John. *Venetian Architecture of the Early Renaissance.* Cambridge, MA, 1980.

McHarg, Ian L. *Design with Nature.* Philadelphia, 1969.

Mellaart, James. *Earliest Civilizations of the Near East.* London, 1965.

Meunier, John, ed. *Language in Architecture: Proceedings of the Association of Collegiate Schools of Architecture 68th Annual Meeting—1980.* Washington, DC, 1981.

Michell, George, ed. *Architecture of the Islamic World—Its History and Social Meaning.* London, 1978.

Mikkola, Kirmo. *Alvar Aalto vs. the Modern Movement.* Jyväskylä, Finland, 1981.

Mondrian, Piet. *De Stijl.* Exhibition catalog, Amsterdam, 1951.

Moore, Charles, and Gerald Allen. *Dimensions—Space, Shape and Scale in Architecture.* New York, 1976.

Morris, A.E.J. *History of Urban Form—Prehistory to the Renaissance.* New York, 1972.

Mumford, Lewis, ed. *Roots of Contemporary American Architecture.* New York, 1952.

Musées Royaux d'Art et d'Histoire. *Inoubliable Petra.* Ghent, Belgium, 1980.

Museum of Finnish Architecture. *Yearbook 2.* Helsinki, 1980.

———. *Yearbook 3.* Helsinki, 1982.

———. *Nordic Classicism 1910–1930.* Helsinki, 1983.

Museum of Modern Art, New York. *The History and the Collection.* New York, 1984.

Norberg-Schulz, Christian. *Intentions in Architecture.* Cambridge, MA, 1968.

———. *Meaning in Western Architecture.* London, 1975.

———. *Genius Loci—Toward a Phenomenology of Architecture.* New York, 1979.

Ojetti, Paola, Fausto Franco, Rodolfo Pallucchini, Alba Medea, and Francesco Cessi. *Palladio Veronese and Vittoria at Maser.* Venice, 1982.

Oliver, Paul, ed. *Shelter, Sign and Symbol.* Woodstock, NY, 1980.

Palladio, Andrea. *The Four Books of Architecture.* [Venice, 1570. Trans. and engraved, Isaac Ware, London, 1738.] Facsimile Reprint, New York, 1965.

Panofsky, Erwin. *Gothic Architecture and Scholasticism.* Latrobe, PA, 1951.

———. *Idea—A Concept in Art Theory.* New York, 1968.

———. *Renaissance and Renascences in Western Art.* London, 1970.
Pearson, Paul David. *Alvar Aalto and the International Style.* New York, 1978.
Pevsner, Nikolaus. *Pioneers of Modern Design—From William Morris to Walter Gropius.* London, 1949.
Picon, Gaëtan. *Surrealists and Surrealism 1919–1939.* New York, 1977.
Pirovano, Carlo, ed. *La Presenza del passato.* The First International Architectural Exhibition at the Venice Biennale, 1980.
Portoghesi, Paolo. *Francesco Borromini.* Zurich, 1977.
Pundt, Hermann G. *Schinkel's Berlin: A Study in Environmental Planning.* Cambridge, MA, 1972.
Quantrill, Malcolm. *Ritual and Response in Architecture.* London, 1974.
———. *Alvar Aalto, A Critical Study.* New York, 1983.
———. *Reima Pietilä: Architecture, Context and Modernism.* New York, 1985.
Rapoport, Amos. *House Form and Culture.* Englewood Cliffs, NJ, 1969.
———. *The Meaning of the Built Environment.* London, 1982.
Rice, David Talbot. *Islamic Art.* London, 1965.
Rice, Eugene F., Jr. *The Renaissance Idea of Wisdom.* Cambridge, MA, 1958.
Rickey, George. *Constructivism: Origins and Evolution.* New York, 1967.
Rosenau, Helen. *The Ideal City.* New York, 1972.
Rossi, Aldo. *A Scientific Autobiography,* trans. Lawrence Venuti. Cambridge, MA, 1981.
———. *The Architecture of the City.* Revised American ed., trans. Diane Ghirardo. Cambridge, MA, 1982.
Rotzler, Willy. *Constructive Concepts: A History of Constructive Art from Cubism to the Present.* New York, 1977.
Rowe, Colin. *The Mathematics of the Ideal Villa and Other Essays.* Cambridge, MA, 1976.
Royal Academy. *The Horses of San Marco.* Exhibition Catalogue, Milan, 1979.
Rubin, William Stanley. *Dada, Surrealism and Their Heritage.* Greenwich, CT, 1968.
Ruskin, John. 1849. *The Seven Lamps of Architecture.* New York, 1977.
Rykwert, Joseph. *On Adam's House in Paradise.* New York, 1972.
Santakari, Esa. *Keskiajan Kivikirkot.* Helsinki, 1979.
Savolainen, Irma. *Mediaeval Stone Churches of Finland.* Helsinki, 1979.
Schildt, Göran. *Valkoinen pöyta—Alvar Allon nuoruus ja taiteelliset perusideat.* Helsinki, 1982. Translated as *The Early Years.* New York, 1984.
Schinkel, K.F. *Collected Architectural Designs.* London, 1982.
Schmalenbach, Werner. *Kurt Schwitters.* New York, 1970.
Scully, Vincent. *American Architecture and Urbanism.* New York, 1969.
Sekler, Eduard F. *Wren and His Place in European Architecture.* New York, 1956.
Smith, John B. *The Golden Age of Finnish Art.* Helsinki, 1975.
Stedelijk Museum, Amsterdam. *De Stijl,* 1951.
Steingruber, Johann David. 1773. *Architectural Alphabet.* Facsimile reprint. New York, 1975.

Stern, Robert A.M. *New Directions in American Architecture.* New York, 1977.

Stroud, Dorothy. *The Architecture of Sir John Soane.* London, 1961.

Sullivan, Louis H. *Kindergarten Chats and Other Writings.* New York, 1965.

Summerson, John. *The Classical Language of Architecture.* London, 1980.

Tafuri, Manfredo. *Theories and History of Architecture.* London, 1980.

Troy, Nancy J. *The De Stijl Environment.* Cambridge, MA, 1983.

Unsal, Behcet. *Turkish Islamic Architecture.* London, 1959.

Venturi, Robert. *Complexity and Contradiction in Architecture.* New York, 1966.

———, Denise Scott Brown and Steven Izenouv. *Learning from Las Vegas: The Forgotten Symbolism of Architectural Form.* Revised ed., Cambridge, MA, 1977.

Vitruvius. *The Ten Books on Architecture.* [Trans. Morris Hicky Morgan. Cambridge, MA, 1914.] Facsimile ed., New York, 1960.

Vuokola, A., and A. Yrjana. *Meidan Kirkkomme.* Porvoo, Finland, 1979.

Walker Art Center, Minneapolis. *De Stijl 1917–1931: Visions of Utopia.* 1982.

Watt, W. Montgomery. *The Majesty That Was Islam.* London, 1974.

Westfall, Carroll William. *In This Most Perfect Paradise.* University Park, MD and London, 1974.

Yates, Frances A. *Giordano Bruno and the Hermetic Tradition.* Chicago, 1964.

———. *The Art of Memory.* Chicago, 1966.

———. *Theatre of the World.* Chicago, 1969.

———. *The Rosicrucian Enlightenment.* London, 1972.

———. *The Occult Philosophy in the Elizabethan Age.* London, 1979.

Zevi, Bruno. *Architecture as Space.* Joseph A. Barry, ed., Milton Gendel, trans. New York, 1974.

Zygas, Kestutis Paul. *Form Follows Form: Source Imagery of Constructivist Architecture 1917–1925.* Ann Arbor, MI, 1981.

ARTICLES

Bandini, Micha. "Typology as a Form of Convention." *AA Files,* no. 6 (May 1984):73–82.

Graves, Michael, "Representation." In *Representation and Architecture,* Ömer Akin and Eleanor F. Weinel, eds. Silver Spring, MD (1982):27–89.

Gullichsen, Kristian. "Neo-Aalto versus Neo-Palladio." *Arkkitehti*—The Future of the Modern Movement. 5–6 (1980):31–33.

Kaufmann, Emil. "Three Revolutionary Architects, Boullée, Ledoux, and Lequeu." *Transactions of the American Philosophical Society.* 42, Pt 3 (1952):474–537. Lancaster, PA: Lancaster Press.

Komonen, Markku. "Wood in Hungary." *Arkkitehti.* 7 (1983): 26–29.

Libeskind, Daniel. "The Eternal Paradox of Eloquence and the Search for Truth." *Arkkitehti*—The Future of the Modern Movement. 5–6 (1980):34–35.

Maxwell, Robert. "The High Museum, Atlanta, Georgia." *AA Files,* no. 7 (September 1984): 68–74.

Moore, Charles. "We Could Make a Richer, More Interesting World Out of the Pieces We Already Have." *Arkkitehti*—The Future of the Modern Movement. 5–6 (1980):30.

Norri, Marja-Riitta. "The Sculpture of Olavi Lanu." *Arkkitehti.* 7 (1983):30–35.

Quantrill, Malcolm. "The World of Victor Newsome." *Art International.* 23 (1979):34–39.

———. "Jack Chambers (1931–1978)." *Art International.* 24 (1980):144–157.

Rykwert, Joseph. "On the Oral Transmission of Architectural Theory." *AA Files,* no. 6 (May 1984):15–27.

Strømnes, Frode. "On the Architecture of Thought." *Abacus No.* 2 (1980):7–29. Museum of Finnish Architecture, Helsinki.

Vidler, Anthony. "The Rhetoric of Monumentality—Ledoux and the Barrières of Paris." *AA Files,* no. 7 (September 1984): 14–29.

INDEX

INDEX

INDEX